D1859453

THE LIFE OF GAUTAMA THE BUDDHA

Owing to the antiquity and rarity of this book, certain pages are regrettably absent, and readability is compromised due to the blurring of the original text. If you possess any insights regarding the availability of these missing sections, kindly inform us. Your assistance is crucial in ensuring the completion of this significant work for the benefit of future generations.

THE LIFE OF GAUTAMA THE BUDDHA:

(COMPILED EXCLUSIVELY FROM THE PALI CANON)

E. H. BREWSTER, C. A. F. RHYS DAVIDS

GYAN

Published by

GYAN

Gyan Publishing House
5, Ansari Road
Daryaganj, New Delhi-110002
Phone: 011-47034999, 9811692060
E-mail: books@gyanbooks.com

Distribution Network
gyanbooks.com
India, USA, Canada, UK, Australia

© Publisher

All rights reserved. No part of this work may be reproduced, stored, adapted, or transmitted in any form or by any means, electronic, mechanical, photocopying, micro-filming, recording or otherwise, or translated in any language, without the prior written permission of the copyright owner and the publisher.

ISBN: 978-93-7014-060-8 (HB)

First Published, 1926

2nd Impression 2025

Printed at: Gyan Press, Delhi.

The book is sold subject to the condition that it shall not, by way of trade or otherwise, be lent, resold, hired out, or otherwise circulated without the prior publisher's written consent.

THE LIFE OF GAUTAMA THE BUDDHA
Author: E. H. BREWSTER, C. A. F. RHYS DAVIDS

TRUBNER'S

ORIENTAL SERIES

THE BUDDHA IN MEDITATION.
(A bronze statue by E. H. Brewster.)

THE LIFE OF GOTAMA THE BUDDHA

(Compiled exclusively from the Pali Canon)

BY

E. H. BREWSTER

With an Introductory Note by

C. A. F. RHYS DAVIDS, D.Lit., M.A.

LONDON

KEGAN PAUL, TRENCH, TRUBNER & CO., LTD.

NEW YORK: E. P. DUTTON & CO.

1926

To

Prof. T. W. Rhys Davids

and

Mrs. C. A. F. Rhys Davids

whose translations and expositions

of the Pali Canon

have made this work possible,

it is gratefully dedicated

by

E. H. B.

CONTENTS

PART IV

The Buddha's Relation with his Disciples and Others

PART V

Last Events in the Life of the Buddha

INTRODUCTORY NOTE

IT is at the request of my good friend Earl Brewster that I write these lines as sponsor to his book. Two years ago I suggested he should undertake it. Henry Warren's worthy *Buddhism in Translations* was, in its materials, too much of a chronological hash to be a safe guide to the general reader. And it covers too wide a field to secure high relief for the special theme which this book seeks to word. It has been no small pleasure to have witnessed, and now and then helped forward the accomplishment of the task.

None of us but must feel a profound regret that when, after the death of their great leader, the Buddhist monk-community, as their records tell, sought to collect in some fixed order and oral form, their common stock of rules and of remembered sayings, they did not make it of equally prime importance to do as much for the story of his whole last life on earth. That we must now piece together scraps of biography and autobiography embedded in those rules and those sayings is the only way left us to make good that negligence. This piecing-together is the aim of the author.

But it were futile to lament over what is lost. There is enough in what we have to form a picture of the man who was, in his life and in his faith, the faith, namely, that true religion lay in the way of daily life growing into noble worth, a very brother-man to men. And we trust that for the readers of these passages such a man will shine forth. I would ask those readers to bear in mind three points :—the picture etched here of Gotama's little world, the winnowing that is necessary as we read, and the picture of the real man that our winnowing yields.

First then, the world about him. A religious teacher and reformer of those days in India was bound to work largely with and on the world of the professionally religious. And I am glad that the compiler has worded these as 'monks'.

Bhikkhu means almsman. But 'monk' is, in what it calls up for us, nearer the truth. It is nearer the truth than 'brethren', much nearer the truth than 'priests'. In 'monks' we have at least the very clue to the world in which the books cited from came to be. We only hide that world when we use other words. It is a world which does not take as its forward view and ideal the *value of life* as such. The monk has turned his back on life as 'growth in the world'. He is cultivating a special, restricted quality of growth. If he be of other creeds he looks, it may be, to growth less hampered when earth life is over. But the Buddhist monk saw *growth* in no worlds beyond earth. He only saw, here or there, a cutting-off of coming-to-be. This cutting off might be here and now, it might be in some other world. If he was in the way to his highest good, he was not as a vigorous growing tree. He was a rotting tree. If he was at the close of that way, he was as a tree-stump with severed roots. He did not believe in the growth of man's life taken as whole. He had a vista of many lives, of many worlds, but he threw away much of the teaching that lay therein.

Now how far do we get a true picture of the founder of 'Buddhism' when we picture him in this monk-world? Was he wholly of it, or was he not wholly of it? Here it is that we must try to winnow wheat from chaff. It is a difficult task, but we must do it, else we come to wrong conclusions. Every reader should do it, for it is only the writer of a romance who will so serve up the past as to bear the reader's imagination passively along. And let him not shrink from charges of 'eclecticism', of winnowing out only 'what does not appeal to him'. Let him seek the very man, the live, the heard, the seen, the fellow 'man'. Let him dwell less on the externals, the imputed speech belonging to that place, that time. So reading he may be surprised to find how much towards a real man these little passages yield wherein at first stands so dim a figure. We have here a very man if we will work him out. Out, that is, from much chaff. Without winnowing, we might conclude he was a mighty talker. But whereas it was a set opening to countless clerical sermons to make them 'word of the Buddha', the more living interviews show him working a great effect by very few words. In the little Nakulapitar Sutta (p. 121) an instance is given. But in the scriptures, when that ailing man has left the teacher's magnetic presence braced and cheered, he is intercepted by disciples, who are made to explain with much formula-talk what the teacher really meant! Was it perhaps thus that the formula-talks came gradually to be put into the mouth of the man of the few winged words? We must not forget that he was as noted for his silence, as for his words, and that he was known as one who was wont to sit in 'the noble silence' with his disciples, as others did not.

Again, with no sifting we might estimate him as a very wonder-man. Yet, looking closer, we see him shrinking from the hopeless effort to influence his tradition-bound world; we see him casting aside his two carefully thought out messages (see p. 54) and preaching on quite other themes when he made his start; we see him arguing against letting women enter his monk-world, then giving way to the loving cousin; we see him claiming to be building a world-creed, yet foretelling its end in 500 years; we see him linking up the way of man closely with other worlds, yet teaching that, 'if there be no other world,' the good life is yet the best; we see him wording the worth of happiness, yet made to say that the wise see happiness 'as ill'.

Again, with no sifting we might accept him as beyond all measure vain and egoistic, speaking of himself, and not 'officially' only, as not even the most blustering Homeric warrior ever spoke. Yet we hear him bidding his followers weigh the moral worth of his teaching before accepting him, take it and not him as their leader, be their own guides and not be merely willed by any teacher.

Out of my own sifting I think of him with deep love and reverence, not as the monk, nor as the weak man, nor as the wonder-man, nor as the vain man. I think of him as the Brother-man, as a willer of the welfare of men, as the worker of the things that are worthy, as the warder of his brethren's will. I think of him as a Helper as few have been, as one who worded for men the 'better' within them which then and there no creed was wording, as a helper of the many folk of his own world, as a helper toward the worlds of man's wayfaring, as a believer, in spite of monkish ideals, in the hope that lies in coming to be. And I think of him as a teacher whose help was given so straightly to this man and to that, that, so far from talking in set forms of words, he was incapable of saying anything in the same words twice.

The Pali canon of the three Pitakas is, as compared with the date of the Teacher, and *as we have it*, not a very old compilation. The piecing of it together took centuries. Nor can it well have passed on in tongues of Ceylon reciters and emerged long after in writing without undergoing much change of complexion and perhaps of contents. Nevertheless no other records as yet seem to yield us any more archaic figure of Gotama. And if it be the oldest figure of him that we can get, it is much to be able to learn what it is, before we consult records more mediaeval, or any more modern idea of him based on these. The collection of life-episodes in these pages makes no claim to be exhaustive of such episodes, but it would not be easy to find much to add from the Canon itself. Responsibility for the English rendering lies more on the shoulders of us older translators than on the author's. His be the credit for a compilation that many will appreciate, from which many may learn.

C. A. F. RHYS DAVIDS.

CHIPSTEAD, SURREY,
1925.

PREFACE

WESTERN students, ever since the beginning of their interest in Buddhism, have felt the need of a compilation of such accounts of the Buddha's life as are scattered through the Pali Canon.

Rhys Davids, some thirty years ago, in his "American Lectures", called attention to this need. To make such a compilation was a matter of the greatest difficulty for these students until the Pali Text Society should have published the necessary documents. This has in our generation been completed; so that now we have printed, and in Roman script, all of the books of the Pali Canon.

We also have translations of a goodly number of these books.

Previous compilations of the life of the Buddha have been culled from sources some of which are not only uncanonical but are so far separate in time and thought that, to those who know the history of Buddhism, they bear such an appearance as would the New Testament, with Milton's Paradise Regained put between St. Luke and St. John, and then maybe some verse of Dante added. It is interesting to observe in the simpler Canonical scriptures the earlier stages of an oral tradition as compared with later writings.

In the Pali Canon is to be found the most reliable account of the Buddha's life; to a few points of which historical research is bringing verification. The Canon in its present form was arranged (though not written), at the Council of Patna, about 250 B.C., from worded memoirs then considered more or less authoritative. These memoirs were of various dates, from those handed down it may be from the sixth century B.C., the Founder's time, to later more discursive matter, compiled, it may be, scarcely earlier than that Council.[1] In India such

[1] Possibly not even before the Council.

preservation by memory of religious teaching has always been considered the best method; and there it is still so considered.

Indeed the Buddha is represented in these ancient memoirs as questioning disciples regarding their memory of some of these very verses; and there also the collection of memoirs is frequently referred to as an existing body of doctrine under different heads. It is thought probable by modern scholars, that at the Council the memoirs in prose, and possibly the anthological memoirs, were re-edited in their present form of refrains in prose and verse, so as to render them easier for memorizing in the more literary diction which had gradually superseded the original lingua franca, usually called Māgadhī, in which they had been handed down. For this subject the reader is referred to books on the history of Buddhism.

Soon before the Council of Patna the famous edicts of the Emperor Asoka were written on stone, numbers of which can still be read; where is found reference to portions of the Anguttără, the Sutta Nipāta, the Iti-Vuttāka, the Majjhīma Nikāya, probably the Dīgha-Nikāya, and what seems to be the Vinăya, e.g. Pātimokkha (see Rhys Davids' Buddhism, page 225). The entire Canon was put in writing in Ceylon about two centuries after the Council of Patna.

It may not be out of place here to state why the Jātakas, which are a Canonical work, are not used in this compilation. That wonderful collection of Folk-Lore consists of prose and verse of varying dates, while the introduction to the Jātaka Commentary, which contains an account of the Buddha's life down to his thirty-sixth year, was written perhaps in the 5th century A.D.—that is, some eight hundred years later than the editing of the Canon. There is in this introduction and in the introductory episodes to the Jātakas a good deal of biographical material, but it belongs to Commentary rather than to Canon, and hence is outside the range of this little book.

I would not wish to give such an emphasis to historical evidence, important as it is, which would confuse it with religious values. All schools of Buddhism, I believe, would maintain that what is important in their religion belongs to personal experience, and should be tested by it. But to combine in one volume the history of its Founder, according to the earliest sources that survive, is a work which cannot fail to be of great value to students of Buddhism, for reasons most obvious, and especially to those who come to the Buddha for guidance. It is attempted to make this present compilation inclusive of all such purely canonical material, avoiding only repetition.

There are three attempts in the Canon at what appears to be consecutive biography and even autobiography of the Buddha: firstly the two accounts in the Majjhīma-Nikāya (No. 26 and 36) giving his search for truth; secondly the fragments in the first part of the Mahāvagga of the Vinaya which relate the commencement of his ministry, and thirdly the Mahā-Parinibbāna-Suttanta of the Dīgha-Nikāya, dealing with the last weeks of his life. These have formed the structure around which I have placed the rest. With reluctance I have had to exclude much inspiring material as not sufficiently relevant to the purpose of this book; especially is this true of many Suttas and of certain 'Psalms' of the Brethren and Sisters.

These ancient scriptures show a considerable literary development, as will be seen from the archaic form of my first selections compared with later ones. The diversity in such material prevents this book from having much literary unity; furthermore I have drawn upon various translators. My own knowledge of Pali is too limited to undertake independently, even if it were desirable, much translation for such a compilation. And when that work has been as well done as the translations of Rhys Davids, which not only have contributed so much to Pali scholarship, but are also an important addition to the riches of English literature, it would be indeed remiss in an English compilation not to profit by this great work. Where I have not followed the translator, the divergence is due to a later translation having been given by that translator himself, or to a choice between later differing authorities. Occasionally I have left several interpretations of the same word, hoping thereby to convey a better understanding of its meaning. For the several selections where I have ventured my own translation, unguided by an English one, I have generally had most valuable aid from Mrs. Rhys Davids. In all other cases mention is given, with the text, of the translator who has been followed, or who has guided me. I have favoured a literal translation.

The study of Pali reminds me of astronomical research; with stronger lenses "dark spots" appear in the firmament of Pali words: the mystery of the language and those ancient days increases.

The material problems then were simpler; perhaps, partly because of that, the mental life was deeper; but however that may be, the mental life was different, and we find words which indicate conceptions that defy translation. One such word is 'dhamma'. It is defined as doctrine, righteousness, condition, phenomenon, thing, reality, truth, ideal, law, order, norm, object, idea, wisdom . . . (see the Pali Text Society's Pali-English Dictionary and expositions by Mrs. Rhys Davids, M. & W. Geiger and others). In this compilation I have left the word generally untranslated, not because it was not easy to choose some one of these many words, but because I believe that by seeing the original word in its contexts the reader is more likely to arrive at that meaning which gives to the word its individuality. Dhamma is often translated doctrine, or truth, but Pali contains other words which must be translated by these words. Mrs. Besant has translated the Sanskrit form (dharma) as duty, or the law of unfolding life ('of unfolding world-order' were better), which seems to me a happy rendering. Comment on other words will be found in the notes accompanying the texts.

I take this opportunity of acknowledging with gratitude my indebtedness to the translators and publishers of books who make this present one possible; very especially to the Pali Text Society, and to Mrs. Rhys Davids who so generously and tirelessly has advised me through many years of study.

May this book serve to increase understanding of the Buddha, the Dhamma and that old world life which was the Sangha!

E. H. Brewster.

Torre dei Quattro Venti,
Capri, Italy.

PART I

THE EARLIEST YEARS

Honour to the Exalted One
The Arahant Buddha Supreme

THE PROPHECY OF ASITA

(FROM THE POEM "NĀLAKASUTTA" OF THE SUTTA-NIPĀTA)

The Seer Asita saw in their leisure hour groups of next-world devas joyful and glad, and the devas of bright garments, holding scarves and eagerly praising their ruler.

Seeing the devas so pleased and uplifted, paying due heed, he thereupon said: "Why is the assembly of devas so greatly pleased, why are you waving scarves?"

"There was not such excitement when in the battle with the Asuras they were defeated and the devas were victorious. What wonder have the devas seen that they rejoice so greatly?"

"They shout and sing and make music, they wave their arms and dance; I ask you, inhabitants of Meru's peaks, O sirs, quickly dispel my doubt."

"The Bodhisatta, the excellent pearl, the incomparable, is born for good and for blessing in the world of men, in the Sakyas' town, in the country of Lumbini. Therefore are we glad and are greatly rejoicing."

"He, the most excellent of all beings, the highest man, the bull of men, the most excellent of all creatures, will turn the wheel (of the Dhamma) in the Wood of the Seers, roaring like a lion, mighty lord of beasts."

(The Saint Asita) having heard those tidings, descended swiftly. Then he went to the dwellings of Suddhodana, and being seated there he thus addressed the Sakyas: "Where is the prince? I too wish to behold him."

Then the Sakyas showed to Asita, the child, their prince, who was like the shining gold, beaten out by a very skilful (smith) in the mouth of a crucible, beaming with glory and of peerless beauty.

Seeing the prince shining like crest of flame, glowing like the bull of stars going through the sky, like the clear sun free from clouds in autumn (Asita) was joyous, he obtained abundant rapture.

The air-devas held in the sky a canopy of a thousand circles, and many branches, and yaks' tails with golden handles were fanned; but those who held the yaks' tails and the canopy were not seen.

Then the Seer (Asita) with matted hair, known as Dark Glory, welcomed him with uplifted heart and happy mind (who was) like a beautiful gem on an orange cloth, the white canopy carried above his head.

And he, having welcomed, as he was fain to do, the bull of the Sakyas, and, as adept in signs and runes, with glad thoughts raised his voice, saying: "This one is peerless, he is chief among those who stand upon two feet."

Then remembering his own forth-faring, he was distressed and wept. The Sakyas seeing the Seer weeping, asked: "Might there be for us danger to the boy?"

Seeing the Sakyas disturbed the Seer said: "I mind me of nothing baneful for the boy, nor will there be for him danger, for he is no inferior. Be without care."

"This prince will touch the height of perfect enlightenment; he will turn the wheel of the dhamma,[1] he seeing the exceedingly pure, feeling compassion for the welfare of the many, spread abroad by him will be the holy life."

"But my life here will soon be at an end, within (his lifetime) there will be death for me; I shall not hear the dhamma of the incomparable Burden-Bearer, therefore I am afflicted woeful and in ill plight."

Having brought forth great joy to the Sakyas, he departed from within the palace, leading the religious life; then having compassion for his own sister's son, he led him to take up the holy life under the incomparable Burden-Bearer,

(Saying): "When thou hearest from others the report of the Buddha, of him who has arrived at perfect enlighten-

[1] On the retention of this word see Preface.

ment, and walks the way of the dhamma ; go there and asking for instructions lead the holy life under that Blessed One."

Thus taught by him of friendly mind, by him who saw into the future, what is exceedingly pure, Nālaka dwelt with his accumulated merits and with guarded senses, looking forward to the Victorious One.

Then when the time of Asita's prophecy had arrived, hearing report as the Victorious One turned the wheel (of the dhamma), he went and saw the Chief of Saints, and after being converted he asked the great Sage for the highest wisdom.

THE THREEFOLD PRIDE (MEMORIES OF YOUTH)

(*ANGUTTARA-NIKĀYA, Vol. I, p.* 145.)

"I was tenderly cared for, monks, supremely so, infinitely so. At my father's home lotus-pools were made for me ; in one place for the blue lotus-flowers, in one place for white lotus-flowers and in one place for red lotus-flowers ; blossoming for my sake. And, monks, I used only unguents from Benares. Of Benares fabric were my three robes. Day and night a white umbrella was held over me, so that I might not be troubled by cold, heat, dust, chaff, or dew. I dwelt in three palaces, monks ; in one for the cold, in one for the summer, and in one for the rainy season."

"When in the palace for the rainy season, surrounded during the four months by female musicians, I did not go down from the palace."

"And, monks, while in another's dwelling only a dish of red rice and rice soup would be offered to the servants and slaves, in my father's house not only rice but a dish with rice and meat was given to the servants and slaves."

"Endowed, monks, with such wealth, being nurtured with such delicacy, there came this thought : "Verily the unenlightened worldling himself subject to old age, without escape from old age, when he sees another grown old, is oppressed, beset and sickened. I too am subject to old age and cannot escape it. If I, who am subject to old age and without escape from it, should see another one who is grown old, and should be oppressed, beset, and sickened, it would not be well with me. While I thought thus, monks, all pride of youth left me."

"Verily the unenlightened worldling himself subject to sickness without escape from sickness, when he sees another sick, is oppressed, beset, and sickened. I too am subject to sickness and cannot escape it. If I, who am subject to sickness without escape from it, should see another one who is sick, and should be oppressed, beset, and sickened, it would not be well with me."

"While I thought thus, monks, all pride in health left me."

"Verily the unenlightened worldling himself subject to death without escape from it, when he sees another dead, is oppressed, beset, and sickened. I too am subject to death, and cannot escape it. If I, who am subject to death without escape from it, should see another one who is dead and should be oppressed, beset, sickened, it would not be well with me."

"While I thought thus, monks, all pride in life left me."

PART II

DISCIPLINE AND ENLIGHTENMENT

The Sublime Story

I

(*FROM DĪGHA NIKĀYA XIV*)

Closely following the Rhys Davids translation

(*This story is presented in the Canon as told by Gotama to his disciples concerning the earliest of the seven Buddhas recognized in the oldest books, Vipassin, "seer," but as true for each of the others. Since it is the Gotama-story that has been applied to the rest, we give it here as such.*)

Now Gotama, when as Bodhisat he ceased to belong to the hosts of the heaven of Delight, descended into his mother's womb, mindful and self-possessed.[1] That, in such a case, is the rule.

It is the rule that, when the Bodhisat ceases to belong to the hosts of heaven of Delight, and enters a mother's womb, there is made manifest throughout the world—including the worlds of the gods, the Māras and the Brahmās and the world (of earth) with its recluses and brahmans, its princes and peoples—an infinite and splendid radiance passing the glory of the gods. Even in those dark spaces which are between the worlds, baseless, murky and dark, and where even the moon and sun, so wondrous and mighty, cannot prevail to give light, even there is made manifest this infinite and splendid radiance, passing the glory of the gods. And those beings who happen to be existing there, perceiving each other by that radiance say: "Verily there be other beings reborn here." And the ten thousand worlds of the universe tremble and shudder and quake. And that this infinite splendid radiance is made manifest in the world, passing the glory of the gods, that, in such a case, is the rule.

It is the rule that, when a Bodhisat is descending into a mother's womb, four sons of the gods go toward the four quarters to protect him saying: "Let no one, be he human,

[1] This and some of the following recur in Majjhima Nikāya iii, 119 f.

or non-human, or whatsoever he be, work harm to the Bodhisat or to the mother of the Bodhisat." That in such a case, is the rule.

It is the rule that, when the Bodhisat is descending into a mother's womb the mother of the Bodhisat is a woman, virtuous through her own nature ; averse from taking life, averse from taking what is not given, averse from unchastity, averse from lying speech, averse from indulgence in strong drinks. That, in such a case, is the rule.

It is the rule that when a Bodhisat is descending into a mother's womb, that mother has no mind for indulgence in the pleasures of sense with men, and is incapable of transgression with any man whatever, who may be enamoured of her. That, in such a case, is the rule.

It is the rule that, when the Bodhisat is descending into a mother's womb, that mother is living in the enjoyment yielded by the five senses, is addicted to it, possessed of it, surrounded by it. That, in such a case, is the rule.

It is the rule that, when the Bodhisat is descending into a mother's womb, no ailment whatever befalls that mother ; at ease is she and unafflicted in body ; and within her womb she sees the Bodhisat complete, in the endowment of all his organs and his limbs. Just as if, brethren, there were a beautiful cat's-eye of purest water, octangular, cut with supreme skill, translucent, and flawless, excellent in every way. And through it were strung a thread, blue or orange, red, white, or yellow. If a man who had eyes to see were to take it into his hand, he would clearly perceive how the one was strung on the other. Even so, brethren, when the Bodhisat is descending into a mother's womb, no ailment whatever befalls that mother, at ease is she and unafflicted in body ; and within her womb she sees the Bodhisat complete in the endowment of all his organs and his limbs. That in such a case, is the rule.

It is the rule that, on the seventh day after the birth of a Bodhisat, the mother of the Bodhisat dies, and is reborn in the heaven of Delight. That in such a case, is the rule.

It is the rule that, whereas other women bring forth after bearing either nine or ten months, the mother of a Bodhisat brings not forth till she has borne the child ten months. That, in such a case, is the rule.

It is the rule that, whereas other women bring forth sitting or reclining, the mother of a Bodhisat brings forth, not so, but standing. That, in such a case, is the rule.

It is the rule that, when a Bodhisat issues from his mother's womb, gods receive him first, afterwards men. That, in such a case, is the rule.

It is the rule that, when a Bodhisat issues from his mother's womb, and has not yet touched the earth, four sons of the gods receive him, and present him to the mother, saying: "Rejoice, lady, for mighty is the son that is born to thee." That, in such a case, is the rule.

It is the rule that, when a Bodhisat issues from his mother's womb, he comes forth stainless, undefiled by watery matter, undefiled by mucus, undefiled by blood, undefiled by any uncleanness whatever, pure, spotless. Just as if, brethren, a jewel were laid down on Benares muslin, the jewel is not stained by the muslin, nor is the muslin stained by it; and why is that? Because of the purity of both. Even so is it at the birth of a Bodhisat. That, in such a case, is the rule.

It is the rule that, when a Bodhisat issues from his mother's womb, two showers of water appear from the sky, one of cold, the other of warm water, wherewith they do the needful bathing of the Bodhisat and of his mother. That, in such a case, is the rule.

It is the rule that, when a Bodhisat has come to birth, he stands firm on both feet, and, with his face to the north, takes seven strides, the while a white canopy is held over him, and, looking around on every side, he utters as with the voice of a bull: "Chief am I in the world, eldest am I in the world, foremost am I in the world. This is the last birth. There is now no more coming to be." That, in such a case, is the rule.

It is the rule that, when a Bodhisat issues from his mother's womb, there is made manifest throughout the universe—including the worlds of the devas, the Māras, and the Brahmās, and this world with its recluses and brahmans, its princes and peoples—an infinite and splendid radiance passing the glory of the devas. Even in those spaces, which are between the worlds, baseless, murky and dark, and where even moon and sun, so wondrous and mighty, cannot prevail to give light, even there is manifest this infinite and splendid radiance, passing the glory of the devas. And those beings who happen to be existing there, perceiving each other by that radiance, say: "Verily there be other beings reborn here." And the ten thousand worlds of the universe tremble, and shudder and quake. And this infinite and splendid radiance is made manifest in the world, passing the glory of the devas. This, in such a case, is the rule.

When the boy Gotama was born, they brought word to Suddhodana the rāja, saying: "A son, my lord, is born to you. May it please you to see him?" Now when Suddhodana, the rāja, had seen the babe, he sent for the brahman soothsayers, saying: "Let the reverend brahman soothsayers see the child." Then, brethren, when the brahman soothsayers had seen the child, they said to the rāja: "Rejoice, sire, for one of the mighty ones is born your son. Fortune is yours, sire, good fortune is yours, in that in your family such a son has come to birth. For this babe, sire, is endowed with the thirty-two marks of the Great Man; and to one so endowed two careers lie open, and none other. If he live the life of the house, he becomes Lord of the Wheel, a righteous Lord of the Right, ruler of the four quarters, conqueror, guardian of the people's good, owner of the Seven Treasures. His do those seven treasures become, to wit: the Wheel Treasure, the Elephant Treasure, the Horse Treasure, the Gem Treasure, the Woman Treasure, the Steward Treasure, the Eldest Son Treasure making seven.[1] More than a thousand sons will be his, heroes, vigorous of frame, crushers of the hosts of the enemy. He, when he has conquered this earth to its ocean bounds, is established not by the scourge, not by the sword, but by righteousness. But if such a boy go forth from the life of the house, into the homeless state, he becomes an Arahant, a Buddha Supreme rolling back the veil from the world.

[1] For explanation of each of these see *Dialogues of the Buddha II*, No. xvii, translated by Rhys Davids.

And what, sire, are the thirty-two marks of the Great Man, wherewith endowed this child hath two careers open to him, and only two: that of the Lord of the Wheel . . . that of Buddha Supreme?

This babe, sire, has feet with level tread. That this is so counts to him as one of the marks of a Great Man.

On the soles of the babe's feet wheels appear with a thousand spokes, with tyre and hub in every way complete. That this is so counts to him as one of the marks of a Great Man.

This babe has projecting heels,
He is long in the fingers and long in the toes,
Soft and tender in hands and feet,
With hands and feet like a net.
His ankles are like rounded shells;
His legs are like an antelope's.
Standing and without bending he can touch and rub his knees with either hand.
His male organs are concealed in a sheath.
His complexion is like bronze, the colour of gold.
His skin is so delicately smooth that no dust cleaves to his body.
The down on it grows in single hairs, one to each pore,
The small hairs on his body turn upward, every hair of it, blue-black in colour like eye-paint, in little curling rings, curling to the right.
This babe has a frame divinely straight.
He has the seven convex surfaces.
The front half of his body is like a lion's.
There is no furrow between his shoulders.
His proportions have the symmetry of the banyan-tree: the length of his body is equal to the compass of his arms, and the compass of his arms is equal to his height.
His bust is equally rounded.
His taste is supremely acute.
His jaw is as a lion's.
He has forty teeth,
Regular teeth,
Continuous.
The eye-teeth very lustrous. His tongue is very long.
He has a divine voice, like a karavīka-bird's.
His eyes are intensely blue.
He has the eyelashes of a cow.
Between the eyebrows appears a hairy mole, white and like soft cotton down.
His head is like a royal turban. This too counts to him as one of the marks of a Great Man.

Endowed, sire, as is this babe with these two-and-thirty marks of the Great Man, two careers and none other are open to him . . . (as above). Thereupon the rāja let the brahman soothsayers be invested with new robes and gratified their every desire.

And the rāja engaged nurses for the babe Gotama. Some suckled him, some washed him, some nursed him, some carried him about on their hip. And a white canopy was held over him day and night, for it was commanded: "Let not cold or heat or straws or dust or dew annoy him." And the boy Gotama became the darling and the beloved of the people, even as a blue or red or white lotus is dear to and beloved of all, so that he was literally carried about from hip to hip.

And when the boy Gotama was born, he had a lovely voice, well modulated and sweet and charming; just as the voice of the karavīka-bird in the mountains of Himâlaya is lovely and sweetly modulated and charming.

And when the boy Gotama was born, there was manifested in him the clairvoyant eye born of the result of his karma, by the which verily he could see as far as a league by day and eke by night.

And when the boy Gotama was born, he looked forward with unblinking eyes, like devas in the heaven of Delight. Now it was because of this, people exclaiming a Seer, a Seer! [1] that this became his name. And again, brethren, while rāja Suddhodana was sitting as a judge, he would take the boy on his hip and so lay down the law as to the causes arising till verily the boy, thus seated on his father's hip, and continually considering, would also determine the points of the matter according to justice. Then at the thought: "It is the babe who is judging cases aright, ever more and more did that word 'A Seer, a Seer', become said of him."

Now rāja Suddhodana had three palaces built for the boy Gotama, one for the rains, one for the winter, and one for the summer, and he had them fitted with every kind of gratification for the five senses. Thus it came to pass

[1] Vipassin! This is the name ascribed to the first of the seven Buddhas, concerning each of whom this legend was held to be true.

that Gotama spent the four months of the rainy season in the rains-palace, ministered to by bands of female musicians; and not once did he come down (from the upper terrace) into the mansion.

Here endeth the Birth Chapter.

II

Now the young lord Gotama when many days had passed by, bade his charioteer make ready the state carriages, saying: "Get ready the carriages, good charioteer, and let us go through the park to inspect the pleasaunce." "Yes, my lord," replied the charioteer, and harnessed the state carriages and sent word to Gotama: "The carriages are ready, my lord; do now what you deem fit." Then Gotama mounted a state carriage, and drove out in state into the park.

Now the young lord saw, as he was driving to the park, an aged man as bent as a roof gable, decrepit, leaning on a staff, tottering as he walked, afflicted and long past his prime. And seeing him Gotama said: "That man, good charioteer, what has he done, that his hair is not like that of other men nor his body?"

"He is what is called an aged man, my lord."

"But why is he called aged?"

"He is called aged, my lord, because he has not much longer to live."

"But then, good charioteer, am I too subject to old age, one who has not got past old age?"

"You, my lord, and we too, we all are of a kind to grow old, we have not got past old age."

"Why then, good charioteer, enough of the park for to-day. Drive me back hence to my rooms."

"Yea, my lord," answered the charioteer, and drove him back. And he, going to his rooms sat brooding sorrowful and depressed, thinking "Shame then verily be upon this thing called birth, since to one born old age shows itself like that!"

Thereupon the rāja sent for the charioteer and asked him:

"Well, good charioteer, did the boy take pleasure in the park? Was he pleased with it?"

"No, my lord, he was not."

"What then did he see on his drive?"

(And the charioteer told the rāja all.)

Then the rāja thought thus: "We must not have Gotama declining to rule. We must not have him going forth from the house into the homeless state. We must not let what the brahman soothsayers spoke of come true."

So, that these things might not come to pass, he let the youth be still more surrounded by sensuous pleasures. And thus Gotama continued to live amidst the pleasures of sense.

Now after many days had passed by, the young lord again bade his charioteer make ready and drove forth as once before . . .

And Gotama saw as he was driving to the park, a sick man, suffering and very ill, fallen and weltering in his own water, by some being lifted up, by others being dressed. Seeing this, Gotama asked: "That man, good charioteer, what has he done that his eyes are not like others' eyes, nor his voice like the voice of other men."

"He is what is called ill, my lord."

"But what is meant by ill."

"It means, my lord, that he will hardly recover from his illness."

"But am I too, then, good charioteer, subject to fall ill; have I not got out of reach of illness?"

"You, my lord, and we too, we all are subject to fall ill, we have not got beyond the reach of illness."

"Why then, good charioteer, enough of the park for to-day. Drive me back hence to my rooms." "Yea, my lord," answered the charioteer and drove him back. And he, going to his rooms sat brooding sorrowful and depressed, thinking: "Shame then verily be upon this thing called birth, since to one born decay shows itself like that, disease shows itself like that!"

Thereupon the rāja sent for the charioteer and asked him: "Well, good charioteer, did the young lord take pleasure in the park and was he pleased with it?"

"No, my lord, he was not."

"What did he see then on his drive?"

(And the charioteer told the rāja all.)

Then the rāja thought thus: "We must not have Gotama declining to rule; we must not have him going forth from the house to the homeless state; we must not let what the brahman soothsayers spoke of come true."

So, that these things might not come to pass, he let the young man be still more abundantly surrounded by sensuous pleasures. And thus Gotama continued to live amidst the pleasures of sense.

Now once again after many days . . . the young lord Gotama . . . drove forth.

And he saw, as he was driving to the park, a great concourse of people clad in garments of different colours constructing a funeral pyre. And seeing this he asked his charioteer: "Why now are all those people come together in garments of different colours, and making that pile?"

"It is because some one, my lord, has ended his days."

"Then drive the carriage close to him who has ended his days."

"Yea, my lord," answered the charioteer, and did so. And Gotama saw the corpse of him who had ended his days and asked: "What good charioteer, is ending one's days?"

"It means, my lord, that neither mother, nor father, nor other kinsfolk will now see him, nor will he see them."

"But am I too then subject to death, have I not got beyond reach of death? Will neither the rāja, nor the rānee, nor any other of my kin see me more or shall I again see them?"

"You, my lord, and we too, we all are subject to death, we have not passed beyond the reach of death. Neither the rāja, nor the rānee, nor any other of your kin will see you any more, nor will you see them."

"Why then, good charioteer, enough of the park for to-day. Drive me back hence to my rooms."

"Yea, my lord," replied the charioteer, and drove him back.

And he, going to his rooms, sat brooding sorrowful and depressed, thinking: "Shame then verily be upon this thing called birth, since to one born the decay of life, since disease, since death shows itself like that!"

Thereupon the rāja (questioned the charioteer as before and as before let Gotama be still more surrounded by sensuous enjoyment). And thus he continued to live amidst the pleasures of sense.

Now once again after many days . . . the lord Gotama . . . drove forth.

And he saw, as he was driving to the park, a shaven-headed man, a recluse, wearing the yellow robe. And seeing him he asked the charioteer: "That man, good charioteer, what has he done, that his head is unlike other men's heads and his clothes too are unlike those of others?"

"That is what they call a recluse, because, my lord, he is one who has gone forth."

"What is that, 'to have gone forth?'"

"To have gone forth my lord, means being thorough in the religious life, thorough in the peaceful life, thorough in good actions, thorough in meritorious conduct, thorough in harmlessness, thorough in kindness to all creatures."

"Excellent indeed, friend charioteer, is what they call a recluse, since so thorough is his conduct in all those respects, wherefore drive me up to that forthgone man."

"Yea, my lord," replied the charioteer and drove up to the recluse. Then Gotama addressed him, saying: "You, master, what have you done that your head is not as other men's heads, nor your clothes as those of other men?"

"I, my lord, am one who has gone forth."

"What, master, does that mean?"

"It means, my lord, being thorough in the religious life, thorough in the peaceful life, thorough in good actions, thorough in meritorious conduct, thorough in harmlessness, thorough in kindness to all creatures."

"Excellently indeed, master, are you said to have gone forth, since so thorough is your conduct in all those respects." Then the lord Gotama bade his charioteer, saying:

"Come then good charioteer, do you take the carriage and drive it hence back to my rooms. But I will even here cut off my hair, and don the yellow robe, and go forth from the house into the homeless state."

"Yea, my lord," replied the charioteer, and drove back. But the prince Gotama, there and then cutting off his hair and donning the yellow robe, went forth from the house into the homeless state.

Now at Kapilavatthu, the rāja's seat, a great number of persons, some eighty-four thousand souls,[1] heard of what prince Gotama had done and thought: "Surely this is no ordinary religious rule, this is no common going forth, in that prince Gotama himself has had his head shaved and has donned the yellow robe and has gone forth from the house into the homeless state. If prince Gotama has done this why then should not we also?" And they all had their heads shaved, and donned the yellow robes, and in imitation of the Bodhisat, they went forth from the house into the homeless state. So the Bodhisat went on his rounds through the villages, towns and cities accompanied by that multitude.

Now there arose in the mind of Gotama the Bodhisat, when he was meditating in seclusion, this thought: "That indeed is not suitable for me that I should live beset. 'Twere better were I to dwell alone, far from the crowd."

So after a time he dwelt alone, away from the crowd. Those eighty-four thousand recluses went one way, and the Bodhisat went another way.

Now there arose in the mind of Gotama the Bodhisat when he had gone to his place,[2] and was meditating in seclusion, this thought: "Verily this world has fallen upon trouble; one is born, and grows old, and dies; and falls from one state, and springs up in another. And from this suffering, moreover, no one knows of any way of escape, even from decay and death. O, when shall a way of escape from this suffering be made known, from decay and from death?"

[1] The number is an usual idiom for a great many.
[2] Under his Wisdom-tree, says the Commentary.

Then to the Bodhisat this thought occurred: "What now being present, is decay and dying also present; what conditions decay and dying?"

Then from attention to the cause arose the conviction through reason: "Where birth is, there is decay and dying; birth is the condition of decay and dying."

Then to the Bodhisat this occurred: "What now being present, is birth also present; what conditions birth?" Then from attention to the cause rose the conviction through reason: "Where becoming is, birth also is; becoming is the condition of birth?"

Then to the Bodhisat this occurred: "What now being present, is becoming also present; what conditions becoming"?

"Where grasping is, there is becoming; grasping is the condition of becoming" . . .

"What now being present, is grasping also present, what conditions grasping?" . . .

"Where craving is, there is grasping; craving is the condition of grasping." . . .

"What now being present, is craving also present; what conditions craving?" . . .

"Where feeling is, there is craving; feeling is the condition of craving." . . .

"What now being present, is feeling also present; what conditions feeling?" . . .

"Where contact is, there is feeling; contact is the condition of feeling." . . .

"What now being present, is contact also present; what conditions contact?" . . .

"Where is the sixfold field, there is contact; the sixfold field is the condition of contact."[1] . . .

"What now being present, is the sixfold field also present; what conditions the sixfold field?" . . .

"Where name-and-form[2] is, there is the sixfold field; name-and-form is the condition of the sixfold field." . . .

"What now being present, is name-and-form also present; what conditions name-and-form?" . . .

[1] Buddhist psychology regards mind as a sixth sense.
[2] Here name-and-form has the signification of mind and body.

"Where cognition is there is name-and-form; cognition is the condition of name-and-form."[1]

"What now being present, is cognition also present; what conditions cognition?" . . .

"Where name-and-form is, there is cognition; name-and-form conditions cognition."

Then to Gotama the Bodhisat this occurred: "Cognition turns back from name-and-form; it goes not beyond. Only as follows can one be born or grow old, or die, or fall from one condition, or reappear in another; that is, in that cognition is conditioned by name-and-form, and name-and-form by cognition, the sixfold field by name-and-form, contact by the sixfold field, feeling by contact, craving by feeling, grasping by craving, becoming by grasping, birth by becoming, decay and dying by birth, and so too grief, lamentation, ill, sorrow and despair come to pass, such is the coming to be of this entire body of ill."

"Coming to be, coming to be." At that thought there arose to Gotama the Bodhisat a vision into things not called before to mind, and knowledge arose, reason arose, wisdom arose, light arose.

Then to Gotama the Bodhisat this occurred: "What now being absent, is decay and dying also absent; by ceasing of what does decay and dying cease?" Then from attention to the cause arose the conviction through reason:—

"Where birth is absent, decay and dying are absent; when birth ceases, decay and dying ceases" . . .

"Where becoming is absent, birth is absent; when becoming ceases, birth ceases" . . .

"Where grasping is absent, birth is absent; when grasping ceases, becoming ceases" . . .

"Where craving is absent, grasping is absent; when craving ceases, grasping ceases" . . .

"Where feeling is absent, craving is absent; when feeling ceases, craving ceases" . . .

[1] Ancient and modern commentators think that the omission here of the two ultimate links in the "Chain of Causation", as elsewhere given, ignorance and effective mental properties (sankhāra), may come from their predominating force being in a previous life: the "chain" here confining itself to the present and the next life.

"Where contact is absent, feeling is absent; when contact ceases, feeling ceases" . . .

"Where the sixfold field is absent, contact is absent; when the sixfold field ceases, contact ceases" . . .

"Where name-and-form is absent, the sixfold field is absent; when name-and-form ceases, the sixfold field ceases" . . .

"Where cognition is absent, name-and-form is absent; when cognition ceases name-and-form ceases" . . .

"Where name-and-form is absent, cognition is absent; when name-and-form ceases, cognition ceases."

Then to Gotama the Bodhisat this occurred: "Lo, I have won to this, the way to enlightenment through insight. And it is this, that from name-and-form ceasing, cognition ceases, and conversely; that from name-and-form ceasing, the sixfold field ceases; from the sixfold field ceasing, contact ceases; from contact ceasing, feeling ceases; from feeling ceasing, craving ceases; from craving ceasing, grasping ceases; from grasping ceasing, becoming ceases; from becoming ceasing, birth ceases; from birth ceasing, decay and dying, grief, lamentation, ill, sorrow and despair cease. Such is the ceasing of this entire body of ill."

"Ceasing to be, ceasing to be," at that thought there arose to Gotama the Bodhisat a vision into things not called before to mind, and knowledge arose, reason arose, wisdom arose, light arose.

Thereafter the Bodhisat dwelt in the discernment of the rising and passing away of the five groups (of individual life) depending on grasping: "Such is form, such is the coming to be of form, such is its passing away; such is feeling, such is the coming to be of feeling, such is its passing away; such is perception, such is its coming to be, such is its passing away; such are the synergies, such is their coming to be, such is their passing away; such is cognition, such is its coming to be, such is its passing away."

And for him, abiding in the discernment of the rising and passing away of the five groups depending on grasping, not long was it before his heart void of grasping, was set free from the cankers.

END OF PART II

(The comparison of this account with the life of Gotama as found in the Vinaya Texts, Majjhima and Saṃyutta Nikāyas, is of much interest to students of Buddhism. But it now follows so closely the narrative of Gotama, elsewhere given in this book, from the Vinaya that we omit the remaining part of this discourse.

It is true that this account has important omissions which are interesting to note. They are the absence of events corresponding to those under the Ajapāla, Muchalinda and Rājâyatana-trees ; mention is not made of previous teachers, or others corresponding to the five ascetics ; nor the sermons preached to them on the " Middle Way " and the " Absence of Self ". But there is the same account given of Gotama's disinclination to teach the Dhamma, his persuasion by a great Brahmā, his first discourse in a place called the " Deer park ", the formula of his discourses to lay-converts on generosity, morality, heaven, the danger of vanity and the defilement of lusts; and that of his discourses to monk-converts on the advantage of renunciation, and the " Truths " which the Buddhas alone have won ;—that is to say, the doctrine of Sorrow, of its origin, of its cessation, and the " Path "—his conversion of great multitudes, the attainment of Arahantship by his disciples, his sending them out to preach the Dhamma, and the regular recitation of the Pātimokkha.)

The Noble Quest[1]

(FROM MAJJHIMA-NIKĀYA, 26th SUTTA)

" Before I was fully enlightened, monks, being not yet the Buddha, only a Bodhisatta, myself subject to birth, old age, disease, death, sorrow and corruption, I sought what was subject to birth, old age, disease, death, sorrow and corruption.

" Then, monks, it occurred to me : ' Why do I seek thus ? '

[1] The translation in some places omits repetitions.

"What if now, perceiving the wretchedness of these states, I were to seek the incomparable security of a Nibbana free from birth, old age, disease, death, sorrow and corruption?

"After a time, monks, while yet of tender age, with the black hair of a lad, in the fulness of my youth, just entering manhood, against the wishes of my weeping parents, I had my hair and beard shaved off, put on the yellow robes and went forth from the home into the homeless life.

"So having become a recluse, searching for what is good, seeking the peerless way of desirable peace, I went to Āḷāra Kālāma and I spoke to him thus:—

'Brother Kālāma, I would like to lead the religious life under your dhamma and discipline.'[1]

"Then, monks, Āḷāra Kālāma addressed me as follows: 'Let your reverence remain. Of such a nature is this dhamma that in a brief time an intelligent man can learn for himself, realize and live in the possession of what is taught.'

"And, monks, in a brief time, I quickly learned that dhamma. And I, and the others with me, just by lip-profession, just by verbal assertion, uttered the Wisdom doctrine and the Elders' doctrine, and claimed that 'I know, I see!' Then, monks, came to me the thought:

"Not by mere faith Āḷāra Kālāma announces that he has learned this dhamma for himself, realized it, and abides in the possession of it. Surely Āḷāra Kālāma knows and understands this dhamma".

"Then I went, monks, to where Āḷāra Kālāma was, and addressed him thus: 'Up to what does this dhamma lead, brother Kālāma, concerning which you say that you have learned it for yourself, realized it and abide in its possession?'

"When I thus questioned Āḷāra Kālāma, he replied that it led to the realm of non-existence. Then, monks, came to me the thought":

"Not only Āḷāra Kālāma has faith; I also have faith. Not only Āḷāra Kālāma has energy, . . . mindfulness, . . . concentration, . . . wisdom. I also have them. What if

[1] The term here is *dhamma-vinaye*; a compound so significant in Buddhist terminology.

I now were to strive for the realization of that dhamma, of which Āḷāra Kālāma declares that he has learned it for himself, realized it, and abides in its possession."

"In a brief time, monks, I quickly learned that dhamma for myself, realized it and abode in its possession. Then, monks, I approached where Āḷāra Kālāma was, and addressed him thus:

"'Brother Kālāma, is this as far as the dhamma leads, of which you declare that you have learned it for yourself, realized it and abide in its possession?'

"'This is as far, brother, as the dhamma leads, of which I have declared that I have learned it for myself, realized it and abide in its possession.'

"'I too, brother Kālāma, have learned this dhamma for myself, realized it and abide in its possession.'

"'Fortunate we are, brother. Supremely favoured, that we should meet such a true ascetic as your reverence. As I have declared the dhamma, so have you learned it; as you have learned it, so have I declared it. As I know the dhamma, so you know the dhamma . . . As I am, so are you; as you are, so am I. Come then, brother, together we will direct this company of disciples.'

"Thus, monks, Āḷāra Kālāma, my teacher, made me his pupil, as equal to himself, and honoured me with very great honour. Then, monks, came to me the thought:

"'This dhamma leads not to detachment, to absence of passion, to cessation, to abatement, to higher knowledge, to full enlightenment, to Nibbana, but only to the attainment of the sphere of nothingness.'

"And I did not find that dhamma sufficient, monks, unsatisfied I went away from there.

"Then, monks, searching for what is good, seeking the peerless way of the desirable peace, I came near to where Uddaka, the disciple of Rāma, was; and approaching, I spoke to Uddaka as follows:

"'Brother Rāma, I would like to lead the religious life under your dhamma and discipline.'

"Then, monks, Uddaka, the disciple of Rāma, addressed me as follows:

"'Let the honourable one remain. Of such a nature is this dhamma, that in a brief time an intelligent man can learn for himself, realize and live in possession of what is taught.'

"Then, monks, in a brief time I quickly learned that dhamma. And I, and others, just by lip-profession, just by verbal assertion, uttered the Wisdom doctrine and the Elders' doctrine, and claimed that 'I know, I see!'

"Then, monks, the thought came to me:

"'Not by mere faith, Rāma announces that he has learned this dhamma for himself, realized it, and lives in the possession of it. Surely Rāma knows and understands this dhamma.'

"Then, monks, I went to where Uddaka, the disciple of Rāma was, and addressed him thus:

"'Up to what does this dhamma lead, brother Rāma, concerning which you say that you have learned it for yourself, realized it, and abide in its possession?'

"When, monks, I thus had questioned Uddaka the disciple of Rāma, he replied, that it led to the realm of neither perception nor non-perception.

"Then, monks, came to me the thought:

"'Not only has Rāma faith, I also have faith. Not only has Rāma energy, . . . mindfulness, . . . concentration, wisdom; I also have them. What if I now were to strive for the realization of the dhamma, of which Rāma declares that he has learned it for himself, realized it and abides in its possession?'

"In a brief time, monks, I quickly learned that dhamma for myself, realized it and abode in its possession. Then, monks, I approached where Uddaka, the disciple of Rāma was, and addressed him thus:—

"'Brother, is this as far as the dhamma leads, of which you declare that you have learned it for yourself, realized it, and abide in its possession?'

"'This is as far, brother, as the dhamma leads, of which I have declared that I have learned it for myself, realized it, and abide in its possession.'

"'I too, brother, have learned this doctrine for myself, realized it, and abide in its possession.'

"'Fortunate we are, brother, supremely favoured, that we should meet such a true ascetic as your reverence. As I have declared the dhamma, so have you learned it; as you have learned it, so have I declared it. As I know the dhamma, so you know the dhamma . . . As I am, so are you; as you are, so am I. Come then, brother, together we will direct this company of disciples.'

"Thus, monks, Uddaka the disciple of Rāma, my teacher, made me, his pupil, as equal to himself, and honoured me with very great honour. Then came to me the thought:

"'This dhamma does not lead to detachment, to absence of passion, to cessation, to abatement, to contemplation, to full enlightenment, to Nibbana, but only as far as the realm of neither perception nor non-perception.'

"And, monks, I did not find that dhamma sufficient; unsatisfied I went away from there. Then, monks, searching for something good, seeking the peerless way of desirable peace, I passed through the land of Magadha from place to place, and came near to the town of Uruvelā. There I saw a well placed plot of ground; a serene dense grove, a clear flowing stream, suitable for bathing, refreshing, all about were villages in which to go for alms. Perceiving this, monks, it occurred to me . . . 'Here is everything necessary for the struggle of a worthy man.'

"And there, monks, as all was suitable for the struggle, I settled down."

Conquest of Fear

(Trans. from a portion of Majjhima-Nikāya, 4th Sutta)

(The Buddha is addressing the Brahman Jāṇussoṇi)

And to me also before my full enlightenment, being still only imperfectly enlightened, but verily seeking to attain enlightenment, I also thought: "Hard is it to live in the depths of the forest, in remote places; difficult to rejoice in solitude and retirement; unsettling to the mind for the monk who has not reached tranquillity."

Then I said within myself: "All those ascetics and brahmans who resort to remote places in the depths of the forest, while they are not pure in body, action, word, thought, or way of life; filled with covetousness, lust, keen passions, hatred and corrupt thought and desires; possessed by sloth and torpor; unbalanced and unpacified in mind; full of doubts and uncertainty; or who resort to the forest in self-conceit and in disparagement of others; terrified, cowardly, with desire for honour and fame; indolent and apathetic, inert, feeble and forgetful; lacking intelligence, uncontrolled, wavering in mind; without reason, stupid, they, because of these impurities, invoke fear and terror. But I resort to the remote places in the lonely depths of the forest, following purity of body, action, word, thought and way of life; freed from covetousness, filled full with loving kindness, with sloth and torpor banished; serene of mind, conquered every doubt, not exalting myself nor disparaging others, gone excitement and fear, satisfied with little, resolved and strenuous, collected in mind, who have won concentration and the blessing of the higher knowledge. Whatsoever Noble Ones there be who resort to remote places in the lonely depths of the forest, thus purified and thus attained, of such am I."

Then perceiving that these purifications and attainments were mine, serenity in the life of the forest arose in me. Then I said within myself: "How now, if upon those noted auspicious nights of the full moons and the eighth of the waxing and waning moon, I should seek the shrines in grove and forest and under the trees, and abide on such a night in those places of horror and hair-raising, so that, forsooth, I might contemplate that fear and horror."

And subsequently on those auspicious nights of the full moons and the eighth of the waxing and waning moons I sought the shrines in grove and forest and under the trees, and abode on such nights in those places of horror and hair-raising. And while I stayed there some beast approached, a peacock caused a twig to fall, the wind rustled among the fallen leaves; and I thought: 'Now comes that fear and terror!'

Then I said within myself: "But why at any rate should I await expecting that fear? How if when that fear and terror really come I indeed should overcome that fear and terror just as I happen to be?"

And that fear and terror came as I walked to and fro, but I neither stood still, nor sat down, nor lay down, until, walking to and fro, I had overcome that fear and terror. And that fear and terror came as I stood still, but I neither walked to and fro, nor sat down, nor lay down, until, standing still, I had overcome that fear and terror: and that fear and terror came over me as I sat; but I neither lay down nor stood up nor walked to and fro, until, sitting, I had overcome that fear and terror. And that fear and terror came over me as I lay down; but I neither sat up nor walked to and fro until, lying down, I had overcome that fear and terror.

There are many ascetics and brahmans who conceive night to be just the same as day, and day just the same as night. This I call delighting in illusion on the part of those ascetics and brahmans. Now I perceive that when night is here, it is night, when day is here, it is day.

Now who can say this truly of anyone, can truly say it also of me: "A being without illusion has been born, for the good of many, for the benefit of many, out of compassion for the world, for the blessing, the welfare and the happiness of gods and men."

There I dwelt, strenuous, serene, attentive, mindful, with body cool and calm, with mind collected and tranquil . . .

Here follows a description of the Enlightenment as in Majjhima-Nikāya 36.

ENLIGHTENMENT ATTAINED

(FROM THE MAHĀSACCAKA SUTTA)

Containing a further description of the Buddha's search for enlightenment, taken from Sutta No. 36 of the Majjhima-Nikāya.

(The Buddha is addressing Aggivessāna.)

"Here there came to me, Aggivessāna, three comparisons spontaneously, not previously heard.

"Thus if, Aggivessāna, a damp, muddy piece of wood should be thrown into the water; and a man come there provided with a piece of wood to rub (thinking): 'I wish to make a fire, to produce light.' What think you now, Aggivessāna, could this man possibly make a fire, produce light by rubbing a damp, muddy piece of wood which had been thrown into the water?"

"Certainly not, Gotama."

"And why not?"

"That piece of wood, Gotama, is damp, muddy and also had been thrown into the water. All the trouble and bother of the man would be in vain."

"Now it is just so, Aggivessāna, with certain ascetics or brahmans, who are not weaned from the body, who are not inwardly rid of, and wholly allayed what in their desires is the wish of desire, the snare of desire, the dizziness of desire, the thirst of desire, and the fever of desire; if now these good ascetics and brahmans experience painful, piercing, terrible sensations that arise in them, then they are incapable of wisdom, of insight, and of the incomparable full awakening; and also if these good ascetics and brahmans do not experience painful, piercing, terrible sensations that arise in them, then also they are incapable of wisdom, of insight, and of the incomparable full awakening. Now this comparison, Aggivessāna, was the first to come to me, spontaneously, not previously heard.

"And then, Aggivessāna, there came to me a second comparison spontaneously, not previously heard. Thus if, Aggivessāna, a damp, muddy piece of wood should be cast far from the water upon the ground, and a man should come provided with a piece of wood to rub (thinking): 'I wish to make fire, to produce light.' What do you think now, Aggivessāna, could this man possibly make fire, produce light, by rubbing the damp and muddy piece of wood cast far from the water on to the ground?"

"Certainly not, Gotama."

"And why not?"

"That piece of wood, Gotama, is damp and muddy and also it has been cast from the water on to the ground, all the trouble and bother of the man would be in vain."

"Now exactly like this, Aggivessāna, it is with certain ascetics or brahmans, who have overcome the body, and also desire, who nevertheless are not inwardly rid of and have not wholly allayed what in their desires is the wish of desire, the snare of desire, the dizziness of desire, the thirst of desire, the fever of desire; if now these good ascetics and brahmans experience painful, piercing, terrible sensations that arise in them, they are incapable of wisdom, of insight, and the incomparable full awakening; and even if these good ascetics and brahmans experience not these painful, piercing, terrible sensations that arise in them, then also they are incapable of wisdom, of insight, and the incomparable full awakening. This comparison, Aggivessāna, was the second to come to me, spontaneously, not previously heard.

"And then, Aggivessāna, there came to me a third comparison, spontaneously, not previously heard. Thus, Aggivessāna, if a dry, clean piece of wood, that (once) had been cast far from the water upon the ground, and a man should come provided with a piece of wood to rub (thinking): 'I wish to make fire, to produce light.' What do you think now, Aggivessāna, could this man possibly make fire, produce light, by rubbing the dry, clean piece of wood cast far from the water upon the ground?"

"Certainly, Gotama."

"And why?"

"That piece of wood is dry and clean and lies on the ground out of the water."

"Now exactly like this is it with certain ascetics and brahmans that have been weaned from the body, and also from desires, that are inwardly rid of and have wholly allayed what in their desires is the wish of desire, the snare of desire, the dizziness of desire, the thirst of desire, the fever of desire, if thus these good ascetics and brahmans feel painful, piercing, terrible sensations, that arise in them, then they are capable of wisdom, of insight, and the imcomparable full awakening; and even if these dear ascetics and brahmans do not feel painful, piercing, terrible sensations, that arise in them, also then they are capable of wisdom, of insight, and of the incomparable full awakening.

"This comparison, Aggivessāna, was the third to come to me, spontaneously, not previously heard.

"These three comparisons, Aggivessāna, came to me spontaneously, not previously heard.

"Then, Aggivessāna, this came to me: 'What if I now with gritted teeth, and my tongue cleaving to my palate, should master, crush, and force my thought by the mind?' And I now, Aggivessāna, with gritted teeth, and tongue cleaving to my palate, mastered, crushed, and forced my thought by the mind. While I thus, Aggivessāna, with gritted teeth, and my tongue cleaving to my palate, mastered, crushed, and forced my thought by the mind, the sweat oozed out from under my arm-pits. Just as, Aggivessāna, a strong man seizing another weaker one by his head or shoulder masters, crushes and forces him, Aggivessāna, so with gritted teeth and tongue cleaving to my palate I mastered, crushed, and forced my thought by the mind until the sweat oozed out from under my arm-pits. Also verily, Aggivessāna, energetic and not weakened was my force, present and irremovable my attention, but my body being driven by such painful effort was agitated and disturbed. However, Aggivessāna, my condition was such that the painful feelings arisen in me could not obsess my thought.

"Then, Aggivessāna, this came to me: 'What if I now concentrate my attention in Jhāna, without breathing?'

"So now, Aggivessāna, I held the inbreathings and outbreathings of the mouth and nose. Then, Aggivessāna, with holding the inbreathings and outbreathings of the mouth and nose there was an extraordinary roar in the ears of the going out of the air. Just as indeed the swollen bellows of a forge make an extraordinary roar, so now, Aggivessăna, with holding the inbreathing and outbreathing of the mouth and nose, was the extraordinary roar in the ears due to the going out of the air.

"Verily, Aggivessăna, energetic and not weakened was my force, present and irremovable my attention, but my body being driven by such painful effort was agitated and disturbed. However, Aggivessăna, my condition was such that the painful feelings arisen in me could not obsess my thought.

"Then, Aggivessăna, this came to me: 'What if I now still more concentrate my attention in Jhāna, without breathing?'

"So now, Aggivessăna, I held the inbreathing and outbreathing of the mouth and nose and ear. Then, Aggivessăna, with the holding the inbreathings and outbreathings of the mouth, and nose and ear, violent airs shook my head. Just as if, Aggivessăna, a strong man should cleave his head with a sharp point of a dagger, also in precisely the same way while I held the inbreathings and outbreathings of the mouth, nose and ear, violent airs shook my head. Verily, Aggivessăna, energetic and not weakened was my force, present and irremovable my attention, but my body being driven by such painful effort was agitated and disturbed. However, Aggivessăna, my condition was such that the painful feelings arisen in me, could not obsess my thought.

"Then, Aggivessăna, this came to me: 'What if I now still more concentrate my attention in Jhāna, without breathing?' And I now, Aggivessăna, held the inbreathing and outbreathing of the mouth, nose and ear. Then, Aggivessăna, with the holding of the inbreathings and outbreathings of the mouth, nose and ear were violent pains in the head. Just as if, Aggivessăna, a strong man should give rapid beatings of a strong piece of leather upon the head, also in precisely the same way, while I held the inbreathings and outbreathings of the mouth, nose and ear were the violent pains in the head.

" Verily, Aggivessāna, energetic and not weakened was my force, present and irremovable my attention, but my body being driven by such painful effort was agitated and disturbed. However, Aggivessāna, my condition was such that the painful feelings arisen in me could not obsess my thought.

" Then, Aggivessāna, this came to me: 'What if I now still more concentrate my attention in Jhāna, without breathing ? '

" So now, Aggivessāna, I held the inbreathings and outbreathings of the mouth, and nose and ear. Then, Aggivessāna, with the holding the inbreathings and outbreathings of the mouth, nose and ear, violent winds tore at my belly. Just as if, Aggivessāna, a deft butcher, or butcher's apprentice, with a sharp carving knife should carve the stomach, so, Aggivessāna, while I held the inbreathings and outbreathings of the mouth, nose and ear, violent winds tore at my belly. Verily, Aggivessāna, energetic and not weakened was my force, present and irremovable my attention, but my body being driven by such painful effort, was agitated and disturbed. However, Aggivessāna, my condition was such that the painful feelings arisen in me could not obsess my thought.

" Then, Aggivessāna, this came to me: 'What if I now still more concentrate my attention in Jhāna, without breathing ? '

" So now, Aggivessāna, I held the inbreathings and outbreathings of the mouth, nose and ear. Then, Aggivessāna, with holding the inbreathing and outbreathing of the mouth, nose and ear, a violent burning was in my body. Just as if, Aggivessāna, two strong men should seize a weaker man by both the arms and roll him and throw him down into a ditch full of burning coals, so, Aggivessāna, while I held the inbreathings and outbreathings of the mouth, nose and ear a violent burning was in my body. Verily, Aggivessāna, energetic and not weakened was my force, present and irremovable my attention, but my body being driven by such painful effort was agitated and disturbed. However, Aggivessāna, my condition was such that the painful feelings arisen in me, could not obsess my thought.

"Then, Aggivessāna, a deva seeing me spoke thus: 'The ascetic Gotama is dead.' Other devas then said: 'The ascetic Gotama is not dead but he is dying,' and other devas said: 'The ascetic Gotama is not dead and he is not dying; an arahant (saint) is the ascetic Gotama, he is even dwelling in the state of arahantship.'

"Then, Aggivessāna, this came to me: 'What if I should entirely abstain from food?' Then Aggivessāna, the devas drew near to me and said: 'Do not now, sir, entirely abstain from food; even if now, sir, you should entirely abstain from food then we shall instil heavenly nourishment through the pores of your skin, indeed you shall remain alive.' Then, Aggivessāna, this came to me: 'What if I now indeed should practise utter fasting, but these devas should instil heavenly nourishment through my pores and thus I should be sustained, then that would be for me a lie.'

"And, Aggivessāna, I rejected the devas and said: 'It is enough.'

"Then, Aggivessāna, came to me the thought: 'What if I now take less and less nourishment, as much as will go in the hollow of two hands, of bean-soup, or of pea-soup, or of lentil-soup?' And, Aggivessāna, I took less and less nourishment, one or two handfuls of bean-soup, or of pea-soup, or of lentil-soup. And while I thus, Aggivessāna, took less and less nourishment, one or two handfuls of bean-soup, or pea-soup, or lentil-soup, my body became exceeding thin. Like dried canes now became my arms and legs, withered through this extremely scanty diet; like the foot of a camel became my buttock, through this extremely scanty diet; like a string of beads became my spinal column; with the vertebrae protruding, through this extremely scanty diet; just as the roof-beams of an old house sharply protrude, so protruded my ribs, through this extremely scanty diet; just as in a deep well the little water-stars far beneath are scarcely seen, so now in my eye-balls the sunken pupils are scarcely seen, through the extremely scanty diet: as a wild gourd, freshly cut, in the hot sun becomes empty and withered, so now became empty and withered the skin of my head, through this extremely scanty diet.

"And when, Aggivesăsna, I wished to touch my belly, I reached to the back of my spine, and when I wished to touch my spine, I again reached to the belly. Thus near, Aggivessăna, had come my belly to the spinal column, through this extremely scanty food. And if I wished, Aggivessăna, to evacuate my bowels and urinate, I fell forward, through this extremely scanty diet. Then to reinforce this body, Aggivessăna, I chafed the limbs with the hand. And while, Aggivessăna, I thus chafed the limbs with the hand, there fell from the skin the badly rooted hair, through this extremely scanty diet.

"Then, Aggivessăna, men beheld me and said: 'The ascetic Gotama is black.' Other men said: 'The ascetic Gotama is not black, the ascetic Gotama is brown.' And other men said: 'The ascetic Gotama is not black and the ascetic Gotama is not brown, the ascetic Gotama is yellow.' So much, Aggivessăna, had the clear pure colour of my skin been smitten by this scanty diet.

"Then, Aggivessăna, this came to me: 'Whatever ascetic or brahman in the past has ever felt such painful, burning, bitter sensations? This is the uttermost, beyond this one cannot go. Whatever ascetics or brahmans in the future ever will feel such painful, burning, bitter sensations? This is the uttermost, beyond this one cannot go.' 'Whatever ascetics or brahmans in the present feel such painful, burning, bitter sensations? This is the uttermost, beyond this one cannot go.' Now not by this terrible asceticism do I win beyond the human, do I win distinction of truly genuine knowledge. There is perhaps another way of enlightenment.

"Then Aggivessăna, this came to me: 'I remember indeed, once, while my father was doing the work [1] of the Sakyan, I, sitting under the shade of a rose-apple tree, aloof from desire, aloof from things not good, with thinking and with thought sustained, entering to have become a dweller in the first Jhāna, born of solitude, full of joy and happiness.' Is not this the way of enlightenment?

[1] That is plowing, see *Buddhist Birth Stories*, 2nd edition, p. 163.

"Then, Aggivessāna, came to me the consciousness following on attention: 'This is the way of enlightenment.'

"Then, Aggivessāna, this came to me: 'Why should I perhaps fear this happiness, this happiness otherwise than by sense-desire, otherwise than by things not good?'

"Then, Aggivessāna, this came to me: 'No, I do not fear this happiness, which is otherwise than by sense-desire, than by things not good.'

"Then, Aggivessāna, this came to me: 'I cannot easily reach this happiness with a body so exceedingly weakened: what if I now take solid food, rice soup?' And then I I took solid food, rice soup.

"At that time, Aggivessāna, five ascetics lived near to me: (thinking) 'When the ascetic Gotama will have gained for us the dhamma, he will share it with us.' But when I now, Aggivessāna, took solid food and cooked rice, then those five ascetics separated from me, and went away saying: 'The ascetic Gotama giving up exertion, falls into luxury.'

"And I now, Aggivessāna, taking solid food, gained strength, aloof from desire, aloof from things not good, with thinking, and with thought sustained, I entered on and became a dweller in the first Jhāna, born of solitude, full of joy and happiness. Yet the feeling of joy which in that way arose in me Aggivessāna, could not obsess my thought.

"After suppressing attention and investigation, Aggivessāna, I entered on and became a dweller in the second Jhāna, born of that interior concentration of mind, when reasoning and investigation cease, tranquil, uplifted, full of joy and happiness. Yet the feeling of joy which in that way arose in me, Aggivessāna, could not obsess my thought.

"By the fading out of joy I remained equable mindful and attentive producing in my body that happy state of insight of which the Ariyans say: 'Equable and mindful, he dwells in happiness,' and I entered and became a dweller in the third Jhāna. Yet the feeling of happy ease which in that way arose in me, Aggivessāna, could not obsess my thought.

"Rejecting joy and sorrow, Aggivessāna, and rejecting

former gladness and sadness, entering, I dwelt in the fourth Jhāna, joy and sorrow perishing, a state of pure lucidity and equanimity. Yet the happy feelings which in that way arose in me, Aggivessăna, could not obsess my thought.

" With the mind thus composed, pure, translucent, straightforward, cleansed of dross, supple, ready for action, firm, incorruptible, I bent down my mind to the memory of former lives. I remembered many former lives: one birth, then two births, then three births, then four births, then five births, then ten births, then twenty births, then thirty births, then forty births, then fifty births, then a hundred, then a thousand, then a hundred thousand, then epochs during various evolutions of the world, then epochs during various dissolutions of the world, then epochs during both evolutions and dissolutions of the world. In such a place, such was my name, such my family, such my state, such my office, I experienced such good or such evil, such was the end of my life; from there I passed away and entered again another life, there I was now, I had such a name, such my family, such my state, such my office, I experienced such good or such evil, such was the end of my life, from there I passed away and entered again another life. Thus I did remember many various forms of previous lives, with all their special details, and with all their special relations. In the first watch of the night came to me this first knowledge. Ignorance was dispelled, knowledge was born, darkness was dispelled, light was born, while I dwelt, alert, ardent and strenuous. Yet the happy feelings which in that way arose in me, Aggivessăna, could not obsess my thought.

With my mind thus composed, pure, translucent, straightforward, cleansed of dross, supple, ready for action, firm, incorruptible, I directed the mind to the knowledge of the decease and rebirth of beings. With pure deva-eye surpassing that of men, I saw beings decease and be reborn, common and noble, beautiful and ugly, happy and sorrowful; I realized how these beings always reappeared according to their actions, and I thought: " These good beings are certainly not right in actions, not right in words, not right in thoughts, they revile what they should honour, they esteem that which is dangerous, they do that which is dangerous; with the dissolution of the body after death they go the baneful way to perdition, to hell. Those good beings, however, who are right in actions, right in words, right in thoughts, who revile not what they should honour, esteem that which is right, do that which is right; with the dissolution of the body after death, go the blissful way to the heavenly world.

"Thus I saw with pure deva-eye, surpassing that of men, beings deceasing and reborn, common and noble, beautiful and ugly, happy and sorrowful; I understood how beings always fared according to their actions. In the middle watch of the night came to me this second knowledge. Ignorance was dispelled, knowledge was born, darkness was dispelled, light was born, while I dwelt alert, ardent, and attentive. Yet the feeling of joy which in that way arose in me could not obsess my thought.

"With my mind thus composed, pure, translucent, straightforward, cleansed of dross, supple, ready for action, firm, incorruptible, I directed my mind to the destruction of the Cankers (Deadly Floods, Delusions):—

"I knew as it really is: 'This is ill.'

I knew as it really is: 'This is the origin of ill.'

I knew as it really is: 'This is the cessation of ill.'

I knew as it really is: 'This is the path that leads to the cessation of ill.'

"I knew as they really are: These are the Cankers.

"I knew as it really is: 'This is the origin of the Cankers.

I knew as it really is: 'This is the cessation of the Cankers.

I knew as it really is: 'This is the Path that leads to the cessation of the Cankers.

"Thus knowing, thus seeing, my mind was set free from the delusion of hankering after sensuous life, was set free from the delusion of hankering after becoming, was set free from the delusion coming from ignorance.

"In this freedom and emancipation this knowledge arose: Rebirth has been destroyed. The higher life has been fulfilled."

An Ancient Path

(*SAMYUTTA-NIKĀYA, Vol. II, p.* 104 (*trans, p.* 72)

(*Mrs. Rhys Davids's trans.*)

While at Sāvatthi the Exalted One said:—

Before I was enlightened, brethren, it came to me, a Bodhisat yet unenlightened, thus: Alas! this world has fallen upon trouble. There is getting born and growing old and dying and falling and arising, but there is not the knowing of an escape from suffering, from decay-and-death. O when shall an escape be revealed from suffering, from decay-and-death? Then, brethren, this came to me: What now being, does decay-and-death come to be? What conditions decay-and-death? To me, brethren, thinking according to law came grasp of insight: Where there is birth, decay-and-death comes to be; decay-and-death is conditioned by birth: To me, brethren, came this: What now being, does birth come to be? does becoming come to be? does grasping come to be? does craving come to be? does feeling come to be? does contact come to be? does sense come to be? does name-and-shape come to be? what conditions name-and-shape? To me, brethren, thinking according to law, came grasp of insight: where there is consciousness, there is name-and-shape; name-and-shape is conditioned by consciousness. To me, brethren, came this: what now being, does consciousness come to be? what conditions consciousness? To me, brethren, thinking according to law came grasp of insight: where there is name-and-shape, there is consciousness; consciousness is conditioned by name-and-shape. To me, brethren, came this: This consciousness turns back, it goes no further than name-and-shape. Thus far are ye born, or grow old, or die, or fall, or arise. Consciousness, namely, comes to pass conditioned by name-and-shape, name-and-shape conditioned by consciousness, sense conditioned by name-and-shape, contact conditioned by sense, whence come to pass, feeling, craving, grasping, becoming, birth, decay-and-death, with grief, lamenting, suffering, sorrow, despair—even such is the coming to be of this entire mass of ill.

Coming to be, coming to be! At the thought, brethren, there arose in me concerning things not taught before vision; knowledge arose, insight arose, wisdom arose, light arose.

To me, brethren, came this: What now not being, does decay-and-death not come to be? From the ceasing of what ceases decay-and-death? To me, brethren, thinking according to law, came grasp of insight: Where there is not birth, decay-and-death is not; from the ceasing of birth ceases decay-and-death. To me, brethren, came this: What now not being does birth not come to be, . . . does becoming, does grasping, craving, feeling, contact, sense, name-and-shape not come to be? From the ceasing of what, does name-and-shape cease? To me, brethren, thinking according to law came grasp of insight: where consciousness is not, name-and-shape come not to be. From the ceasing of consciousness ceases name-and-shape.

To me, brethren, came this: Won have I to the path of enlightenment, to this, that from the ceasing of name-and-shape consciousness ceases; from the ceasing of consciousness name-and-shape ceases; from the ceasing of name-and-shape sense ceases; from the ceasing of sense contact ceases . . . yea, feeling, craving, grasping, becoming, birth, decay-and-death, with grief, lamenting, suffering, sorrow, despair cease. Even such is the ceasing of this entire mass of ill.

Ceasing, ceasing! At that thought, brethren, concerning things not taught before there arose in me vision, knowledge arose, insight arose, wisdom arose, light arose.

Just as if, brethren, a man faring through the forest, through the great wood should see an ancient path, an ancient road traversed by men of former days. And he were to go along it, and going along it he should see an ancient city, an ancient prince's domain, wherein dwelt men of former days, having gardens, groves, pools, foundations of walls, a goodly spot. And that man, brethren, should bring word to the prince or to the prince's minister: "Pardon, lord, know this. I have seen as I fared through the forest, through the great wood, an ancient path, an ancient road traversed by men of former days, I have been along it and going along it I have seen an ancient city, an ancient prince's domain, wherein dwelt men of former days, having gardens, groves, pools, foundations of walls, a goodly spot. Lord, restore that city." And, brethren, the prince or his minister should restore that city. That city should thereafter become prosperous and flourishing, populous, teeming with folk, grown and thriven.

Even so have I, brethren, seen an ancient path, an ancient road traversed by the rightly enlightened ones of former times.

And what, brethren, is that ancient path, that ancient road traversed by the rightly enlightened ones of former times ?

Just this Ariyan eightfold path, to wit, right views, right aims, right speech, right action, right livelihood, right effort, right mindfulness, right concentration. This, brethren, is that ancient path, that ancient road, traversed by the rightly enlightened ones of former times. Along that have I gone, and going along it I have fully come to know decay-and-death, I have fully come to know the uprising of decay-and-death. I have fully come to know the ceasing of decay-and-death, I have fully come to know the way going to the ceasing of decay-and-death. Along that have I gone, and going along it I have fully come to know birth, yea, and becoming and grasping, and craving, and feeling, and contact, and sense, and name-and-shape, and consciousness. Along that have I gone, and going along it I have fully come to know activities, I have fully come to know the uprising of activities, I have fully come to know the ceasing of activities, I have fully come to know the way going to the ceasing of activities. This that I have fully come to know I have declared to the brethren, to the sisters, to laymen, to laywomen, even this divine life, brethren, that is prosperous, and flourishing, wide-spread, and to be known by many, and multiplied so far as it is well made manifest by devas and men.

The Going Forth for a Religious Life

(VERSES FROM THE SUTTA NIPĀTA, 405-24)

I will praise the going forth, even as the far-seeing One went forth, even as, considering, he approved of going forth.

Cramped is this household life, the home of dust.

Free as air is going forth. Thus seeing he went forth.

Going forth he rejected wrong-doing in action, and having put away wrong-doing in speech, he wholly purified his way of living.

To the mountain fortress of the Magadhese, to Rājagaha came the Buddha.

Rich in the signs of worth, he accepted alms for food.

Standing on the upper terrace of his palace, Bimbisāra saw him.

On recognizing these signs, he spoke of this matter.

"Sirs, mark this man, he is handsome, great and pure, guarded in conduct he looks but as far as a plow."

With downcast eyes, and self-possessed is he, verily of no mean birth.

Let the king's messenger make haste (and find out) where the monk will go?

Thus sent, the messengers followed after him, and asked: "Where will the monk go? where does he abide?"

He going from house to house, guarded and well restrained the door (of sense), calm and self-possessed, his bowl was quickly filled.

His round for alms completed, the Sage departed from the town. He reached Pandăva. There he will abide.

As soon as they had seen him stop, there the messengers drew near, and one messenger returned to the king, announcing:

"This monk, Sire, like a great tiger, like a lion in his mountain cave, has seated himself on the eastern slope of Mount Pandăva."

On hearing the messengers' words the Khattiya hastening in a fine chariot went out to the Pandăva mountain.

The Khattiya (after) driving where a chariot might go, alighted and drawing near on foot saluted him.

After having greeted him with courteous speech and being seated, the king said :

" Young and of tender years art thou, a young man in his first youth, thy colour is as fine as that of a high-born Khattiya.

" To you leading a band of heroes, causing the vanguard to shine, I would give wealth. Accept this then, and tell us your lineage."

" Close upon the slopes of the Himâlayas, O king, there lives a people endowed with wealth and energy, folk of Kosāla.

" By race descendants from the Sun, by birth Sakyas are they.

" From that family have I gone forth, no longer craving sensual pleasures.

" Seeing the danger in sensual pleasures, considering the going forth as safe, I shall go on in the struggle, for in that my mind rejoices."

The Chronicle of Gotama, Twenty-fifth Exalted One

(*FROM THE BUDDHAVAṂSA, XXVI* [1])

Translated by Mrs. Rhys Davids

I am the Buddha of to-day, Gotama of Sakyan growth, striving in my striving I won the uttermost enlightenment.

Asked by Brahmā and calmed I set rolling the Norm-wheel, first understood among eighteen myriads.

Thereafter teaching, I had a concourse past reckoning of men and devas, among whom was the second understanding.

Just here have I admonished my own offspring ; not to be counted are they of the third understanding.

As one is the concourse of my disciples ; there was a coming together of twelve hundred and fifty monks, great seers.

[1] According to commentarial tradition, the whole of this little poem was uttered by Gotama when visiting his home after becoming Buddha.

Shining and flawless from the midst of the company of monks I give everything wished for as a gem giving all that men desire.

To them who are fain for fruit, to them who seek to give up desire for rebirth I have set forth the fourfold truth, in compassion for living things.

There was understanding of the Norm by ten times twenty thousand, an understanding by one of two, in number incalculable.

Made clear and for the multitude, potent and prosperous and in full bloom: here is the holy teaching of me, Sage of the Sakyas.

Some hundreds of monks, canker-free, their passions gone, their hearts at peace and minds intent, all and ever ward me round.

They now who at this time put off man's estate, these monks in training, not yet ripe in mind, by wise men revered,

Praising the Ariyan Way a folk ever delighting in the Norm, men self-possessed, wayfarers through the worlds, they will awaken.

My city is called Kapilavatthu, my father prince Suddhôdana, my mother who bore me the lady Māyā.

For nine and twenty years I dwelt at home, in three peerless mansions, Rāma, Surāma, Subhata,

Adorned by forty thousand women, Bhaddakacchā the woman, Rāhula the son.

When by chariot and horse I went out and saw the four signs, I for six years fared a faring of painful striving.

The Wheel by me set rolling at Benares in the Isipatăna, I Gotama the Buddha am the refuge of all living things.

Kolĭta and Upatissa the two monks are my chief disciples, Ānanda is my attendant ever near me.[1]

Khemā and Uppalavannā are my chief women disciples, Chitta and Hatthâlavaka are my chief attendant laymen.

Nanda's mother and Uttarā are my chief attendant laywomen. At the root of the aspen tree I won uttermost enlightenment.

[1] Commentarial tradition assigns this post to Ānanda during the last twenty-five years of Gotama's life.

Glory of a fathom long reaching to sixteen cubits ever is mine. A short century is my life that now goes on.

So long abiding I make many folk to cross over, fixing the torch of the Norm for them that are to come.

I, no long time with my disciple band, shall here go out utterly as a fire when fuel is destroyed.

Both these incomparable ardours and these ten powers and this body of many virtues, structure of two and thirty features,

Casting a splendour unique six-rayed like the sun, all will wholly fade away—are not all things empty.

PART III

FIRST EVENTS AFTER THE ENLIGHTENMENT

First Events after the Enlightenment

FROM THE MAHĀVAGGA OF THE VINAYA TEXTS

(Adapted from Rhys Davids's and Oldenberg's translation, S.B.E.)

I

The Buddha Enjoys the Bliss of Emancipation Under the Bodhi-tree he Meditates on the Chain of Causation

At that time the Blessed Buddha dwelt at Uruvelā, on the bank of the River Neranjarā, at the foot of the Bodhi-tree just after he had become enlightened. And the Blessed Buddha sat cross-legged at the foot of the Bodhi-tree during seven days, enjoying the bliss of emancipation.

Then the Blessed One (on the seventh night) during the first watch of the night fixed his mind upon how things come to be (that is upon the " causal chain ") in direct and in reverse order :—

Because of ignorance, synergies (or activities).
Because of synergies, consciousness.
Because of consciousness, mind and body.
Because of mind and body, the sixfold provinces (of the senses).
Because of the sixfold provinces, contact.
Because of contact, feeling.
Because of feeling, craving.
Because of craving, grasping.
Because of grasping, becoming.
Because of becoming, birth.
Because of birth, decay, and death, sorrow, lamentation, ill, grief, and despair.

Such is the coming to pass of this entire body of ill. Again, from the ceasing of ignorance, which consists in the complete absence of lust, synergies cease :

From the ceasing of synergies, consciousness ceases.
From the ceasing of consciousness, mind and body cease.
From the ceasing of mind and body, the sixfold provinces cease.
From the ceasing of the sixfold provinces, contact ceases.

E

From the ceasing of contact, feeling ceases.
From the ceasing of feeling, craving ceases.
From the ceasing of craving, grasping ceases.
From the ceasing of grasping, becoming ceases.
From the ceasing of becoming, birth, decay and death, sorrow, lamentation, ill, grief, and despair cease. Such is the cessation of this entire body of ill.

Knowing this the Blessed One then on that occasion pronounced this solemn utterance: "Verily when things become manifest to the ardent, meditating brahman then all doubts fade away, since he understands thing-with-cause."

Then the Blessed One during the middle watch of the night, again fixed his mind upon, how things come to be (i.e. "the causal chain") in direct and reverse order: (as above) . . . Such is the cessation of this entire body of ill.

Knowing this the Blessed One then on that occasion pronounced this solemn utterance: "Verily when things become manifest to the ardent, meditating brahman, then all his doubts fade away, since he has understood the cessation of causes."

Then the Blessed One during the third watch of the night (again) fixed his mind upon the "Causal chain", in direct and in reverse order: (as above).

Knowing this the Blessed One then on that occasion pronounced this solemn utterance: "Verily when things become manifest to the ardent, meditating brahman, he stands dispelling the hosts of Mara, like the sun that illuminates the sky."

Here ends the account of what passed under the Bodhi-tree.

II

Under the Ajapāla-tree

Then the Blessed One, at the end of those seven days, arase from the state of meditation, and went from the foot of the Bodhi-tree to the Ajapāla banyan-tree (banyan tree of the goat-herds). And when he had reached it, he sat cross-legged at the foot of the Ajapāla banyan-tree for seven days, enjoying the bliss of emancipation.

Now a certain brahman, who was of a haughty disposition, went to the place where the Blessed One was; having approached him, he exchanged greetings with the Blessed One; having exchanged with him greetings and complaisant words, he stationed himself near him; then standing near him, that brahman thus spoke to the Blessed One: "By what, Gotama, does one become a brahman, and what are the characteristics that make a man a brahman?"

And the Blessed One, having heard that, on this occasion pronounced this solemn utterance: "That brahman, who has pushed out[1] evil, who is not haughty, not impure, self-restrained, who is a master of knowledge, who has led the holy life, that brahman may rightly speak the holy word, he who is puffed up about nothing in the world."

Here ends the account of what passed under the Ajapāla-tree.

III

Under the Muchalinda-tree

Then the Blessed One at the end of those seven days, arose from that state of meditation, and went from the foot of the Ajapāla banyan-tree to the Muchalinda-tree. And when he had reached it, he sat cross-legged at the foot of the Muchalinda-tree uninterruptedly during seven days, enjoying the bliss of emancipation.

At that time a great cloud appeared out of season, rainy weather which lasted seven days, cold weather, storms and darkness. And the Naga (or Serpent) king Muchalinda came out from his abode, and seven times encircled the body of the Blessed One, with his windings, and kept extending his large hood over the Blessed One's head, thinking to himself: "May no cold (come to) the Blessed One; May no heat (come to) the Blessed One; May no touch

[1] The usual play on the words *brāh*mano, *bāh*-ita.

of gadflies and gnats, storms and sunheat and reptiles (come to) the Blessed One."

And at the end of those seven days, when the Naga king Muchalinda saw the open, cloudless sky, he loosened his windings from the body of the Blessed One, made his own appearance disappear, created the appearance of a youth, and stationed himself in front of the Blessed One, raising his clasped hands, and paying reverence to the Blessed One.

And the Blessed One perceiving that, on this occasion, pronounced this solemn utterance: "Happy the solitude of him who is content, who has heard the Truth, who sees. Happy is non-malice in this world, (self) restraint toward all beings that have life. Happy is passionlessness in this world, the getting beyond all sense-desires. The suppression of that 'I am' conceit, this truly is the highest happiness."

Here ends the account of what passed under the Muchalinda-tree.

IV

Under the Rājâyatana-tree

Then the Blessed One, at the end of those seven days, arose from the state of meditation, and went from the foot of the Muchalinda-tree to the Rājâyatana (tree); when he had reached it, he sat cross-legged at the foot of the Rājâyatana-tree during seven days, enjoying the bliss of emancipation.

At that time Tapussa and Bhallika, two merchants, came travelling on the road from Ukkala (Orissa) to that place. Then a deva who had been (in a previous life) a blood-relation of the merchants Tapussa and Bhallika, thus spoke to the merchants Tapussa and Bhallika: "Here, my noble friends, at the foot of the Rājâyatana-tree, is staying the Blessed One, who has just become a Buddha. Go and show your reverence to him, the Blessed One, by (offering) ricecake and honeycomb. Long will this be to you for a good and for a blessing."

And the merchants took the rice cake and honeycomb,

and went to the place where the Blessed One was; having approached him and respectfully saluted the Blessed One, they placed themselves near him; standing there, the merchants thus addressed the Blessed One: "May, Lord, the Blessed One accept from us rice cake and honeycomb, that this may long be to us for a good and for a blessing."

Then the Blessed One thought: "The Tathāgatas do not accept (food) with their hands. Now with what shall I accept the rice cake and the honeycomb?" Then the four Mahārāja gods, understanding by the power of their minds the reflection, which had arisen in the mind of the Blessed One, offered to the Blessed One from the four quarters (of the horizon) four bowls made of stone (saying): "May, Lord, the Blessed One accept herewith the rice cake and honeycomb." The Blessed One accepted those new stone bowls; and therein he received the rice cake and honeycomb, and these, when he had received, he ate.

And Tapussa and Bhallika, the merchants, when they saw that the Blessed One had cleansed his bowl and his hands, bowed down in reverence at the feet of the Blessed One and thus addressed the Blessed One: "We take our refuge, lord, in the Blessed One and in the Dhamma; may the Blessed One receive us as disciples who from this day forth while our life lasts, have taken their refuge (in him)."

These were the first in the world to become lay disciples of the Two Words.[1]

Here ends the account of what passed under the Rājâyatana-tree.

V

Under the Ajapāla Banyan-tree

Then the Blessed One, at the end of those seven days, arose from that state of meditation, and went from the foot of the Rajâyatana-tree to the Ajapāla banyan-tree. And when he had reached it the Blessed One stayed there at the foot of the Ajapāla banyan-tree.

[1] Buddha, Dhamma, not yet Sangha.

Then in the mind of the Blessed One, who was alone, and had retired into solitude, the following thought arose: "I have penetrated this dhamma which is profound, difficult to perceive and to understand, which brings quietude of heart, which is exalted, which is unattainable by reasoning, is abstruse, intelligible only to the wise. This people on the other hand, is given to habit, intent upon habit, delighting in habit. To these people therefore hard to see is this matter, to wit, that this is caused by that, how things come to be; most hard also to see is this matter, to wit, the tranquillization of all synergies, the renouncing of all the grounds (of re-birth) the destruction of craving, the absence of passion, ceasing, Nibbana."

Now if I teach the dhamma, and other men are not able to understand my preaching there would result but weariness and annoyance for me.

And then the following stanzas, unheard before, occurred to the Blessed One: "With great pains have I acquired it. Enough of making known! This doctrine will not be easy to understand for beings that are oppressed by lust and hatred. Steeped in lust, shrouded in thick darkness, they will not see what goes against the stream, abstruse, deep, difficult to perceive, and subtle."

When the Blessed One had pondered over this matter, his mind became inclined to remain in quietude, and not to preach the dhamma.

Then Brahmā Sahampāti, understanding by the power of his mind the reflection which had arisen in the mind of the Blessed One, thought: "Alas! The world perishes. Alas! the world is destroyed if the mind of the Tathāgata, of the holy, of the fully ever Enlightened One inclines itself to remain in quietude and not to preach the dhamma."

Then Brahmā Sahampati disappeared from the Brahmā world, and appeared before the Blessed One, (as quickly) as a strong man might stretch his bent arm out, or draw back his outstretched arm.

And Brahmā Sahampati adjusted his upper robe so as to cover one shoulder, and putting his right knee on the ground, raised his joined hands towards the Blessed One, and said to the Blessed One : " Lord, may the Blessed One preach the dhamma ! May the Perfect One preach the dhamma ! There are beings whose mental eyes are darkened by scarcely any dust ; but if they do not hear the dhamma, they cannot attain salvation. There will be they who understand the dhamma."

Thus spoke Brahmā Sahampati ; and when he had thus spoken, he further said : " The dhamma hitherto manifested in the country of Magadha had been impure, thought out by contaminated men. But do thou now open the door of the Immortal ; let them hear the dhamma of the Spotless One."

" As a man standing on a rock, on a mountain's top, might overlook the people all around, thus Wise One, ascending to the highest abode of dhamma look down, all-seeing One, upon the people lost in suffering, overcome by birth and decay, thou who hast freed thyself from suffering."

" Arise, hero, victorious one ! Wander through the world, leader of the caravan, who thyself art free from debt. May the Blessed One preach the dhamma ! There will be they who will understand."

When he had thus spoken the Blessed One said to Brahmā Sahampati : " The following thought, Brahmā, has occurred to me : I have penetrated this dhamma which is profound, difficult to perceive and to understand, which brings quietude of heart, which is exalted, which is unattainable by reasoning, is abstruse, intelligible (only) to the wise. This people, on the other hand, is devoted to things settled, intent upon things settled, delighting in things settled. To these people therefore hard to see is this matter, i.e., that this is caused by that, to see how things come to be ; most hard also to see is this matter, i.e., the tranquillization of all synergies, the renouncing of all the grounds (of re-birth), the destruction of craving, the absence of passion, ceasing, Nibbana. Now if I proclaim the dhamma, and other men are not able to understand my preaching there would result but weariness and annoyance for me. And also, Brahmā, the following strange stanzas have come to my mind, unheard of before : 'With great pains have I acquired it,

Enough of making known! This doctrine will not be easy to understand for beings that are lost in lust and hatred. Steeped in lust, shrouded in thick darkness, they will not see what goes against the stream, abstruse, deep, difficult to perceive, and subtle.' I have pondered over this matter, Brahmā, and my mind has become inclined to remain in quietude and not to preach my dhamma."

. . . (A second and third time Brahmā Sahampati made the same supplication; twice the Blessed One made the same reply.

Then the Blessed One, when he had heard Brahmā's (third) solicitation, looked full of compassion towards sentient beings over the world with the Buddha-eye. And the Blessed One, looking over the world with the Buddha-eye saw beings whose mental eyes were darkened by scarcely any dust, and beings whose eyes were covered by much dust, beings sharp of sense and blunt of sense, of good disposition and of bad disposition, easy to instruct and difficult to instruct, some of them seeing the dangers of future life and of sin.

As in a pond of blue red or white lotuses, some born in the water, grown up in the water, do not emerge over the water, but thrive hidden under the water; and other lotuses, born in the water, grown up under the water, reach to the surface of the water; and other lotuses, born in the water, grown up in the water, stand emerging out of the water, and the water does not touch them,

Thus the Blessed One, looking over the world with the eye of a Buddha saw beings whose mental eyes were different, . . . and when he had thus seen them, he addressed Brahmā Sahampati in the following stanza: "Wide opened is the door of the undying to all who are hearers; let them send forth faith to meet it. The dhamma sweet and good I spake not to men, Brahmā, ware of the weary task."

Then Brahmā Sahampati understood: "The Blessed One grants my request that he should preach the dhamma." And he bowed down before the Blessed One, and passed round him with his right side towards him; and then he straightway disappeared.

Here ends the story of Brahmā's request.[1]

VI

The First Sermon and First Disciples—The Attainment of Arahantship

Now the Blessed One thought: "To whom shall I preach the dhamma first? Who will understand this dhamma readily?"

And the Blessed One thought: "There is Āḷāra Kālāma; he is clever, wise, and learned; long since has the eye of his mind been darkened by scarcely any dust. What if I were to preach the dhamma first to Āḷāra Kālāma? He will readily understand this dhamma."

Then an invisible deva said to the Blessed One: "Āḷāra Kālāma died, lord, seven days ago." And knowledge sprang up in the Blessed One's mind that Āḷāra Kālāma had died seven days ago. And the Blessed One thought: "Highly noble was Āḷāra Kālāma. If he had heard my dhamma, he would readily have understood it."

Then the Blessed One thought: "To whom shall I preach the dhamma first? Who will understand this dhamma readily?" And the Blessed One thought: "There is Uddaka Rāmaputta; he is clever, wise, and learned; long since has the eye of his mind been darkened by scarcely

[1] This account of Brahmā Sahampati's request and the following account up to the Buddha's *first sermon* is also given in Sutta 26 of the Majjhima Nikāya. Physiologists tell us that we live because we wish to live: in the above account we have a profound change in the Buddha's life. His search had been realized: from now on the only basis of his life is compassion.

any dust. What if I were to preach the dhamma first to Uddaka Rāmaputta? He will easily understand this dhamma."

Then an invisible deva said to the Blessed One: "Uddaka Rāmaputta died, Lord, yesterday evening." And knowledge arose in the Blessed One's mind that Uddaka Rāmaputta had died the previous evening. And the Blessed One thought: "Highly noble was Uddaka Rāmaputta. If he had heard my doctrine, he would readily have understood it."

Then the Blessed One thought: "To whom shall I preach the dhamma first? Who will understand this dhamma readily?" And the Blessed One thought: "The five monks have done many services to me; they attended on me during the time of my ascetic discipline. What if I were to preach the dhamma first to the five monks?"

Now the Blessed One thought: "Where do the five monks dwell now?" And the Blessed One saw by the power of his divine, clear vision, surpassing that of men, that the five monks were living at Benares, in the deer-park Isipatana. And the Blessed One, after having remained at Uruvelā as long as he thought fit, went forth to Benares.

Now Upaka, a man belonging to the Ājīvaka sect (i.e., the sect of naked ascetics), saw the Blessed One travelling on the road, between Gaya and the Bodhi-tree; and when he saw him, he said to the Blessed One: "Your countenance, friend, is serene, your complexion is pure and bright. In whose name, friend, have you retired from the world? Who is your teacher? Whose dhamma do you profess?"

When Upaka the Ājīvaka had spoken thus, the Blessed One addressed him in the following stanzas: "I have overcome all foes; I am all-wise; I am free from stains in all things; I have left everything; and have obtained emancipation of craving. Having myself gained knowledge, whom should I call my master? I have no teacher; no one is equal to me; in the world of men and of devas no being is like me. I am the holy one in this world, I am the highest teacher, I alone am the perfectly ever enlightened one (sammāsambuddho); I have gained coolness and have obtained Nibbana. To set in motion the wheel of the dhamma, I go to the city of the Kāsis (Benares); I will beat the drum of the Immortal in the darkness of this world."

(Upaka replied): "You profess then, friend, you are worthy to be Victor everlasting?"

(Buddha said): "Like me are all Victorious Ones who have reached extinction of the cankers; I have overcome sinful states; therefore, Upaka, am I the Victorious One."

When he had spoken thus, Upaka the Ājīvaka replied: "It may be so, friend"; shook his head, took another road, and went away.

And the Blessed One, wandering from place to place, came to Benares, to the deer park Isipatana, to the place where the five monks were. And the five monks saw the Blessed One coming from afar; when they saw him, they took counsel with each other, saying: "Friends, there comes the samana Gotama, a man of full habit, who has wavered in his exertions, and who has turned away to luxury. Let us not salute him, nor rise from our seats when he approaches, nor take his bowl and his robe from his hands. But let us put there a seat; if he likes, let him sit down."

But when the Blessed One gradually approached near unto those five monks, the five monks kept not their agreement. They went forth to meet the Blessed One; one took his bowl and his robe, another prepared a seat, a third one brought water for the washing of the feet, a foot-stool, and a towel. Then the Blessed One sat down on the seat they had prepared; and when he was seated, the Blessed One washed his feet: Now they addressed the Blessed One by his name, and with the appellation "Friend".[1]

When they spoke to him thus, the Blessed One said to the five monks: "Do not address, monks, the Tathāgata by his name, and with the appellation 'Friend'. The Tathāgata, monks, is the holy, perfectly ever Enlightened One. Give ear, O monks. The immortal (Amata) has been won by me: I will teach you; to you I preach the dhamma. Do you walk in the way I show you, and you

[1] *Āvuso*, the word used by one religieux to another as an equal or inferior.

will live ere long, even in this life, having fully known yourselves, having seen face to face, that incomparable goal of the holy life, for the sake of which clansmen rightly give up the world and go forth into the houseless state."

When he had spoken thus, the five monks said to the Blessed One: "By those observances, friend Gotama, by those practices, by those austerities, you have not won to power surpassing that of men, nor to higher knowledge and vision. How will you now, living with full habit, having given up your exertions, having turned to luxury, be able to obtain power surpassing that of men, and the higher knowledge and vision?"

When they had spoken thus, the Blessed One said to the five monks: "The Tathāgata, O monks, does not live with full habit, he has not given up exertion, he has not turned to luxury. The Tathāgata, monks, is the holy, most fully Enlightened One. Give ear, O monks, the immortal has been won; I will teach you; to you I will preach the dhamma. Do you walk in the way I show you; you will live ere long, even in this life, having fully known yourselves, having seen face to face that incomparable goal of the holy life, for the sake of which clansmen rightly give up the world and go forth into the houseless state."

. . . (*The five monks repeat twice the same remonstrances, to which the Blessed One makes the same replies.*)

When they had spoken thus, the Blessed One said to the five monks: "Do you admit, monks, that I have never spoken to you in this way before this day?"

"You have never spoken so, lord."

"The Tathāgata, monks, is the holy, fully Enlightened One. Give ear, O monks . . . (as above).

And the Blessed One was able to convince the five monks; and the five monks again listened willingly to the Blessed One; they gave ear, and fixed their mind on the knowledge (imparted to them).

The Buddha's First Sermon, known as the Foundation of the Kingdom of Righteousness or the Setting in Motion of the Wheel of the Dhamma.

The Mahāvagga continues:

And the Blessed One thus addressed the five monks: "There are two extremes, monks, which he who has given up the world, ought to avoid.

What are these two extremes? A life given to pleasures, devoted to pleasures and lusts; this is degrading, sensual, vulgar, ignoble, and profitless.

And a life given to mortifications; this is painful, ignoble, and profitless.

By avoiding these two extremes, monks, the Tathāgata has gained the knowledge of the Middle Path which leads to insight, which leads to wisdom, which conduces to calm, to knowledge, to Sambodhi (Supreme Enlightenment), to Nibbana.

Which, monks, is this Middle Path the knowledge of which the Tathāgata has gained, which leads to insight, which leads to wisdom, which conduces to calm, to knowledge, to Sambodhi, to Nibbana?

It is the Noble Eightfold Path, namely: right views, right intent, right speech, right conduct, right means of livelihood, right endeavour, right mindfulness, right meditation.

This, monks, is the Middle Path the knowledge of which the Tathāgata has gained, which leads to insight, which leads to wisdom, which conduces to calm, to knowledge, to perfect enlightenment, to Nibbana.

This, monks, is the Noble Truth of Suffering[1]; birth is suffering; decay is suffering; illness is suffering; death is suffering; presence of objects we hate, is suffering; separation from objects we love, is suffering; not to obtain what we desire, is suffering.

In brief, the five aggregates which spring from grasping, they are painful.

This, monks, is the Noble Truth concerning the Origin of Suffering; verily it originates in that craving, which causes the renewal of becomings, is accompanied by sensual

[1] The Pali word is *dukkha* which in some places we have more accurately translated as *Ill.*—Compiler.

delight, and seeks satisfaction now here, now there; that is to say, craving for pleasures, craving for becoming, craving for not becoming.

This, monks, is the Noble Truth concerning the Cessation of Suffering. Verily, it is passionlessness, cessation without remainder of this very craving; the laying aside of, the giving up, the being free from, the harbouring no longer of, this craving.

This, monks, is the Noble Truth concerning the Path which leads to the Cessation of Suffering. Verily, it is this Noble Eightfold Path, that is to say, right views, right intent, right speech, right conduct, right means of livelihood, right endeavour, right mindfulness and right meditation.

This is the Noble Truth concerning Suffering; thus, monks, in things which formerly had not been heard of have I obtained insight, knowledge, understanding, wisdom, intuition. This Noble Truth concerning Suffering must be understood; thus, monks, in things which formerly had not been heard of have I obtained insight, knowledge, understanding, wisdom, and intuition. This Noble Truth concerning Suffering I have understood. Thus, monks, in things which formerly had not been heard of have I obtained insight, knowledge, understanding, wisdom, and intuition.

This is the Noble Truth concerning the Origin of Suffering; thus, monks, in things which had formerly not been heard of have I obtained insight, knowledge, understanding wisdom, intuition. This Noble Truth concerning the Cause of Suffering must be abandoned . . . has been abandoned by me. Thus, monks, in things which formerly had not been heard of have I obtained knowledge, understanding, wisdom, and intuition.

This is the Noble Truth concerning the Cessation of Suffering, thus, monks, in things which formerly had not been heard of, have I obtained insight, knowledge, understanding, wisdom, intuition.

This Noble Truth concerning the Cessation of Suffering must be seen face to face . . . has been seen by me face to face, thus, monks, in things which formerly had not been heard of, have I obtained insight, knowledge, understanding, wisdom, intuition.

This is the Noble Truth concerning the Path which leads to the cessation of suffering, thus, monks, in things which formerly had not been heard of, have I obtained insight, knowledge, understanding, wisdom, intuition. This Noble Truth concerning the Path which leads to the cessation of suffering must be realized . . . has been realized by me, thus, monks, in things which formerly had not been heard of, have I obtained insight, knowledge, understanding, wisdom, intuition.

As long, monks, as I did not possess with perfect purity this true knowledge and insight into these four Noble Truths, with its three modifications and its twelve constituent parts, so long, monks, I knew that I had not yet obtained the highest absolute enlightenment in the world of men and gods, in Māra's and in Brahmā's world, among all beings, samanas, and brahmans, gods and men.

But since I possessed, monks, with perfect purity this true knowledge and insight into these four Noble Truths, with its three modifications and its twelve constituent parts, then I knew, monks, that I had obtained the highest, universal enlightenment in the world of men and gods. . . . . (etc., as above.)

And this knowledge and insight arose in my mind: 'The emancipation of my mind cannot be shaken; this is my last birth; now shall I not be born again.'"

Thus the Blessed One spoke. The five monks were delighted, and they rejoiced at the words of the Blessed One. And when this exposition was propounded, the venerable Kondañña obtained the pure and spotless Dhamma-eye (that is to say, the following knowledge): "Whatsoever is an arising thing, all that is a ceasing thing."

And as the Blessed One had set going the wheel of the dhamma, the earth-inhabiting devas shouted: "Truly the Blessed One has set going at Benares, in the deer park Isipatana, the wheel of the dhamma, which may be opposed neither by a samanā, nor by a brahman, neither by a deva, nor by Māra, nor by Brahmā, nor by any being in the world."

Hearing the shout of the earth-inhabiting devas, the four firmament-devas shouted . . . (etc., as above). Hearing their shout the Tāvatiṃsa devas, . . . the Yāma devas, . . . the Tusita devas, . . . the Nimmānarati devas, . . . the Paranimmitavasavatti devas, . . . the Brahmā-world devas shouted : "Truly the Blessed One has set going at Benares, in the deer park Isipatana, the wheel of the dhamma, which may be opposed neither by a samanā nor by a brahman, neither by a deva, nor by Māra, nor by Brahmā, nor by any being in the world."

Thus in that moment, in that instant, in that second the shout reached the Brahmā world ; and this whole system of ten thousand worlds quaked, was shaken, and trembled ; and an infinite, mighty light was seen through the world, which surpassed the light that can be produced by the divine power of the devas.

And the Blessed One pronounced this solemn utterance : "Truly Kondañña has perceived it (aññāsi) truly Kondañña has perceived it." Hence the venerable Kondañña received the name Aññātakondañña (Kondañña who has perceived the doctrine).

And the venerable Aññātakondañña, having seen the dhamma, having mastered the dhamma, having understood the dhamma, having penetrated the dhamma, having overcome uncertainty, having dispelled all doubts, having gained full knowledge, dependent on nobody else for knowledge of the doctrine of the Teacher, thus spoke to the Blessed One : "Lord let me become a recluse under the Blessed One, let me receive ordination." "Come, monk," said the Blessed One, "well taught is the dhamma ; lead a holy life for the sake of the complete ending of suffering."

Thus this venerable person received ordination.

And the Blessed One administered to the other monks exhortation and instruction by discourses relating to the dhamma. And the venerable Vappa and the venerable Bhaddiya, when they received from the Blessed One such exhortation and instruction by discourses relating to the dhamma, obtained the pure and spotless dhamma-eye (that is to say, the following knowledge): "Whatsoever is a beginning thing, all that is an ending thing."

And having seen the dhamma, having mastered the dhamma, having understood the dhamma, having penetrated the dhamma, having overcome uncertainty, having dispelled all doubts, having won confidence, dependent on nobody else for knowledge of the religion of the teacher, they thus spoke to the Blessed One: "Lord, let us become a recluse under the Blessed One and receive ordination."

"Come, monks," said the Blessed One, "well taught is the dhamma, lead a holy life for the sake of the complete ending of Ill." Thus these venerable persons received ordination.

And the Blessed One, living on what the monks brought him, administered to the other monks exhortation and instruction by discourses relating to the dhamma; in this way the six persons lived on what the three monks brought home from their alms.

And the venerable Mahānāma and the venerable Assaji, when they received from the Blessed One such exhortation and instruction by discourses relating to the dhamma, obtained the pure and spotless dhamma-eye (that is to say, the following knowledge). "Whatsoever is a beginning thing all that is an ending thing."

And having seen the dhamma, having mastered the dhamma, having understood the dhamma, having penetrated the dhamma, having overcome uncertainty, having dispelled all doubts, having gained full knowledge, dependent on nobody else for knowledge of the doctrine of the Teacher, they thus spoke to the Blessed One: "Lord, let us become a recluse under the Blessed One and receive ordination."

"Come, monks," said the Blessed One, "well taught is the dhamma, lead a holy life for the sake of the complete ending of Ill." Thus these venerable persons received ordination.

Anattalakkhaṇa Sutta or Discourse on Not Having Signs of the Self.

And the Blessed One spoke thus to the five Bhikkhus: "The body (rūpa), monks, is not the self. If the body, monks, were the self, the body would not be subject to disease, and we should be able to say: 'Let my body be such and such a one, let my body not be such and such a one.' But since the body, monks, is not the self, therefore the body is subject to disease, and we are not able to say, 'let my body be such and such a one, let my body not be such and such a one.' "

Sensation (vedanā), monks, is not the self . . . (as above); perception (saññā) is not the self . . . synergies (sankhāra's) are not the self . . . consciousness (viññāṇa) is not the self . . . (as above).

"Now what do you think, monks, is the body permanent or perishable?"

"It is perishable, lord."

"And that which is perishable, does that cause pain or joy?"

"It causes pain, lord."

"And that which is perishable, painful, subject to change, is it possible to regard that in this way? This is mine, this am I, this is myself?"

"That is impossible, lord."

(Here follows the same dialogue regarding sensation, perception, synergies, and consciousness) . . .

"Therefore, monks, whatever body has been, will be, and is now, belonging or not belonging to sentient beings, gross or subtle, inferior or superior, distant or near, all that body is not mine, is not me, is not my self; thus it should be considered by right knowledge according to the truth.

(*The same is stated of sensation, perception, synergies and consciousness.*)

Considering this, monks, the wise and noble disciple turns

away from[1] the body, turns away from sensation, turns away from perception, turns away from the synergies, turns away from body and mind.

Turning away he loses passion, losing passion he is liberated, in being liberated the knowledge comes to him: 'I am liberated,' and he knows rebirth is exhausted, the holy life is completed, duty is fulfilled; there is no more living in these conditions."

Thus the Blessed One spoke. The five monks were delighted, and rejoiced at the words of the Blessed One. And when this exposition had been propounded, the minds of the five monks became free from attachment to the world, and were released from the cankers.

At that time there were six Arahants (persons who had reached absolute holiness) in the world.

(End of the first portion for recitation)

VII

The Story of Yasa

At that time there was in Benares a youth of good family, Yasa by name, the son of a seṭṭhi (leading burgess) and delicately nurtured. He had three palaces, one for winter, one for summer, one for the rainy season. In the palace for the rainy season he lived during the four months (of that season) surrounded with musicians among whom no man was, and he did not descend from that palace (all that time). Now one day Yasa, the clansman, who

[1] I have ventured to use "turns away from" for nibbindati: although I find Rhys Davids and Oldenberg use: "becomes weary," Warren translates: "conceives an aversion for," the Pali Text's Society's "Pali-English Dictionary" sanctions: "turns away from." Since the Buddhist seeks to gain a state of equanimity above aversion and weariness, I have chosen a translation which seems to me more consistent. Perhaps: "becomes free from," or "finds a way out from." would have been permissible. Nibbindati is derived from nir + vindati. Nir means out, away. Vindati means to find, and to know.

(See the Pali Text Society's Pali-English Dictionary or Andersen's Pali Glossary.)

was endowed with, and possessed of the five pleasures of sense, while he was attended (by those female musicians), fell asleep, sooner than usual; and after him his attendants also fell asleep. Now an oil lamp was burning through the whole night.

And Yasa, the clansman, awoke sooner than usual; and he saw his attendants sleeping; one had her lute leaning against her arm-pit; one had her tabor leaning against her neck; one had her drum leaning against her arm-pit; one had dishevelled hair; one had saliva flowing from her mouth; and they were muttering in their sleep. One would think it was a cemetery one had fallen into. When he saw that, the evils manifested themselves to him; his mind became weary. And Yasa gave utterance to this solemn exclamation "Alas, what distress! alas, what danger!"

And Yasa, the clansman, put on his gilt slippers, and went to the gate of his house. Non-human beings opened the gate, in order that no being might prevent Yasa leaving the world, and going forth into the houseless state. And Yasa went to the gate of the city. Non-human beings opened the gate, in order that no being might prevent Yasa leaving the world, and going forth into the houseless state. And Yasa went to the deer park Isipatana.

At that time the Blessed One, having arisen in the night, at dawn was walking up and down in the open air. And the Blessed One saw Yasa, the clansman, coming from afar. And when he saw him, he left the place where he was walking, and sat down on a seat laid out. And Yasa gave utterance near the Blessed One to that solemn exclamation: "Alas, what distress! alas, what danger!" And the Blessed One said to Yasa, "Here is no distress, Yasa, here is no danger. Come here, Yasa, sit down; I will teach you the dhamma."

And Yasa, the clansman, when he heard that there was no distress and that there was no danger, became glad and joyful; and he put off his gilt slippers,[1] and went to the place where the Blessed One was; having approached

[1] The Tibetan version makes him wade through a stream. Rockhill's *Life of the Buddha*, p. 38.

him and having respectfully saluted the Blessed One, he sat down near him. When Yasa was sitting near him, the Blessed One, preached to him in due course: that is to say; he delivered the discourse on giving, the discourse on morals, the discourse on heaven, about the evils, the vanity, and the sinfulness of desires, and about the blessings of the abandonment of desire.

When the Blessed One perceived that the mind of Yasa was prepared, impressible, free from obstacles (to understanding the dhamma), elated, and believing, then he preached what is the original doctrine of the Buddhas, namely Ill, the Cause of Ill, the Cessation of Ill, the Path. Just as a clean cloth free from black specks properly takes the dye, thus in Yasa, even while sitting there, arose the pure and flawless dhamma-eye (that is the knowledge); "Whatsoever is an arising thing, that is a ceasing thing."

Now the mother of Yasa having gone up to his palace, and not seeing Yasa, went to the seṭṭhi, the householder, her husband, and having approached him, she said to the seṭṭhi, the householder: "Your son Yasa, householder, has disappeared." Then the seṭṭhi, the householder, sent messengers on horseback to the four quarters of the horizon; and he went himself to the deer park Isipatana. Then the seṭṭhi, the householder, saw on the ground the marks of the gilt slippers; and when he saw them, he followed them up.

And the Blessed One saw the seṭṭhi, the householder, coming from afar. On seeing him, he thought: "What if I were to effect such an exercise of miraculous power that the seṭṭhi, the householder, sitting here, should not see Yasa who is sitting here also." And the Blessed One effected such an exercise of his miraculous power.

And the seṭṭhi, the householder, went to the place where the Blessed One was; having approached him, he said to the Blessed One: "Pray, lord, has the Blessed One seen Yasa, the clansman?"

"Well, householder, sit down. Perhaps, sitting here, you may see Yasa, the clansman, sitting here also."

And the seṭṭhi, the householder, thinking: "Indeed, sitting here I shall see Yasa sitting here also," became glad and joyful, and having respectfully saluted the Blessed One, he sat down near him.

When the seṭṭhi, the householder, was sitting near him, the Blessed One preached to him in due course; that is to say; he delivered the discourse on giving, the discourse on morals, the discourse on heaven, about the evils, the vanity and the sinfulness of desires and about the blessing of the abandonment of desire.

And the seṭṭhi, the householder, having seen the dhamma, having mastered the dhamma, having penetrated the dhamma, having overcome uncertainty, having dispelled all doubts, having gained full knowledge, dependent on nobody else for the knowledge of the doctrine of the Teacher, said to the Blessed One: "Glorious, lord, glorious, lord! Just as if one should set up lord what had been overturned, or should reveal what had been hidden, or should point out the way to one who had lost his way, or should bring a lamp into the darkness, in order that those who had eyes might see visible things, thus has the Blessed One preached the dhamma in many ways. I take my refuge, lord, in the Blessed One, and in the Dhamma, and in the Fraternity of monks; may the Blessed One receive me from this day forth while my life lasts as a lay-disciple who has taken refuge."

This was the first person in the world who became a lay-disciple by the threefold word (Buddha, Dhamma, Sangha).

And Yasa the clansman while instruction was administered (by the Buddha) to his father, contemplated the stage of knowledge which he had seen with his mind and understood; and his mind became free from attachment to the world, and was released from the cankers.

Then the Blessed One thought: "Yasa the clansman, while instruction was administered to his father has contemplated the stage of knowledge which he had seen with his mind and understood; and his mind has become free from attachment to the world, and has become released from the cankers. It is impossible that Yasa the clansman should return to the world and enjoy pleasures, as he did before, when he lived in his house. What if I were now to put an end to that exertion of my miraculous power." And the Blessed One put an end to that exertion of his miraculous power.

Then the seṭṭhi, the householder, saw Yasa sitting there. On seeing him he said to Yasa: "My son Yasa, your mother is mourning and grieving; give life to your mother."

Then Yasa looked at the Blessed One. And the Blessed One said to the seṭṭhi, the householder: "What do you think then, householder? That Yasa has won only an imperfect degree of knowledge and insight into the dhamma as you have yourself? Or rather that he was contemplating the stage of knowledge which he had seen with his mind and understood; and that his mind has thus become free from attachment to the world, and has become released from the cankers? Now would it then be possible, householder, that Yasa should return to the world and enjoy pleasures as he did before, when he lived in his house?"

"Not so lord."

"Yasa, householder, had won, like yourself, an imperfect degree of knowledge and insight into the dhamma. But when he was contemplating the stage of knowledge which he had seen with his mind and understood, his mind became free from attachment to the world, and became released from the cankers. It is impossible, householder, that Yasa should return to the world and enjoy pleasures as he did before, when he lived in his house."

"It is all gain, lord, to Yasa, it is high bliss, lord, for Yasa, that the mind of Yasa has become free from attachment to the world, and has become released from the cankers. Might lord the Blessed One consent to take his meal with me to-day together with Yasa as his attendant?"

The Blessed One expressed his consent by remaining silent. Then the seṭṭhi, the householder, when he understood that the Blessed One had accepted his invitation, rose from his seat, respectfully saluted the Blessed One. and passing round him with his right side towards him, departed thence.

And Yasa, soon after the seṭṭhi, the householder, was gone, said to the Blessed One: "Let me be made under the Master, the Blessed One, a recluse and be ordained."

"Come, Monk," said the Blessed One, "well taught is the dhamma; lead the holy life for the sake of the entire endmaking of Ill."

Thus this venerable person received the upasampadā ordination. At that time there were seven Arahants in the world.

End of the story of Yasa's leaving the world.

VIII

The First Women Lay-disciples

And in the forenoon the Blessed One, having put on his under-robes, took his alms-bowl, and, with his robe on, went with the venerable Yasa as his attendant to the house of the seṭṭhi, the householder. When he arrived there he sat down on a seat laid out for him. Then the mother and the former wife of the venerable Yasa went to the place where was the Blessed One; having approached him and having respectfully saluted the Blessed One, they sat down near him.

Then the Blessed One preached to them in due course; that is to say, he delivered the discourse on giving, . . . (as in chap. 7, 5, 6, down to:); thus there arose in them, while sitting there, the pure and spotless dhamma-eye (that is the knowledge): "Whatsoever is an arising thing all that is a ceasing thing."

And having seen the dhamma, having mastered the dhamma, having understood the dhamma, having penetrated the dhamma, having overcome uncertainty, having dispelled all doubts, having gained full knowledge, dependent on nobody else for the knowledge of the Teacher's doctrine, they thus spoke to the Blessed One: "Glorious, lord, glorious, lord! Just as if one should set up what has been overturned, or should reveal what had been hidden, or should point out the way to one who had lost his way, or should bring a lamp into the darkness, in order that those who had eyes might see visible things, thus has the Blessed One preached the doctrine in many ways. We take our refuge, lord, in the Blessed One, and in the Dhamma, and in the Order of monks; may the Blessed One receive us from this day forth, while our life lasts, as disciples who have taken their refuge in him.

These were the first women in the world who became lay-disciples by the three words (Buddha, Dhamma, Sangha).

And the mother and the father and the former wife of the venerable Yasa with their own hands served and offered excellent food, both hard and soft, to the Blessed One and to the venerable Yasa; and when the Blessed One had finished his meal, and cleansed his bowl and his hands, they sat down near him. Then the Blessed One taught, incited, animated, and gladdened the mother, and father, and the former wife of the venerable Yasa by religious discourse; and then he rose from his seat and went away.

IX

Further Ordinations and Attainment of Arahantship

Now four lay persons, friends of the venerable Yasa, belonging to the seṭṭhi families of Benares, and to the highest after the seṭṭhi families, by name Vimala, Subāhu, Puṇṇaji, and Gavampati heard: "Yasa the clansman has cut off his hair and beard, and has put on yellow robes, and has given up the world, and gone forth into the houseless state." When they had heard that, they thought: "Surely that cannot be a common dhamma and discipline, that cannot be a common renunciation of the world, if Yasa the clansman has cut off his hair and beard, and has put on yellow robes, and has given up the world, and gone forth into the houseless state."

Those four persons went to the place where the venerable Yasa was; having approached him and having respectfully saluted the venerable Yasa they stood by his side. And the venerable Yasa went with his four lay friends to the place where the Blessed One was; having approached him and having respectfully saluted the Blessed One, he sat down near him. Sitting near him, the venerable Yasa said to the Blessed One: "Lord, here are four lay friends of mine, belonging to the seṭṭhi families of Benares and to the highest after the seṭṭhi families; their names are Vimala, Subāhu, Puṇṇaji, and Gavampati. May the Blessed One administer exhortation and instruction to these four persons."

Then the Blessed One preached to them . . . (as above).

And having seen the dhamma . . . (even as with Yasa, they became) dependent on nobody else for the knowledge of the Teacher's doctrine, they thus spoke to the Blessed One: "Lord, let us receive the first and the complete ordinations from the Blessed One."

"Come, monk," said the Blessed One, "well taught is the dhamma; lead a holy life for the sake of the entire endmaking of Ill."

Thus these venerable persons received the upasampadā ordination. And the Blessed One administered to these monks exhortation and instruction by discourse relating to the dhamma. While they received exhortation and instruction from the Blessed One by discourse relating to the dhamma, their minds became free from attachment to the world, and were released from the cankers.

At that time there were eleven Arahants in the world.

Here ends the story of the ordination of the four laymen.

X

Now fifty lay persons, friends of the venerable Yasa, belonging to the highest families in the country and to those next to the highest, heard . . . (as above in chap. 9).

While they received exhortation and instruction from the Blessed One by discourse relating to the dhamma, their minds became free from attachment to the world, and were released from the cankers.

At that time there were sixty-one Arahants in the world.

XI

Sending Forth the First Missionaries, and a Story of Mara

And the Blessed One said to the monks : "I am delivered, monks, from all fetters, human and divine. You, monks, are also delivered from all fetters, human and divine. Go ye now, monks, and wander for the gain of the many, for the welfare of the many, out of compassion for the world, for the good, for the gain, and for the welfare of gods and men. Let not two of you go the same way. Preach, monks, the dhamma which is lovely in the beginning, lovely in the middle, lovely at the end, in the spirit and in the letter ; proclaim a consummate, perfect, and pure life of holiness. There are beings whose mental eyes are covered by scarcely any dust, but if the dhamma is not preached to them, they cannot attain salvation. They will understand the dhamma. And I will go, monks, to Uruvelā, to Senāni-town, in order to preach the dhamma.

And Māra the Wicked One went to the place where the Blessed One was ; having approached him, he addressed the Blessed One in the following stanza : "Thou art bound by all fetters, human and divine. Thou art bound by strong fetters. Thou wilt not be delivered from me, recluse ! "

Buddha replied : "I am delivered from all fetters, human and divine. I am delivered from the strong fetters. Thou art struck down, O Death."

(Māra said) . "The fetter which pervades the air, with which mind is bound, with that fetter I will bind thee. Thou wilt not be delivered from me, O recluse."

(Buddha replied) : "Whatever forms, sounds, odours, tastes, or contacts there are which please the senses, in me desire for them has ceased. Thou art struck down, O Death."

Then Māra the Wicked One understood: "The Blessed One knows me, the Well-farer knows me." And, sad and afflicted, he vanished away.

Here ends the story of Māra.

XII

Ordination by the Threefold Refuge

At that time the monks brought (to Buddha), from different regions and different countries, persons who desired to leave the world and be ordained, thinking: "The Blessed One will confer on them the one and the other ordination." But the monks became tired (from the journey), and those also who desired to obtain the ordination. Now when the Blessed One was alone and had retired into solitude, the following consideration presented itself to his mind: "The monks now bring to me from different regions and different countries persons who desire to obtain ordination, thinking: 'The Blessed One will confer on them the ordination.' Now both the monks become tired, and those also who desire to obtain ordination. What if I were to grant permission to the monks, saying: 'Confer henceforth, monks, in the different regions, and in different countries, both modes of ordination yourselves.'"

And the Blessed One, having left his solitude in the evening, in consequence of that, and on this occasion, after having delivered a religious discourse, thus addressed the monks: "When I was alone, monks, and had retired into solitude, the following consideration presented itself to me:—What if I were to permit . . . (as above).

I grant you, monks, this permission: Confer henceforth in the different regions and in the different countries both modes of ordination yourselves (on those who desire to receive them.) And you ought monks, to confer them in this way: Let him (who desires to receive ordination), first have his hair and beard cut off, let him put on yellow robes, adjust his upper robe so as to cover one shoulder, salute the feet of the monks (with his head), and sit down squatting; then let him raise his joined hands and tell him to say:

'I take my refuge in the Buddha, I take my refuge in the Dhamma, I take my refuge in the Sangha. And for the second time I take (as above . . . Sangha). And for the third time I take my refuge in the Buddha, and for the third time I take my refuge in the Dhamma, and for the third time I take my refuge in the Sangha!'

I prescribe, O monks, that the world be left and ordination given by the three times repeated declaration of taking refuge."

End of the account of ordination by the three-fold declaration of taking refuge.

XIII

THE BUDDHA DECLARES HIS FREEDOM FROM FETTERS

And the Blessed One, after having kept the rains-residence, thus addressed the monks: "By wise contemplation, monks, and by wise right exertion have I attained the highest emanicipation, have I realised the highest emancipation. Attain ye also, monks, the highest emancipation, realise the highest emancipation, by wise contemplation, and by wise right exertion."

And Māra, the Wicked One, went to the place where the Blessed One was; having approached him, he addressed the Blessed One by the following stanza: "Thou art bound by Māra's fetter's, human and divine. Thou art bound by strong fetters. Thou wilt not be delivered from me, recluse!"

(Buddha replied): "I am delivered from Māra's fetters, human and divine. I am delivered from the strong fetters. Thou art struck down, O Death."

Then Māra the Wicked One understood: "The Blessed One knows me, the Wellfarer knows me"; and, sad and afflicted he vanished away.

XIV

Story of the Thirty Rich Young Companions

And the Blessed One, after having dwelt at Benares as long as he thought fit, went forth to Uruvelā. And the Blessed One left the road and went to a certain grove; having gone there, and having entered it, he sat down at the foot of a tree. At that time there was a party of thirty friends, rich young men, who were sporting in that same grove together with their wives. One of them had no wife; for him they had procured a harlot. Now while they did not pay attention, and were indulging in their sports; that harlot took up the articles belonging to them and ran away.

Then those companions, doing service to their friend, went in search of that woman; and roaming about that grove, they saw the Blessed One sitting at the foot of a tree. Seeing him they went to the place where the Blessed One was; having approached him, they said to the Blessed One: "Pray lord, has the Blessed One seen a woman passing by?"

"What have you to do, young men, with the woman?"

"We were sporting, lord, in this grove, thirty friends, rich young men, together with our wives. One of us had no wife; for him we had procured a harlot. Now, lord, while we did not pay attention, and were indulging in our sports, that harlot has taken up the articles belonging to us, and has run away. Therefore, lord, we companions, doing service to our friend, go in search of that woman, and roam about the grove."

"Now what think you, young men? Which would be

the better for you; that you should go in search of a woman, or that you should go in search of yourself?"[1]

"That, lord, would be the better for us, that we should go in search of ourself."

If so, young men, sit down, I will preach to you the dhamma. The rich young companions replied: "Yes, lord," and respectfully saluted the Blessed One, and sat down near him.

Then the Blessed One preached to them . . . (as above in chap. 8, or 9).

And having seen the dhamma . . . (as above in chap. 9 down to:) Thus these venerable persons received ordination.

Here ends the story of the thirty rich young companions.
End of the second portion for recitation.

XV

Concerning Magical Powers and the Jaṭilas

(In this chapter the same story is told in two somewhat different forms I have omitted the first one: . . . 2–5).—Compiler.

And the Blessed One, wandering from place to place, came to Uruvelā. At that time there lived in Uruvelā three Jaṭilas, Uruvelā Kassapa, Nadī Kassapa (Kassapa of the River, i.e. the Neranjarā), and Gaya Kassapa (Kassapa of the village Gaya). Of these the Jaṭila Uruvelā Kassapa was chief, leader, foremost, first, and highest over five hundred Jaṭilas; Nadī Kassapa was chief, leader, foremost, first and highest over three hundred Jaṭilas, Gaya Kassapa was chief, leader, foremost, first, and highest over two hundred Jaṭilas.

Near the Neranjarā river the Blessed One said to the Jaṭila Uruvelā Kassapa: "If it is not disagreeable to you, Kassapa, let me dwell one night in your fire room."

[1] Or "of the Self" (*attānaṃ gaveseyyātha*). "Self" in India might also mean "spirit" and "World-Soul".

"It is not agreeable to me, great recluse. There is a savage snake king there, possessed of magical power, a dreadfully venomous serpent; let him do no harm to you."

"He is not likely to do any harm to me; pray, Kassapa, allow me a place in your fire room."

When he saw that Kassapa had given his permission, fearlessly he, who had overcome all fear, entered. When the chief of serpents saw that the Sage had entered; he became irritated, and sent forth a cloud of smoke. Then the chief of men,[1] joyful and unperplexed, also sent forth a cloud of smoke.

Unable to master his rage, the chief of serpents sent forth flames like a burning fire. Then the chief of men, the perfect master of the element of fire, also sent forth flames. When they shone forth both with their flames, the Jaṭilas looked at the fire room (saying): "Truly the countenance of the great recluse is beautiful, but the Nāga will do harm to him."

And when that night had elapsed, the flames of the Nāga were extinguished but the various-coloured flames of him who is possessed of magical powers remained. Dark blue and red, light red, yellow, and crystal-coloured flames of various colours appeared on the Aṅgīrasa body.[2] Having put the chief of serpents into his alms-bowl, he showed him to the brahman (saying): "Here you see the Nāga, Kassapa; his fire has been conquered by my fire.

And the Jaṭila Uruvelā Kassapa, having conceived great faith in the Blessed One in consequence of this wonder, said to the Blessed One: "Stay with me, great recluse, I will daily provide you with food."

End of the first Wonder.

[1] Manussanāgo can be literally either "The Snake among men" or "The Elephant among men".

[2] The Gautamas, according to Vedic tradition, belong to the Aṅgīrasa tribe.

XVI

(*Continued*)

And the Blessed One resided in a certain grove near the hermitage of the Jaṭila Uruvelā Kassapa. And on a beautiful night the four firmament devas, filling the whole grove with light by the brilliancy of their complexion, went to the place where the Blessed One was; having approached him and respectfully saluted the Blessed One, they stood in the four quarters like great firebrands.

And when that night had elapsed, the Jaṭila Uruvelā Kassapa went to the place where the Blessed One was; having approached him, he said to the Blessed One: "It is time, great Samaṇa,[1] the meal is ready. Who were they, great Samaṇa, who came this beautiful night, filling the whole grove with light by the brilliancy of their complexion, to the place where you were, and having approached you and respectfully saluted you, stood in the four quarters like great firebrands?"

"They were the four firmament devas, Kassapa, who came to me in order to hear my preaching."

Then the Jaṭila Uruvelā Kassapa thought: "Truly the great Samaṇa possesses high magical powers and great faculties, since even the four firmament devas come to hear his preaching. He is not, however, holy[2] like me."

And the Blessed One ate the food offered by the Jaṭila Uruvelā Kassapa and continued to stay in that same grove.

End of the second Wonder.

(Chapter XVII and XVIII contain accounts as above of the appearance of Sakka, ruler of the devas, and Brahmā Sahampati.)

XIX

(*Continued*)

At that time a great sacrifice which the Jaṭila Uruvelā Kassapa used to celebrate was approaching, and all the people of Anga and Magadha wished to go to that sacrifice

[1] Pronounce sămănă, = recluse.
[2] Lit.: worthy: arahā.

carrying abundant food, both hard and soft. Now the Jaṭila Uruvelā thought: "Presently my great sacrifice is approaching, and all the people of Anga and Magadha will come and bring with them abundant food, both hard and soft. If the great Samaṇa should perform a wonder before that great assembly, gain and honour would increase to the great Samaṇa, and my gain and honour would diminish. O that the great Samaṇa might not come here to-morrow!"

Then the Blessed One, understanding by the power of his mind this reflection which had risen in the mind of the Jaṭila Uruvelā Kassapa, went to Uttarakuru; having begged alms there, he took the food (he had received) to the Anotatta lake; there he took his meal and rested during the heat of the day at the same place.

And when the night had elapsed, the Jaṭila Uruvelā Kassapa went to the place where the Blessed One was; having approached him, he said to the Blessed One: "It is time, great Samaṇa, the meal is ready. Why did you not come yesterday, great Samaṇa? We were thinking of you: 'Why does the great Samaṇa not come?' and your portions of food, both hard and soft, were served for you."

(Buddha replied): "Did you not think, Kassapa: 'Presently my great sacrifice (as above down to:) O that the great Samaṇa might not come here to-morrow?'

"Now I understood, Kassapa, by the power of my mind this reflection which had risen in your mind, and I went to Uttarakuru; having begged alms there, I took the food to the Anotatta lake; there I took my meal and rested during the heat of the day at the same place."

Then the Jaṭila Uruvelā Kassapa thought: "Truly the great Samaṇa possesses high magical powers and great faculties, since he is able to understand by the power of his mind the thoughts of other people. He is not, however, holy like me."

And the Blessed One ate the food offered by the Jaṭila Uruvelā Kassapa, and continued to stay in that grove.

End of the fifth Wonder.

XX

(Continued)

At that time the Blessed One had rags taken from a dust heap (of which he was going to make himself a robe). Now the Blessed One thought: "Where shall I wash these rags?" Then Sakka the king of the devas, understanding in his mind the thought which had risen in the mind of the Blessed One, dug a tank with his own hand, and said to the Blessed One: "Lord, might the Blessed One wash the rags here."

And the Blessed One thought: "What shall I rub the rags upon?" Then Sakka king of the devas, understanding in his mind the thought which had arisen in the mind of the Blessed One, put there a great stone and said: "Lord, let the Blessed One rub the rags upon this stone."

. . . (The Blessed One on this occasion was aided in several similar ways which he related to Kassapa.)

Then the Jaṭila Uruvelā Kassapa thought: "Truly the great Samaṇa possesses high magical powers and great faculties, since Sakka the ruler of the devas does service to him. He is not, however, holy like me."

And the Blessed One ate the food offered by the Jaṭila Uruvelā Kassapa, and continued to stay in that same grove.

And when that night had elapsed, the Jaṭila Uruvelā Kassapa went to the place where the Blessed One was; having approached him, he announced to the Blessed One that it was time, by saying: "It is time, great Samaṇa, the meal is ready."

(Buddha replied): "Go you, Kassapa; I will follow you." Having thus sent away the Jaṭila Uruvelā Kassapa, he went to pluck a fruit from the rose-apple tree in which India lies; then arriving before Kassapa he sat down in the room where Kassapa's (sacred) fire was kept.

Then the Jaṭila Uruvelā Kassapa saw the Blessed One sitting in the fire room; seeing him he said to the Blessed One: "By what way have you come, great Samaṇa?

I have departed before you, and you have arrived before me and are sitting in the fire room."

"When I had sent you away, Kassapa, I went to pluck a fruit from the rose-apple tree in which India lies; then I arrived before you and sat down in the fire room. Here is the jambu fruit, Kassapa, it is beautiful, fragrant, and full of flavour; you may eat it, if you like."

"Nay, great Samaṇa, to you alone it is becoming to eat it; eat it yourself."

And the Jaṭila Uruvelā Kassapa thought: "Truly the great Samaṇa possesses high magical powers and great faculties, since he is able, having sent me away before him, to go and pluck a fruit from there, and then to arrive before me and to sit down in the fire room. He is not, however, holy like me."

And the Blessed One ate (as above described).

And when that night had elapsed (as above described). Having thus sent away the Jaṭila Uruvelā Kassapa, he went to pluck a fruit from a mango tree growing near the rose-apple tree (as above described). He went to pluck a fruit from an emblic myrobalan tree (as above described). He went to pluck a fruit from a yellow myrobalan tree growing near the rose-apple tree (as above). He went to the next world to pluck a pāricchattaka flower; then arriving before Kassapa he sat down in the fire room. Then the Jaṭila Uruvelā Kassapa saw . . . (as above).

"When I had sent you away, Kassapa, I went to the next world to pluck a pāricchattaka flower; then I arrived before you, and sat down in the fire room. Here is the pāricchattaka flower, Kassapa; it is beautiful and fragrant; you may take it if you like."

"Nay, great Samaṇa, to you alone it is becoming to keep it; keep it yourself."

And the Jaṭila . . . (thought as above). "He is not, however, holy like me."

At that time one day the Jaṭilas, who wished to attend on their sacred fires, could not succeed in splitting fire-wood. Now these Jaṭilas thought: "Doubtless this is the great psychic power of the great Samaṇa, that we cannot succeed in splitting fire-wood." Then the Blessed One said to the Jaṭila Uruvelā Kassapa: "Shall the fire-wood be split, Kassapa?"

"Let it be split, great Samaṇa."

Then in a moment the five hundred pieces of fire-wood were split. And the Jaṭila Uruvelā Kassapa thought: "Truly the great Samaṇa possesses great psychic power, and great authority, since even the fire-wood splits itself (at his command). He is not, however, holy like me."

At that time the Jaṭilas, who wished to attend on their sacred fires, could not succeed in lighting up the fires. (As in the preceding story.)

At that time the Jaṭilas after having attended on their sacred fires, could not succeed in extinguishing the fires (as above).

At that time in the cold winter nights, in the time between the Ashṭaka festivals, when snow falls, the Jaṭilas plunged into the river Neraṇjarā, and emerged again, and repeatedly plunged into the water and emerged. And the Blessed One created five hundred vessels with burning fire; at those the Jaṭilas coming out of the river warmed themselves. And the Jaṭilas thought: "Doubtless this is the great psychic power of the great Samaṇa that these vessels with fire have been caused to appear here." Then the Blessed One said to Kassapa: "Let the fires warm you, Kassapa! Let them warm you, great recluse!" And the Jaṭila Uruvelā Kassapa thought: "Truly the great Samaṇa possesses high magical powers and great faculties, since he can create such great vessels with fire. He is not, however, holy like me."

At that time a great rain fell out of season; and a great inundation rose. The place where the Blessed One lived was covered with water. Then the Blessed One thought: "What if I were to cause the water to recede round about and if I were to walk up and down in the midst of the water on a dust-covered spot." And the Blessed One caused the water to recede round about, and he walked up and down in the midst of the water on a dust-covered spot.

And the Jaṭila Uruvelā Kassapa, who was afraid that the

water might have carried away the great Samaṇa, went with a boat together with many Jaṭilas to the place where the Blessed One lived. Then the Jaṭila Uruvelā Kassapa saw the Blessed One, who caused the water to recede round about, walking up and down in the midst of the water on a dust-covered spot. Seeing him, he said to the Blessed One : " Are you there, great Samaṇa ? "

" Here I am, Kassapa," replied the Blessed One, and he rose in the air and stationed himself in the boat.

And the Jaṭila Uruvelā Kassapa thought : " Truly the great Samaṇa possesses great psychic power and great authority, since the water does not carry him away. He is not, however, holy like me."

Then the Blessed One thought : " This foolish man will still for a long time be thinking thus : 'Truly the great Samaṇa possesses great psychic power, great authority ; he is not, however, holy like me.' What if I were to agitate this Jaṭila ? "

And the Blessed One said to the Jaṭila Uruvelā Kassapa : " *You* are not holy (arahā), Kassapa, nor have you even entered the path of Arahantship, nor do you live in such a way of life by which you will become holy, or enter the path of Arahantship."

Then the Jaṭila Uruvelā Kassapa prostrated himself, inclining his head to the feet of the Blessed One and said to the Blessed One : " Lord, let me receive ordination from the Blessed One."

(Buddha replied) : " You, Kassapa, are chief, leader, foremost, first, and highest of five hundred Jaṭilas ; go first and inform them of your intention, and let them do what they think fit."

Then the Jaṭila Uruvelā Kassapa went to those Jaṭilas ; having gone to them, he said to those Jaṭilas : " I wish, sirs, to lead a religious life under the direction of the great Samaṇa ; you may do, sirs, what you think fit."

(The Jaṭilas replied) : " We have won faith, sir, in the great Samaṇa long since ; if you will lead, sir, a religious life under the great Samaṇa's direction, we will all lead a religious life under the great Samaṇa's direction."

Then the Jaṭilas flung their hair, their braids, their provisions, and the things for the agnihotra sacrifice into the river, and went to the place where the Blessed One was; having approached him and prostrated themselves before him, inclining their heads to the feet of the Blessed One, they said to the Blessed One: "Lord, we would receive ordination from the Blessed One."

"Come, monks," said the Blessed One, "well taught is the dhamma; lead a holy life for the sake of the complete extinction of ill."

Thus these venerable persons received the upasampadā ordination.

And the Jaṭila Nadī Kassapa saw the hair, the braids, the provisions, the things for the agnihotra sacrifice, which were carried down by the river; when he saw that, he became afraid that some misfortune might have befallen his brother. He sent some Jaṭilas, saying: "Go and look after my brother," and went himself with his three hundred Jaṭilas to the venerable Uruvelā Kassapa; having approached him, he said to the venerable Uruvelā Kassapa: "Now, Kassapa, is this better?"

(Uruvelā Kassapa replied): "Yes, friend, this is better."

. . . (*The same is recounted of Nadī Kassapa and Gaya Kassapa and the Jaṭilas under them.*)

At the command of the Blessed One the five hundred pieces of fire-wood could not be split and were split, the fires could not be lit up and were lit up, could not be extinguished and were extinguished; beside he created five hundred vessels with fire. Thus the number of these miracles amounts to three thousand five hundred.

XXI

The Fire Sermon

And the Blessed One, after having dwelt at Uruvelā as long as he thought fit, went forth to Gayasīsa, accompanied by a great number of monks, by the thousand monks who all had been Jaṭilas before. There near Gaya, at Gaya-Head, the Blessed One dwelt together with those thousand monks.

There the Blessed One thus addressed the monks:

"Every thing, monks, is burning.

And how, monks, is every thing burning?

The eye, monks, is burning; visible things are burning; eye-consciousness is burning; eye-contact is burning; and whatever sensation produced by the cause of eye-contact, be it pleasant, or painful, or neither pleasant or painful, that also is burning.

With what is it burning?

I declare unto you, that it is burning with lust, with hatred, with delusion, it is burning with birth, decay, death, grief, lamentation, suffering, dejection and despair.

The ear is burning, sounds are burning . . . [1]

The tongue is burning, tastes are burning . . .

The body is burning, tangibles are burning . . .

The mind is burning, things are burning . . .

The mind-consciousness is burning, mind-contact is burning, and whatever sensation produced by the cause of mind-contact, be it pleasant or painful, or neither pleasant nor painful, that also is burning. With what is it burning?

I declare unto you that it is burning with lust, with hatred, with delusion, it is burning with birth, decay, death, grief, lamentation, suffering, dejection, and despair.

Considering this, O monks, a learned disciple, walking in the Noble Path, turns [2] away from the eye, turns away from the visible things, turns away from mental impressions based on the eye, turns away from the eye-contact, be it pleasant or painful, or neither pleasant nor painful.

. . . (Similarly he turns away from all the senses.) Turning away, he divests himself of passion; passionless

[1] The omissions in this paragraph follow the same line of relationship as that given above concerning the eye.

[2] See previous note on Nibbindati, p. 66.

he is liberated. Being liberated he is aware that he is liberated; and he knows that rebirth is exhausted, that the holy life is completed, that duty is fulfilled, and that there is no further return to this world."

When this exposition was propounded, the minds of those thousand monks became free from attachment to the world, and were released from the cankers!

Here ends the sermon on "The Burning".

End of the third portion for recitation concerning the Wonders done at Uruvelā.

XXII

The Conversion of King Bimbisāra and the Brahmans of Magadha

And the Blessed One, after having dwelt at Gaya-Head as long as he thought fit, went forth to Rājagaha, accompanied by a great number of monks, by the thousand monks who all had been Jaṭilas before. And the Blessed One, wandering from place to place came to Rājagaha. There the Blessed One dwelt near Rājagaha, in the Laṭṭhivana pleasure garden, near the shrine of Supatiṭṭha.

Then the Magadha king Seniya Bimbisāra heard: "The Samaṇa Gotama the son of the Sakyans, an ascetic of the Sakya tribe, has just arrived at Rājagaha and is staying near Rājagaha, in the Laṭṭhivana pleasure garden, near the sacred shrine of Supatiṭṭha. Of him, the blessed Gotama, such a glorious fame is spread abroad:—Truly he is the blessed, holy, absolute Buddha, proficient in knowledge and conduct, the Wellfarer, who understands all worlds, the highest one, who guides men that are teachable, the teacher of gods and men, the blessed Buddha. He makes known the truth, which he has understood himself and seen face to face, to this world-system with its devas, its Māras, and its Brahmās; to all beings, samaṇas and brahmans, gods and men; he preaches that dhamma which is lovely in the beginning, lovely in the middle, lovely at the end, in the spirit and in the letter; he proclaims the consummate perfect, and pure holy life." It is good to obtain the sight of holy men (Arahants) like that.

And the Magadha king Seniya Bimbisāra, surrounded by twelve myriads of Magadha brahmans and householders, went to the place where the Blessed One was; having approached him and respectfully saluted the Blessed One, he sat down near him. And of those twelve myriads of Magadha brahmans and householders some also respectfully saluted the Blessed One and sat down near him; some exchanged greeting with the Blessed One, having exchanged with him greeting and complaisant words, they sat down near him; some bent their clasped hands towards the Blessed One and sat down near him; some made known their name and family name before the Blessed One and sat down near him; some sat down near him silently.

Now those twelve myriads of Magadha brahmans and householders thought: "How now is this? Does the great Samaṇa follow the holy life under Uruvelā Kassapa, or does Uruvelā Kassapa follow the holy life under the great Samaṇa?"

And the Blessed One, who understood in his mind the reflection which had arisen in the minds of those twelve myriads of Magadha brahmans and householders, addressed the venerable Uruvelā Kassapa in verse: "What hast thou seen, O dweller of Uruvelā, that thou who art called the gaunt one hast forsaken the fire? I ask thee, Kassapa, this matter: How is it thou hast forsaken the fire sacrifice?"

(Kassapa replied): "It is sights and sounds, and also tastes, and women of sense-desire that the sacrifices promise; because I understood that whatever belongs to the grounds of rebirth is impure, I took no more delight m sacrifices and offerings."

"But if your mind, Kassapa," said the Blessed One, "found there no more delight—either in sights, or sounds, or tastes—what forsooth is it in the world of men or gods in which your mind, Kassapa, now finds delight? Tell me that."

(Kassapa replied): "I have seen the good state where is no ground (of rebirth), and no hindrance, which cleaves not to sensual life, which changes not, whence is no straying from; therefore I took no more delight in sacrifices and offerings."

Then the venerable Uruvelā Kassapa rose from his seat, adjusted his upper robe so as to cover one shoulder, prostrated himself, inclining his head to the feet of the Blessed One, and said to the Blessed One: "My teacher, lord, is the Blessed One, I am his pupil; my teacher, lord, is the Blessed One, I am his pupil." Then those twelve myriads of Magadha brahmans and householders understood: "Uruvelā Kassapa follows the holy life under the great Samaṇa."

And the Blessed One, who understood in his mind the reflection that had arisen in the minds of those twelve myriads of Magadha brahmans and householders, preached to them in due course (as above in Chap. 7). Just as a clean cloth free from black specks properly takes the dye, thus eleven myriads of those Magadha brahmans and householders with Bimbisāra at their head, while sitting there, obtained the pure and spotless eye of the dhamma (that is the knowledge): "Whatsoever is an arising thing all that is a ceasing thing." One myriad announced their having become lay-followers.

Then the Magadha king Seniya Bimbisāra having seen the dhamma, having mastered the dhamma, having penetrated the dhamma, having overcome uncertainty, having dispelled all doubts, having gained full knowledge dependent on nobody else for the knowledge of the Teacher's doctrine, said to the Blessed One: "In former days, lord, when I was a prince, I entertained five aspirations; these are now fulfilled. In former days, lord, to me when I was a prince, came this thought: 'O that I might be inaugurated as king!' That was my first aspiration, lord; that is now fulfilled. 'And might then a holy one, a fully Enlightened One come over into my kingdom!' This was my second aspiration, lord; that is now fulfilled. 'And might I minister to that Blessed One!' That was my third aspiration, lord; that is now fulfilled. 'And might he, the Blessed One, preach the dhamma to me!' This was my fourth aspiration, lord; and that is now fulfilled. 'And might I understand the dhamma of that Blessed One!' This was my fifth aspiration, lord; this is now fulfilled. These were my five aspirations, lord, which I entertained in former days when I was a prince; these are now fulfilled.

"Wonderful, lord! Wonderful, lord! Just as if one should set up, lord, what had been overturned, or should reveal what had been hidden, or should point out the way to one who had lost his way, or should bring a lamp into the darkness, in order that those who had eyes might see visible things, thus has the Blessed One preached the dhamma in many ways. I take refuge, lord, in the Blessed One, and in the dhamma, and in the fraternity of bhikkhus (monks); may the Blessed One receive me from this day forth, while my life lasts, as a lay-disciple who has taken refuge in him. And might the Blessed One, lord, consent to take his meal with me to-morrow together with the fraternity of monks."

The Blessed One expressed his consent by remaining silent.

Then the Magadha king Seniya Bimbisāra, when he understood that the Blessed One had accepted his invitation, rose from his seat, respectfully saluted the Blessed One, and, passing round him with his right side towards him, went away. And when the night had elapsed, the Magadha king Seniya Bimbisāra ordered excellent food, both hard and soft, to be prepared, and had dinner-time announced to the Blessed One in the words: "It is time, lord, the meal is ready." And in the forenoon the Blessed One, having put on his under-robe, took his alms-bowl, and with his robe on, entered the city of Rājagaha accompanied by a great number of monks, by the thousand monks who all had been Jaṭilas before.

At that time Sakka the ruler of the devas, assuming the appearance of a young brahman, walked in front of the fraternity of monks with Buddha at its head, singing the following stanzas: "The Tamed One with the tamed, with the former Jaṭilas, the Liberated One with the liberated, the Blessed One, in colour like fine wrought gold, hath entered Rājagaha."

"The Freed One with the freed, with the former Jaṭilas (etc., as above).

"He who has crossed over with them who have crossed over, with the former Jaṭilas, the Released One with the released, the Blessed One, in colour like fine wrought gold, hath entered Rājagaha."

"He who is possessed of the ten noble states and of the ten Powers, who understands the tenfold dhamma and who in ten ways hath won (his goal), he the Blessed One, surrounded by ten hundred of followers hath entered Rājagaha."

The people when they saw Sakka the king of the devas, said: "This youth indeed is handsome, this youth indeed has a lovely appearance, this youth indeed is pleasing. Whose attendant may this youth be?" When they talked thus, Sakka the king of the devas, addressed those people in this stanza: "He who is wise, entirely tamed, the unrivalled Buddha, the Arahant, the Wellfarer in the world, his attendant am I."

And the Blessed One went to the palace of the Magadha king Seniya Bimbisāra. Having gone there, he sat down with the monks who followed him, on seats laid out for them. Then the Magadha king Seniya Bimbisāra with his own hands served and offered excellent food, both hard and soft, to the fraternity of monks with the Buddha at its head; and when the Blessed One had finished his meal and cleaned his bowl and his hands, he sat down near him.

Sitting near him the Magadha king Seniya Bimbisāra thought: "Where may I find a place for the Blessed One to live in, not too far from the village and not too near, suitable for going and coming, easily accessible for people who keep on seeking (him), by day not too crowded, where there is little sound, little noise by night, sequestered, hidden from men, well fitted for a retired life?"

And the Magadha king Seniya Bimbisāra thought: "There is the Veḷuvana, my pleasure garden, which is not too far from the town and not too near, suitable for going and coming . . . What if I were to make an offering of the Veḷuvana pleasure garden to the fraternity of monks, with the Buddha at its head ? "

And the Magadha king Seniya Bimbisāra took a golden vessel (with water in it, to be poured over the Buddha's hand) ; and made a pure gift to the Blessed One, saying, " I give this Veḷuvana pleasure garden, lord, to the fraternity of monks with the Buddha at its head." The Blessed One accepted the park. Then the Blessed One, after having taught, incited, animated, and gladdened the Magadha king Seniya Bimbisāra by religious discourse, rose from his seat and went away.

And in consequence of this event the Blessed One, after having delivered a religious discourse addressed the monks : " I allow you, monks, to receive the donation of a park."

XXIII

The Conversion of the Two Chief Disciples, Sāriputta and Moggallāna

At that time Sanjaya a wandering ascetic (paribbājaka) resided at Rājagaha with a great retinue of wandering ascetics, with two hundred and fifty wandering ascetics. At that time Sāriputta and Moggallāna (two young brahmans) led a religious life as followers of Sanjaya, the wandering ascetic ; these had given their word to each other : " He who first attains to the immortal shall tell the other one."

Now one day the venerable Assaji in the forenoon, having put on his under-robes, and having taken his alms-bowl and outer robe, entered the city of Rājagaha for alms ; his walking, turning back, regarding, looking, drawing (his arms) back, and stretching (them) out was decorous ; he turned his eyes to the ground, and was dignified in deportment. Now the wandering ascetic Sāriputta saw the venerable Assaji, who went through Rājagaha for alms, whose walking, etc., was decorous, who kept his eyes to the ground, and was dignified in deportment. Seeing him, he thought: "Indeed this person is one of those monks who are the worthy ones (Arahants) in the world, or who have entered the path of Arahantship. What if I were to approach this monk and to ask him: 'In whose name, friend, have you retired from the world? Who is your teacher? Whose dhamma do you profess?'"

Now the wandering ascetic Sāriputta thought: "This is not the time to ask this monk; he has entered the inner yard of a house, walking for alms. What if I were to follow this monk step by step, according to the course recognised by those who want something?"

And the venerable Assaji, having finished his alms-pilgrimage through Rājagaha, went back with the food he had received. Then the wandering ascetic Sāriputta went to the place where the venerable Assaji was; having approached him, he exchanged greetings with the venerable Assaji; having exchanged with him greetings and complaisant words, he stationed himself at his side; standing at his side the wandering ascetic Sāriputta said to the venerable Assaji: "Your countenance, friend, is serene; your complexion is pure and bright. In whose name, friend, have you retired from the world? Who is your teacher? Whose dhamma do you profess?"

(Assaji replied): "There is, friend, the great recluse the Sakya's son, who has retired from the world, out of the Sakya clan; in this Blessed One's name, have I retired from the world; this Blessed One is my teacher, and of the dhamma of this Blessed One do I approve."

"And what, venerable Sir, is the doctrine which your teacher holds? And what does he preach to you?"

"I am only a young disciple, friend; I have but recently received ordination; and I have newly adopted this dhamma and discipline. I cannot explain to you the dhamma in detail; but I will tell you in short what it means."

Then Sāriputta, the wandering ascetic, said to the venerable Assaji: "So be it, friend, tell me as much or as little as you like, but tell me the meaning, I want just the meaning. Why make so much of the letter?"

Then the venerable Assaji pronounced to the wandering ascetic Sāriputta the following teaching of the dhamma · " Of all objects which proceed from a cause, the Tathāgata has explained the cause, and he has explained their cessation also ; this is the doctrine of the great Samaṇa."

And Sāriputta, the wandering ascetic, after having heard this dhamma-text obtained the pure and spotless dhamma-eye (namely) : " Whatsoever is an arising thing, all that is a ceasing thing." (And he said) : " Even if this alone be the dhamma, you have indeed seen the sorrowless way, lost sight of and passed over for many myriads of aeons."

Then the wandering ascetic Sāriputta went to the place where the wandering ascetic Moggallāna was. And the wandering ascetic Moggallāna saw the wandering ascetic Sāriputta coming from afar ; seeing him, he said to the wandering ascetic Sāriputta : " Your countenance, friend, is serene ; your complexion is pure and bright. Have you then really reached the immortal, friend ? "

" Yes, friend, I have attained to the immortal."

" And how, friend, have you done so ? "

. . . (Then Sāriputta told him of his meeting with Assaji).

And the wandering ascetic Moggallāna, after having heard this dhamma-text, obtained the pure and spotless dhamma-eye (that is the following knowledge) : " Whatsoever is an arising thing, all that is a ceasing thing." (And Moggallāna said) : " Even if this alone be the dhamma, indeed you have seen the sorrowless way, lost sight of and passed over for many myriads of aeons."

XXIV

(Continued)

Then the wandering ascetic Moggallāna said to the wandering ascetic Sāriputta, " Let us go, friend, and join the Blessed One ; that he, the Blessed One, may be our teacher."

(Sāriputta replied): "It is on our account, friend, that these two hundred and fifty wandering ascetics live here, and it is we whom they regard; let us first take leave of them; they will do what they think fit."

Then Sāriputta and Moggallāna went to the place where those wandering ascetics were; having approached them they said to the wandering ascetics: "Friends, we are going to join the Blessed One; he, the Blessed One, is our teacher."

(The wandering ascetics replied): "It is on your account, sirs, that we live here, and it is you whom we regard; if you, sirs, will lead the holy life under the great Samaṇa, we all will lead the holy life under the great Samaṇa."

Then Sāriputta and Moggallāna went to the place where the wandering ascetic Sañjaya was; having approached him, they said to the wandering ascetic Sañjaya: "Friend, we go to join the Blessed One; he, the Blessed One, is our teacher."

(Sañjaya replied): "Nay, friends, do not go; we will all three look after this company."

. . . (And a second and third time Sāriputta and Moggallāna said this and Sañjaya answered as before.)

But Sāriputta and Moggallāna took with them those two hundred and fifty wandering ascetics and went to the Veḷuvana. And the wandering ascetic Sañjaya began on the spot to vomit hot blood from his mouth.

And the Blessed One saw them, Sāriputta and Moggallāna, coming from afar; on seeing them he thus addressed the monks: "There, monks, arrive two companions, Kolita and Upatissa;[1] these will be my chief pair of disciples, an auspicious pair."

When they who were unsurpassed for depth and breadth of knowledge and who were set free by the perishing of the grounds of becoming, had arrived at the Bamboo grove, then the Teacher declared concerning them: "There arrive two

[1] Their family names.

companions, Kolita and Upatissa, these will be my chief pair of disciples, an auspicious pair."

Then Sāriputta and Moggallāna went to the place where the Blessed One was; having approached him, they prostrated themselves, with their heads at the feet of the Blessed One, and said to the Blessed One: "Lord, let us receive ordination from the Blessed One."

"Come, monks," said the Blessed One, "well taught is the dhamma; lead a holy life for the sake of the complete ending of ill." Thus these venerable persons received the upasampadā ordination.

At that time many distinguished young Magadha noblemen led a holy life under the direction of the Blessed One. The people were annoyed, murmured, and became angry (saying), "The Samaṇa Gotama causes parents to be childless; the Samaṇa Gotama causes wives to become widows; the Samaṇa Gotama causes the uprooting of families. Now he has ordained one thousand Jaṭilas, and he has ordained these two hundred and fifty wandering ascetics who were followers of Sañjaya, and these many distinguished young Magadha clansmen are now leading a holy life under the Samaṇa Gotama. And moreover, when they saw the monks they chid them in the following stanza: "The great Samaṇa has come to Giribbaja (i.e. Rāgagaha) of the Magadha people, leading with him all the followers of Sañjaya; who will be the next to be led by him?"

The monks heard those people that were annoyed, murmured, and had become angry; these monks told this thing to the Blessed One. (He replied): "This noise, monks, will not last long; it will last only seven days; after seven days it will be over. And if they chide you, monks, in this stanza: 'The great Samaṇa has come, etc.,' you should rebuke them in the following stanza: 'It is truly by a good dhamma that the great heroes the Tathāgatas, lead. Who will murmur at the wise, why grudge the wise men leading righteously?'"

At that time when the people, seeing the monks, chid them in the following stanza: "The great Samaṇa has come, etc.," then the Bhikkhus replied to the revilers . . . (as the Blessed One had directed).

Then the people understood: "It is by dhamma, and not unrighteously, that the Sakyaputtiya Samaṇas lead men"; and thus the noise lasted only seven days, and after seven days it was over.

PART IV

THE BUDDHA'S RELATIONS WITH HIS DISCIPLES AND OTHERS

ORDINATION OF RĀHULA

(*VINAYA TEXTS, I. p.* 207)

(*Adapted from Rhys Davids's and Oldenberg's trans.*)

Then the Blessed one after having resided at Rājagaha as long as he thought fit, went forth to Kapilavatthu. Wandering from place to place he came to Kapilavatthu. There the Blessed One dwelt in the Sakya country, near Kapilavatthu, in the Nigrodhârāma (Banyan Grove).

And in the forenoon the Blessed One, having put on his under-robes, took his alms-bowl and with his robe on went to the residence of the Sakyan Suddhôdănă (his father). Having gone there he sat down on a seat made ready.

Then the princess, who was the mother of Rāhula, said to young Rāhula: "This is your father, Rāhula; go and ask him for your inheritance."

Then young Rāhula went to the place where the Blessed One was; having approached him, he stationed himself before the Blessed One and said: "Your shadow, Sămăṇa, is a place of bliss."

Then the Blessed One rose from his seat and went away, and young Rāhula followed the Blessed One from behind and said: "Give me my inheritance, Samaṇa; give me my inheritance, Samaṇa."

Then the Blessed One said to the venerable Sāriputta: "Well, Sāriputta confer ordination on young Rāhula."

(Sāriputta replied): "How shall I confer, lord, ordination on young Rāhula?"

Because of that and on this occasion the Blessed One, after having delivered a religious discourse, thus addressed the monks: "I prescribe, monks, the ordination of novices by the threefold declaration of taking refuge.

"And you ought, monks, to confer ordination (on a novice) in this way: Let him first have his hair and beard cut off; let him put on yellow robes, adjust his upper robe so as to cover one shoulder, salute the feet of the monks (with his head), and sit down squatting, then let him raise his joined hands and tell him to say: 'I take my refuge in the Buddha, I take my refuge in the Dhamma, I take my refuge in the Samgha. And for the second time, etc. And for the third time, etc.'

"I prescribe monks, the ordination of novices by this threefold declaration of taking refuge."

Thus the venerable Sāriputta conferred ordination on young Rāhula.

Then the Sakyan Suddhodana went to the place where the Blessed One was; having approached him and having respectfully saluted the Blessed One, he sat down near him. Sitting near him the Sakyan Suddhodana said to the Blessed One: "Lord, I ask one boon of the Blessed One." (The Buddha replied): "The perfect ones, Gotama, are beyond granting boons." (Suddhodana said): "Lord it is proper and blameless." (The Buddha): "Speak, Gotama."

"Lord, when the Blessed One gave up the world, it was a great pain to me; so it was when Nanda did the same; my pain was excessive when Rāhula too did so. The love for a son, lord, cuts into the skin; having cut into the skin it cuts into the hide; having cut into the hide, it cuts into the flesh . . . the ligaments . . . the bones; having cut into the bones, it reaches the marrow and dwells in the marrow. Pray, lord, let their reverences not confer ordination on a son without his father's and mother's permission."

Then the Blessed One taught the Sakyan Suddhodana (etc., see Chap. 39). "Let no son, monks, receive ordination without his father's and mother's permission. He who confers ordination (on a son without that permission), is guilty of a misdeed."

The Well-Tuned Lute

A Parable of the Middle Way

(*FROM VINAYA TEXTS, MAHĀVAGGA V, p.* 194 *f.*)

. . . The venerable Soṇa (Soṇa Koḷivisa) soon after his higher ordination resided in the Sītavana grove.

While he with zealous determination was walking to and fro, his feet were wounded, and the place where he walked became covered with blood, like a slaughter-house for oxen. Then when the venerable Soṇa had gone apart and was deep in meditation, there arose this consideration: "Though I live as one of those disciples of the Blessed One in the practice of strenuous effort, yet my mind has not been set free from the cankers through absence of craving.

"And at my home much wealth is stored up for me. It is both possible to enjoy that wealth and to do good deeds. Let me now, then, returning to the lower state, enjoy my wealth and do good deeds."

Now the Blessed One perceived the thought of the venerable Soṇa; and as quickly as a strong man can stretch forth his arm, or can draw it back again, when it has been stretched forth, he disappeared from the hill of the Vulture's Peak, and appeared in the Sītavana grove. Then the Blessed One as he was going through the sleeping-quarters, arrived with many monks where the venerable Soṇa had walked to and fro.

When the Blessed One saw that the place where the venerable Soṇa had walked to and fro was covered with blood, he said to the monks: "Whose walking place is this, monks, which is covered with blood, like a slaughter-house for oxen?"

"Lord, while the venerable Soṇa was walking to and fro here with zealous determination, his feet were wounded; and so this place has become covered with blood . . ."

Then the Blessed One went to the house in which the venerable Soṇa was living, and there he sat down on a seat prepared for him. And the venerable Soṇa bowed down before the Blessed One, and seated himself at one side. Then the Blessed One said to the venerable Soṇa: "Is it not true Soṇa that in your mind, when you had gone apart and were deep in meditation, there arose this thought: 'Though I have become one of those disciples of the Blessed One in the practice of strenuous effort, yet my mind has not been set free from the cankers through absence of craving. And at my house much wealth is stored up for me. It is both possible to enjoy that wealth and to do good deeds. Let me now, then, returning to the lower state enjoy my wealth and do good deeds?'"

"Yes, Lord."

"Now what think you, Soṇa? You were skilled, were you not, in the strings of the lute, when you used to live in the world?"

"That is true, Lord."

"What think you, Soṇa? When your lute strings were stretched too much, then had your lute any sound, was it in a fit condition to be played upon?"

"No, Lord."

"What think you, Soṇa? When the strings of your lute were too loose then had your lute any sound, was it in a fit condition to be played upon?"

"No, Lord."

"What think you, Soṇa? When the strings of your lute were neither too much stretched nor too loose, but fixed in even quality, had your lute sound then, was it in a fit condition then to be played upon?"

"Yes, Lord."

"Thus, Soṇa, does too strenuous effort lead to overstrain, and too weak effort to sloth. Therefore, O Soṇa, be you steadfast in evenness of effort, press through to evenness of your mental powers. Let that be the object of your thought."

"Just so, Lord," said the venerable Soṇa, and he harkened to the word of the Blessed One.

Residence During the Rainy Season—Vassa

(VINAYA TEXTS I, p. 298.)

(*Mainly from Rhys Davids's and Oldenberg's trans.*)

At that time the Blessed One dwelt at Rājagaha, in the Bamboo Grove, in the Squirrels' Feeding Ground. At that time the retreat during the rainy season had not yet been instituted by the Blessed One for the monks. Thus the monks went on their travels alike during winter, summer, and the rainy season.

People were annoyed, murmured, and became angry, saying: "How can the Sakya Samaṇas go on their travels alike during winter, summer, and the rainy season? They crush the green herbs, they hurt vegetable life, they destroy the life of many small living things. Shall the ascetics who belong to other schools, whose doctrine is ill preached, retire during the rainy season and arrange places for themselves to live in; shall the birds make their nests on the summits of the trees; and retire during the rainy season, and arrange themselves places to live in; and yet the Sakya Samaṇas go on their travels alike during winter, summer, and the rainy season, crushing the green herbs, hurting vegetable life, and destroying the life of many small things?"

Now some monks heard those people that were annoyed, murmured, and had become angry.

These monks told this thing to the Blessed One.

In consequence of that and on this occasion the Blessed One, after having delivered a religious discourse, thus addressed the monks:—

"I prescribe, monks, that you enter upon retreat in the rains."

Advice Regarding Vassa

(VINAYA TEXTS I, p. 325 f.)

(*Adapted from Rhys Davids's and Oldenberg's trans.*)

At that time the Blessed Buddha dwelt at Sāvatthi; in the Jetavana, the garden of Anāthapiṇḍika. At that time a number of monks, companions and friends of each other, entered upon retreat in a certain district of the Kosala country. Now those monks thought: "What shall we do in order that we may keep retreat well, in unity and in concord and without quarrel, and that we may not suffer from want of food?"

Then those monks thought: "If we do not speak to or converse with each other, if he who comes back first from the village, from his alms-pilgrimage, prepares seats, gets water for washing the feet, a footstool, and a towel, cleans the slop-basin and gets it ready, and puts there (water to) drink and food.

"And if he who comes back last from the village, from his alms-pilgrimage, eats, if there is any food left (from the dinner of the other monks) and if he desires to do so; and if he does not desire (to eat) throws it away, at a place free from grass, or pours it away into water in which no living things are; puts away the water for washing the feet, the foot-stool, and the towel; cleans the slop-basin, and puts it away, puts the water and the food away, and sweeps the dining-room.

"And if he who sees a water-pot, or a bowl for food, . . . empty and void, puts it (into its proper place), and if he is not able to do so single-handed, calls someone else and puts it away with their united effort without uttering a word on that account, thus shall we keep Vassa well, in unity, and in concord, and without quarrel, and not suffer from want of food."

And those monks did not speak to or converse with each other. He who came back from the village from his alms-pilgrimage first, prepared seats (etc., as above) . . . without uttering a word on that account.

Now it is the custom of the monks who have finished their rains residence, to go to see the Blessed One. Thus those monks, when they had finished their retreat, and when the three months had elapsed, set their places of rest in order, took their alms-bowls, and robes, and went on their way to Sāvatthi. Walking from place to place they came to Sāvatthi, to the Jetavana, the garden of Anāthapiṇḍika, to the Blessed One; having approached the Blessed One and respectfully saluted him they sat down near him.

Now it is the custom of the Blessed Buddhas to exchange greetings with incoming monks. And the Blessed One said to those monks: "Do things go well with you, monks? Do you get enough to support yourselves with? Have you kept the rain-retreat well, in unity, and in concord, and without quarrel? and have you not suffered from want of food?"

"Things go well with us, lord; we get enough, lord, wherewith to support ourselves; we have kept retreat well, in unity, in concord, and without quarrel; and have not suffered from want of food."

The Tathāgatas sometimes ask about what they know; sometimes they do not ask about what they know. They understand the right time when to ask, and they understand the right time when not to ask. The Tathāgatas put questions full of sense, not void of sense; to what is void of sense the bridge is pulled down for the Tathāgatas. For two purposes the blessed Buddhas put questions to the monks, when they intend to preach the doctrine, or when they intend to institute a rule of conduct to their disciples.

And the Blessed One said to those monks: "In what way, monks, have you kept retreat well, in unity, and in concord, and without quarrel and not suffered from want of food?"

"We entered upon retreat, lord, a number of monks, companions and friends of each other, in a certain district of the Kosala country. Now, lord, we thought: 'What shall we do (etc., p. 108, l. 3)?' Then we thought, lord: 'If we do not speak (etc., *ibid.*).' Thus, lord, we did not speak to or converse with each other (etc., down to:) without uttering a word on that account. In that way, lord, we have kept retreat well, in unity, and in concord, and without quarrel; and have not suffered from want of food."

Then the Blessed One thus addressed the monks: "Indeed, monks, these foolish men who profess to have kept retreat well, have kept it badly; indeed, monks, these foolish men who profess to have kept retreat well, have kept it like a herd of cattle; indeed have kept it like a herd of rams;

indeed have kept it like a company of indolent people. How can these foolish persons, monks, take upon themselves the vow of silence, as other sects do?

"This will not do, monks, for converting the unconverted . . . they will be repulsed, and the converted estranged."

And when he had rebuked them he delivered a religious discourse, he thus addressed the monks:

"Let no one, monks, take upon himself the vow of silence, as other sects do. He who does commits a misdeed.

"I prescribe, monks, that the monks, when they have finished their rains residence, hold ward-mote [1] with each other in these three ways: by what has been seen, or by what has been heard, or by what is suspected.

"Hence it will result that you live in accord with each other, that you atone for the offence (you have committed), and that you keep the rules of discipline before your eyes.

"And you ought, monks, to hold ward-mote in this way: Let a learned, competent monk make this known before the Sangha: 'Let the Sangha, reverend sirs, hear me. To-day is the ward-mote day. If the Sangha is ready, let the Sangha hold ward-mote.'

"Then let the senior monk adjust his upper robe so as to cover one shoulder, sit down squatting, raise his joined hands, and say: 'I pronounce my warding, friends, before the Sangha, by what has been seen, or by what has been heard, or by what is suspected; may you speak to me, sirs, out of compassion towards me; if I see (an offence), I will atone for it. And for the second time, etc. And for the third time I pronounce my warding . . . (etc., down to) . . . if I see (an offence), I will atone for it.'

"Then let (each) younger monk adjust his upper robe . . . (etc.)."

[1] Pavāranā.

The Blessed One Waits upon a Deserted Monk

(Vinaya Texts II, p. 240.)

At one time a certain monk had an illness of the bowels, and he lay fallen in his own excrement. Now when the Blessed One, followed by the venerable Ānanda, was passing by the sleeping quarters he came to the cell of that monk and saw him in such a condition. And seeing he went to him and said : " What is it, monk, are you ill ? "

" I have an illness of the bowels, lord."

" Have you no one to wait upon you, monk ? "

" No, lord."

" Why do not the monks wait upon you ? "

" Because, lord, I am of no service to the monks."

Whereupon the Blessed One said to the venerable Ānanda : " Go, Ānanda, and bring some water, let us bathe this monk."

" Yes, lord," replied the venerable Ānanda to the Blessed One, and brought the water. Then the Blessed One poured the water, while the venerable Ānanda washed him. And the Blessed One holding him by the head, and the venerable Ānanda by the feet, they lifted him and laid him down upon his bed.

Then on that occasion and in that connection, the Blessed One called a gathering of the Order, and asked the monks : " Monks, in such and such a quarter is there a monk who is sick ? "

" Yes, lord."

" And, monks, what is the matter with that monk ? "

" He has an illness of the bowels, lord."

" And is there no one to wait upon him, monks ? "

" No, lord."

" But why do not the monks wait upon him ? "

" That monk, lord, is of no service to the monks, hence they do not wait upon him."

" Monks, you have no mothers or fathers who might wait upon you. If, monks, you do not wait upon one another, who forsooth will wait upon you ? Whosoever, monks, would wait upon me, he should wait upon the sick.

"If he have a preceptor his preceptor should wait upon him as long as his life lasts until he is recovered, and the same if he have a teacher, a co-disciple of the same vihāra or a disciple lodging with his teacher. And if he have none of these, then the Sangha should wait upon him; and whosoever does not do so, shall be guilty of offence."[1]

The Helper of the Individual

(FROM MAJJHIMA NIKĀYA II, p. 197 f.)

(*Mrs. Rhys Davids's translation*)

Then the young brahman Subha visited the Exalted One and greeted him and took his seat beside him and said: "The brahmans, master Gotama, say thus: 'A man who lives in the world can lead a life of rectitude, of righteousness, of moral worth; a man who leaves the world does not lead such a life. Here what has Master Gotama to say?'"

"I am one who here distinguishes, young brahman, I do not here generalise. Whether it be of the layman or of the recluse, wrong practices I do not praise. Neither the layman not the recluse, if he lead a wrong life can live rightly, righteously, worthily, because of his wrong practices. Whether it be of the layman or of the recluse right practices I praise. Both the layman and the recluse if they lead the right life, can live rightly, righteously, worthily, because of their right practices?"

"The brahmans, Master Gotama, say thus: 'The business of domestic life which is important, of many interests, of much enterprise, of much toil brings much reward; the business of life out of the world is unimportant, of few interests, of little enterprise, of little toil brings little reward. Here what says Master Gotama?'"

"Here too, young brahman, I distinguish, I do not generalise. There is business which is of great importance, many interests, much enterprise, much toil which brings little reward. Other such business brings much reward.

[1] It is noteworthy that this touching episode occurs not under *The Duties*, but under The Dress, of the Monks.—ED.

There is business of little importance, small interests, little enterprise, little toil which brings little reward. Other such business brings much reward. Of the first two kinds is tilling the land. Of the other two kinds is trade. And domestic life is like tilling the land; life out of the world is like trade."

Tissa

(*SAṂYUTTA-NIKĀYA III*)

(*Trans. by F. L. Woodward, in* Kindred Sayings, *Vol. III*)

At Sāvatthī . . . In the Park.

Now at that time the venerable Tissa, nephew to the Exalted One's father, thus spoke to a number of brethren:

"Truly, friends, my body has become as if drugged; the four quarters are become dim in my eyes, and the teachings are no longer clear to me. Sloth and torpor possess my heart; joyless to me is the righteous life, and I waver in the teachings."

Thereupon a number of brethren went to the Exalted One, saluted him and sat down at one side.

So seated, those brethren said to the Exalted One: "Lord, the venerable Tissa, nephew to the Exalted One's father, speaks thus to a number of brethren: 'Truly friends, my body is become as if drugged. The four quarters are dim to my eyes, and the teachings are no longer clear to me. Sloth and torpor possess my heart: joyless to me is the righteous life, and I waver in the teachings.'"

At that, the Exalted One, called to a certain brother:

"Come thou, brother, and in my name bid hither brother Tissa, saying: 'Friend Tissa, the Master would speak to you.'"

"Even so, lord," said that brother in reply to the Exalted One, and he went to the venerable Tissa and said to him: "Friend Tissa, the Master would speak to you."

"Even so, brother," said the venerable Tissa in reply to that brother, and came to the Exalted One, saluted him and sat down at one side.

As he thus sat the Exalted One thus spake unto the venerable Tissa: "Is it true, as they say, Tissa, that you said this to a number of brethren: 'Truly, friends, my body is become as if drugged . . . and so on . . . and I waver in the teachings?'"

"True, lord."

"Now as to that, what think you Tissa? In a body that is not rid of lust, rid of desire, of love, of thirst, of fever, and craving, in such a body do there arise states of change and instability? Do sorrow and grief, woe, lamentation and despair arise?"

"Yes, lord."

"Well said, well said, Tissa. And is it so likewise with feeling . . . with perception, with the activities and with consciousness?"

"Yes, lord."

"Well said, well said, Tissa. So it is likewise with a mind that is not rid of lust, of desire, of love, thirst, craving and fever: in such a mind there do arise sorrow and grief, woe, lamentation and despair. Now what think you, Tissa? In a body that is rid of all these, in such a body do there arise sorrow, grief, woe, lamentation and despair?"

"Surely not, lord."

"Well said, well said, Tissa. And as with body, so also with feeling, perception, the activities and consciousness, do they arise?"

"Surely not, lord."

"Well said, well said, Tissa. So it is with a mind that is rid of lust. Now what think you, Tissa? Is body permanent or impermanent?"

"Impermamament, lord."

"Is feeling, is perception, the activities, is consciousness permanent or impermanent?"

"Impermanent, lord."

"Wherefore, he who seeth this . . . he knows: . . . 'for life in these conditions there is no hereafter.'

"Suppose now, Tissa, there be two men, one unskilled and the other skilled in wayfaring. And the one who is unskilled asks the way of the other who is skilled in that way. And that other replies: 'Yes, this is the way good man. Go on for a while and you will see the road divide into two. Leave the path to the left and take the right-hand path. Go on for a little, and you will see a thick forest. Go on for a little and you will see a great marshy swamp. Go on for a little and you will see a steep precipice. Go on for a little and you will see a delightful stretch of level ground.'

"Such is my parable, Tissa, to show my meaning; and this is the meaning thereof. By 'the man who is unskilled in the way' is meant the many-folk. By 'the man who is skilled in the way' is meant a Tathāgata, an Arahant, a Fully Enlightened One. By 'the divided way' Tissa, is meant 'the state of wavering'. The left-hand path is a name for this false eightfold path, to wit: the path of wrong views, wrong intentions and so forth. The 'right-hand path', Tissa, is a name for this Aryan Eightfold Path, to wit: right views, and so forth. The 'thick forest', Tissa, is a name for ignorance. The 'great marshy swamp', Tissa, is a name for the sense-desires. The 'steep precipice', Tissa, is a name for vexation and despair. The 'delightful stretch of level ground', Tissa, is a name for Nibbana.

"Be of good cheer, Tissa! Be of good cheer, Tissa! I to counsel (you)! I to uphold! I to teach!"

Thus spake the Exalted One, and the venerable Tissa was comforted and welcomed the words of the Exalted One.

Admission of Women to an Order of Nuns

(From the Chullavagga. Tenth Khandhaka. Vinaya Texts)

(Following mostly Rhys Davids's and Oldenberg's translation, S.B.E.)

I

Now at that time the Blessed Buddha was staying among the Sakyas in Kapilavatthu, in the Nigrodhârāma. And Mahā-Pajāpatī[1] the Gotamī went to the place where the

[1] Mahā-Pajāpatī was sister to the Buddha's mother, and was also married to his father: after his mother's death she was foster-mother to the young Gotama.

Blessed One was, and on arriving there, bowed down before the Blessed One, and remained standing on one side. And so standing she spake thus to the Blessed One:

"It would be well, lord, if women should be allowed to renounce their homes and enter the homeless state under the doctrine and discipline proclaimed by the Tathāgata."

"Enough, Gotamī. Let it not please thee that women should be allowed to do so."

(And a second and a third time did Mahā-Pajāpatī the Gotamī make the same request in the same words, and receive the same reply.) . . .

Then Mahā-Pajāpatī the Gotamī, sad and sorrowful for that the Blessed One would not permit women to enter the homeless state, bowed down before the Blessed One, and keeping him on her right hand as she passed him, departed thence weeping and in tears.

Now when the Blessed One had remained at Kapilavatthu as long as he thought fit, he set out on his journey towards Vesālī; and travelling straight on he in due course arrived thereat. And there at Vesālī the Blessed One stayed, in the Mahā-vana in the Kūtāgāra Hall.

And Mahā-Pajāpatī the Gotamī cut off her hair, and put on orange-coloured robes, and set out, with a number of women of the Sakya clan, towards Vesālī; and in due course she arrived at Vesālī, at the Mahāvana, at the Kūtāgāra Hall. And Mahā-Pajāpatī the Gotamī, with swollen feet and covered with dust, sad and sorrowful, weeping and in tears, took her stand outside under the entrance porch.

And the venerable Ānanda saw her so standing there, and on seeing her so he said to Mahā-Pajāpatī: "Why standest thou there, outside the porch, with swollen feet and covered with dust, sad and sorrowful, weeping and in tears?

"Inasmuch, Ānanda, as the lord, the Blessed One, does not permit women to renounce their homes and enter the homeless state under the doctrine and discipline proclaimed by the Tathāgata."

Then did the venerable Ānanda go up to the place where the Blessed One was, and bow down before the Blessed

One, and take his seat on one side. And, so sitting, the venerable Ānanda said to the Blessed One :

" Behold, lord, Mahā-Pajāpatī the Gotamī is standing outside under the entrance porch, with swollen feet and covered with dust, sad and sorrowful, weeping and in tears, inasmuch as the Blessed One does not permit women to renounce their homes and enter the homeless state under the doctrine and discipline proclaimed by the Blessed One.

" It were well, lord, if women were to have permission granted to them to do as she desires."

" Enough, Ānanda. Let it not please thee that women should be allowed to do so."

(And a second and a third time did Ānanda make the same request, in the same words, and receive the same reply.) . . .

Then the venerable Ānanda thought : " The Blessed One does not give his permission, let me now ask the Blessed One on another ground." And the venerable Ānanda said to the Blessed One :

" Are women, lord, capable when they have gone forth from the household life and entered the homeless state, under the doctrine and discipline proclaimed by the Blessed One—are they capable of realising the fruit of conversion, or of the second Path, or of the third Path, or of Arahantship ? "

" They are capable, Ānanda."

" If then, lord, they are capable thereof, since Mahā-Pajāpatī the Gotamī has proved herself of great service to the Blessed One, when as aunt and nurse she nourished him and gave him milk, and on the death of his mother suckled the Blessed One at her own breast, it were well, lord, that women should have permission to go forth from the household life and enter the homeless state under the doctrine and discipline proclaimed by the Tathāgata."

" If then, Ānanda, Mahā-Pajāpatī the Gotamī take upon herself the Eight Chief Rules, let that be reckoned to her as her ordination."

(They are these) : " A nun, even if of a hundred years standing, shall make salutation to, shall rise up in the presence of, shall bow down before, and shall perform all proper duties towards a monk, if only just initiated. This is a rule to be revered and reverenced, honoured and observed, and her life long never to be transgressed.

"A nun is not to spend the rainy season in a district in which there is no monk.

"This is a rule . . . never to be transgressed.

"Every half month a nun is to await from the Bhikkhu-sangha two things, the asking as to (the date of) the Uposatha ceremony, and the (time when the monk) will come to give the Exhortation.

"This is a rule . . . never to be transgressed.

"After keeping the rainy season the nun is to hold Pavārana (to enquire whether any fault can be laid to her charge) before both Sanghas—as well that of the monks as that of nuns—with respect to three matters, namely, what has been seen, and what has been heard, and what has been suspected.

"This is a rule . . . never to be transgressed.

"A nun who has been guilty of a serious offence is to undergo suitable discipline towards both the Sanghas (monks and nuns).

"This is a rule . . . never to be transgressed.

"When a nun, as novice, has been trained for two years in the Six Rules, she is to ask leave for the upasampadā ordination from both the Sanghas (as well that of monks as that of nuns).

"This is a rule . . . never to be transgressed.

"A nun is on no pretext to revile or abuse a monk.

"This is a rule . . . never to be transgressed.

"From henceforth official admonition by nuns of monks is forbidden, whereas the official admonition of nuns by monks is not forbidden. This is a rule . . . never to be transgressed.

"If Ānanda, Mahā-Pajāpatī the Gotamī take upon herself these Eight Chief Rules, let that be reckoned to her as her ordination."

Then the venerable Ānanda, when he had learnt from the Blessed One these Eight Chief Rules, went to Mahā-Pajāpatī the Gotamī and (told her all that the Blessed One had said, to which she replied):

"Just, Ānanda, as a man or a woman, when young and of tender years, accustomed to adorn himself, would, when he had bathed his head, receive with both hands a garland of lotus flowers or jasmine flowers or atimuttaka flowers, and place it on the top of his head; even so do I, Ānanda, take upon me these Eight Chief Rules never to be transgressed my life long."

Then the venerable Ānanda returned to the Blessed One, and bowed down before him, and took his seat on one side. And, so sitting, the venerable Ānanda said to the Blessed One: "Mahā-Pajāpatī the Gotamī, lord, has taken upon herself the Eight Chief Rules, the aunt of the Blessed One has received the upasampadā ordination."

"If, Ānanda, women had not received permission to go out from the household life and enter the homeless state, under the doctrine and discipline proclaimed by the Tathāgata, then would the pure religion, Ānanda, have lasted long, the good law would have stood fast for a thousand years. But since, Ānanda, women now have received that permission, the pure religion, Ānanda, will not now last so long, the good law will now stand fast for only five hundred years. Just, Ānanda, as houses in which there are many women and but few men, are easily violated by robbers, by burglars; just so, Ānanda, under whatever doctrine and discipline women are allowed to go out from the household life into the homeless state, that religion will not last long.

"And just, Ānanda, as when disease, called mildew, falls upon a field of rice in fine condition, that field of rice does not continue long; just so, Ānanda, under whatsoever doctrine and discipline women are allowed to go forth from the household life into the homeless state, that religion will not last long. And just, Ānanda, as when disease, called blight, falls upon a field of sugar-cane in good condition, that field of sugar-cane does not continue long; just so, Ānanda, under whatsoever doctrine and discipline women are allowed to go forth from the household life into the homeless state; that religion does not last long. And just,

Ānanda, as a man would in anticipation build an embankment to a great reservoir, beyond which the water should not overpass; just even so, Ānanda, have I in anticipation laid down these Eight Chief Rules for the nuns, their life long not to be overpassed."

Here ends the Eight Chief Rules for the Nuns.

II

Now Mahā-Pajāpatī the Gotamī went up to the place where the Blessed One was, and bowed down before him, and stood respectfully on one side.

And, so standing, Mahā-Pajāpatī the Gotamī spake thus to the Blessed One: "What course, lord, should I pursue towards these women of the Sakya clan?" Then the Blessed One taught Mahā-Pajāpatī the Gotamī and incited her and aroused her, and gladdened her with religious discourse; and she, so taught, incited, aroused, gladdened, bowed down before the Blessed One and keeping him on her right hand as she passed him, she departed thence. Then the Blessed One, in that connection, delivered a religious discourse, and said to the monks:

"I allow nuns, O monks, to receive the upasampadā ordination from monks."

Now those nuns said to Mahā-Pajāpatī the Gotamī: "Neither have you received the upasampadā ordination, nor have we; for it has thus been laid down by the Blessed One: 'Nuns are to be ordained by monks.'"

Then Mahā-Pajāpatī the Gotamī went to the venerable Ānanda, and (repeated their words to him). And the venerable Ānanda, went to the Blessed One and (repeated them to him; to which the Blessed One replied):

"In that moment, Ānanda, when Mahā-Pajāpatī the Gotamī took upon herself the Eight Chief Rules, that was to her as the upasampadā ordination."

Now Mahā-Pajāpatī the Gotamī went to where the Blessed One was, and bowed down before him, and stood respectfully on one side. And so standing, Mahā-pajāpatī the Gotamī said: "May the Blessed One preach to me the dhamma in outline; so that, having heard the doctrine of the Blessed One I may remain alone and separate, earnest, zealous, and resolved."

"Of whatsoever doctrines thou shalt be conscious, Gotamī, that they conduce to passion, and not to peace, to pride and not to veneration, to wishing for much and not to wishing for little, to love of society and not to seclusion, to sloth and not to the exercise of zeal, to being hard to satisfy and not to content—verily mayest thou then, Gotamī, bear in mind that that is not dhamma, that that is not the discipline, that that is not the teaching of the Master. But of whatsoever doctrines thou shalt be conscious, Gotamī, that they conduce to peace and not to passion, to veneration and not to pride, to wishing for little and not to wishing for much, to seclusion, and not to love of society, to the exercise of zeal and not to sloth, to content and not to querulousness—verily mayest thou then bear in mind that that is dhamma, and that is the discipline, and that the teaching of the Master."

NAKULAPITAR

(FROM SAṂYUTTA-NIKĀYA III)

Trans. by F. L. Woodward, Kindred Sayings, *Vol. III*

Thus have I heard: The Exalted One was once staying among the Bhaggi, at Crocodile-Haunt in Bhesakalā Grove in the Deer-Park. Then the housefather Nakulapitar came to the Exalted One, saluted him, and sat down at one side.

As he sat there, the housefather Nakulapitar addressed the Exalted One, saying: "Master, I am a broken-down old man, aged, far-gone in years, I have reached life's end, I am sick and always ailing. Moreover, Master, I am one to whom rarely comes the sight of the Exalted One and the worshipful brethren. Let the Exalted One cheer and comfort me, so that it be a profit and a blessing unto me for many a long day."

" True it is, true it is, housefather, that your body is weak and cumbered. For one, carrying this body about, housefather, to claim but a moment's health would be sheer foolishness. Wherefore, housefather, thus you should train yourself: 'Though my body is sick, my mind shall not be sick.' Thus, housefather, must you train yourself."

Meghiya

(*FROM THE UDĀNA IV*)

(*Adapted from the trans. by Maj. D. M. Strong*)

Thus have I heard. On a certain occasion the Blessed One dwelt at Chalaka on the Chalaka mountain.

Now at that time the venerable Meghiya was the servitor of the Blessed One. And the venerable Meghiya went to where the Blessed One was and, drawing near, he saluted the Blessed One and stationed himself respectfully apart, and while thus standing the venerable Meghiya said to the Blessed One: " I wish, lord, to enter the village of Jantu to go on my rounds for alms."

" Very well, Meghiya, do as you think fit."

And the venerable Meghiya clothing himself in the forenoon and taking his alms-bowls and tunic entered the Jantu village for alms. And when he had gone his rounds and finished his meal, he went to the banks of the Kimikālā-river, and as he wandered from place to place along the banks of the river, he beheld an enchanting and delightful grove of mango trees. And when he saw it, he exclaimed: " How beautiful, how lovely is this mango grove. Truly this is a fitting place for a scion of good family to struggle and strive (after holiness). If the Blessed One consents, I will return to this mango grove and there struggle and strive (after holiness)." And the venerable Meghiya went to where the Blessed One was and, drawing near, he saluted the Blessed One and sat down respectfully apart and while thus sitting, he said to the Blessed

One: "In the forenoon, lord, having put on my garments and taking my alms-bowl and tunic, I entered the Jantu village for alms, and when I had gone my rounds and finished my meal, I went to the banks of the Kimikālā-river and wandering on foot from place to place, I beheld an enchanting and delightful grove of mango-trees, and when I saw it, I exclaimed: 'How lovely, how beautiful is this mango grove. Surely this is a fitting place for a son of good family, to struggle and strive. If the Blessed One will consent, I will return to this mango grove, and struggle and strive (after holiness).' If, lord, the Blessed One consents I will go to that mango grove and enter into the struggle."

When these words had been spoken, the Blessed One said to the venerable Meghiya: "Wait a while. Meghiya, we are alone, wait at least till some other monk arrives."

And a second time the venerable Meghiya spoke to the Blessed One, saying: "No further duties, lord, have to be performed by the Blessed One, to what is done nought is to add. But I, lord, have duties still to perform, to what is done there is to be added. If, lord, the Blessed One consents, I would go to that mango grove, and enter upon the struggle."

A second time, the Blessed One said to the venerable Meghiya: "Wait a while, Meghiya, we are alone now, wait at least till some other monk arrives."

A third time the venerable Meghiya said to the Blessed One: (as above . . .).

"As to the struggle, Meghiya, what may we say about it? Do now as you think best."

And the venerable Meghiya arose from his seat, and saluted the Blessed One, and passing round keeping his right side to him, he went to the mango grove, and entering it sat down during the heat of the day at the foot of a tree.

And while living in that mango grove, the venerable Meghiya was constantly assailed by three kinds of evil and unlawful thoughts, namely lustful thoughts, malicious thoughts, and cruel thoughts.

And the venerable Meghiya thought to himself: "How strange is it, how marvellous is it, that I, who through faith have abandoned my home for the homeless state, should be filled with these evil and unlawful thoughts, namely lustful thoughts, malicious thoughts, and cruel thoughts."

And the venerable Meghiya arose from his solitary communings and went to where the Blessed One was and having saluted the Blessed One, he sat down respectfully apart and while thus sitting he said to the Blessed One: "While living in that mango grove, lord, I was assailed by three evil and unlawful thoughts, namely lustful thoughts, malicious thoughts, and cruel thoughts and I thought how strange, how marvellous is it, that I who through faith have abandoned my home for the homeless state, should be assailed by these three evil and unlawful thoughts."

"For the immaturely released heart, O Meghiya, five conditions conduce to maturity. What are these five?

"1. In this world, Meghiya, a monk should have a virtuous friend, a virtuous companion. For the immaturely released heart, Meghiya, this is the first condition which conduces to maturity.

"2. Further, Meghiya, a monk should be pious, should live a life of restraint according to the precepts, and be endued with right conduct, perceiving danger in the least fault, and adopting the moral precepts should exercise himself therein. For the immaturely released heart, Meghiya, this is the second condition which conduces to maturity.

"3. Further, Meghiya, there should be discourses such as tend to the eradication of evil, to the opening up of purpose, to an utter weariness of the world, to passionlessness, to cessation, to tranquillity, to the higher knowledge, to supreme enlightenment, to Nibbana, that is, discourses on frugality, on contentment, solitude, exclusiveness, effort, and exertion, piety, self-concentration, wisdom and emancipation as resulting from insight acquired by knowledge—by means of such discourses satisfaction is obtained, and trouble and difficulties are overcome.

"For the immaturely released heart, Meghiya, this is the third condition which conduces to maturity.

"4. Further, Meghiya, the monk should live a life of effort and exertion, abandoning unlawful practices, he should practise what is lawful, he should be resolute, put forth his strength, not throwing down the burden in the practice of those things that are lawful.

"For the immaturely released heart, Meghiya, this is the fourth condition which conduces to maturity.

"5. Further, Meghiya, the monk should have wisdom, should be endowed with the knowledge of the 'rise and set' of things, of sublime penetration, and of that which leads to the complete cessation of sorrow.

"For the immaturely released heart, Meghiya, this is the fifth condition which conduces to maturity.

"For the immaturely released heart, Meghiya, these are the five conditions which conduce to maturity.

"Thus, Meghiya, when a monk has provided himself with a virtuous friend, a virtuous companion, a virtuous associate, it is to be expected that he will become pious, that he will live a life of restraint according to the precepts and be endued with right conduct, and seeing danger in the least of sins, will adopt the moral precepts and exercise himself therein; and those discourses which tend to the eradication of evil, to a beneficial expansion of the heart, to an utter weariness of the world, to the cessation of all desire, to tranquillity, to the higher knowledge, to supreme enlightenment, to Nibbana, namely, discourses on frugality, contentment, solitude, exclusiveness, effort and exertion, piety, self-concentration, wisdom and emancipation, resulting from insight acquired by knowledge, by the means of such discourses satisfaction is obtained and trouble and difficulties overcome.

"Thus the monk with a virtuous friend, a virtuous companion, a virtuous associate will live a life of effort and exertion, and abandoning unlawful practices, will practise what is lawful, he will be resolute, put forth his strength and not throw down the burden in the practise of what is lawful.

"Thus the monk with a virtuous friend, a virtuous companion, a virtuous associate, will become wise, will be endowed with the knowledge of the 'rise and set' of things, of sublime penetration and of that which conduces to the complete cessation of sorrow.

"Moreover, Meghiya, the monk who holds to these five conditions, must give special attention to four other conditions; in order to abandon lust he must dwell on the impurity (of the body), in order to forsake malice, he must dwell on kindness, with a view to the excision of (evil) thoughts he must practise meditation by inhalations and exhalations; for the removal of the pride which says: 'I am,' he must exercise himself in the consciousness of impermanence. By the consciousness of impermanence, the consciousness of non-self is established, he who is conscious of non-self succeeds in the removal of the notion 'I am,' and in this very existence attains to Nibbana."

And the Blessed One, in this connection, on that occasion, breathed forth this solemn utterance:

"He who judges not aright these mean and subtle thoughts
Whereby the mind is puffed up and inflated
Wanders from birth to birth with wavering mind.
But the awakened, ardent and mindful, who keeps such thoughts in subjection
'Has rid him of the thoughts which puff up and inflate the mind.'"

SOṆA-KOṬIKANNA

(*FROM THE UDĀNA, V, 6*)

(*Adapted from the trans. by Maj. Strong*)

Thus have I heard: On a certain occasion the Blessed One dwelt at Sāvatthi, in the Jetavana, the garden of Anāthapiṇḍika.

Now at that time the venerable Mahākaccāna [1] was living in the Avanti country, on the hill called the Precipice, in Kuraraghara. And at that time the lay-disciple Soṇa-Koṭikaṇṇa was the servitor of the venerable Mahākaccāna.

While enjoying the bliss of solitude, this thought arose in the mind of the lay-disciple Soṇa-Koṭikaṇṇa: "According to the doctrine taught by the venerable Mahākaccāna it is

[1] Pronounce -kacchāna.

not easy for the man who dwells at home, to live the higher life, in entire fulfilment, in complete purity, in all its bright perfection. What if I were to shave my head and beard, assume the yellow-robe, and go forth from my home into the homeless ? "

And the lay-disciple Soṇa Koṭikaṇṇa went to where the venerable Mahākaccāna was and drawing near, he saluted the venerable Mahākaccāna and sat down apart, and while thus sitting he said to the venerable Mahākaccāna : " Just now, sir, as I was enjoying the bliss of solitude, this thought arose in my mind. 'According to the doctrine, etc. (as above transl.).' May it please the lord Mahākaccāna to receive me into the Order of those who have renounced the world."

When these words had been spoken, the venerable Mahākaccāna said to the lay-disciple Soṇa Koṭikaṇṇa : " Hard is it, O Soṇa, to live for a life-time the higher life, to partake of one meal a day, to sleep apart. I pray you, Soṇa, to remain for the present in the condition of a householder, while practising the precepts of the Buddhas, and partaking of one meal a day, and sleeping apart."

And the fancy which the lay-disciple Soṇa Koṭikaṇṇa had for the ascetic life subsided.

A second time, as the lay-disciple Soṇa Koṭikaṇṇa was enjoying the bliss of solitude, this thought arose : " According to the doctrine, etc. (as above . . .) What if I were to, etc. (as above . . .) and go forth from my home into the homeless ? "

A second time the venerable Mahākaccāna said : " Hard is it, O Soṇa, etc. (as above . . .)."

A third time, as the lay-disciple Soṇa Koṭikaṇṇa was enjoying the bliss, etc. (as above . . .) : " May it please the lord Mahākaccāna to receive me into the Order of those who have renounced the world ? "

And the venerable Mahākaccāna received the lay-disciple Soṇa Koṭikaṇṇa into the Order of those who have renounced the world.

Now at that time there were very few monks in the Southern districts of the Avanti country.

At the end of three years, the venerable Mahākaccāna with

difficulty and trouble, collecting monks from here and there, managed to form a Chapter of ten monks. And the venerable Soṇa was admitted into the higher ranks of the Order.

As the venerable Soṇa was passing the rainy season in solitude, there occurred to him the thought: "I have not seen the Blessed One, face to face, but I have heard he is such and such. If my teacher approves, I will go and see the Exalted One, that Arahant, the Supreme Buddha."

And the venerable Soṇa, arising at eventide from his solitary communings went to where the venerable Mahākaccāna was, and drawing near saluted him and sat down apart and while thus sitting the venerable Soṇa said to him: "Just now, lord, while passing the rainy season in solitude this thought occurred to me: 'I have not seen the Blessed One (as above . . .). I will go and see . . . the Supreme Buddha.'"

"It is well, Soṇa, it is well, go and see the Exalted One, that Saint, the Supreme Buddha. You will behold the holy, the gracious one, the dispenser of joy, whose senses are placid, whose spirit is at rest, who has attained to supreme self-conquest, he who has won, the subdued, the guarded one, whose senses are stilled; and when you behold him, in my name, bow down, in salutation at his feet and say: 'My master, lord, the venerable Mahākaccāna bows his head in salutation at the feet of the Exalted One, and asks: If there is any slight ailment, if there is freedom from bodily fatigue, if he is vigorous, strong and in good health?'"

"Be it so," said the venerable Soṇa and praising the words spoken by the venerable Mahākaccāna, and giving thanks, he put his sleeping place in order, and taking his alms-bowl and robe departed on his way to Sāvatthi. And wandering from place to place he came at the Jetavana, the garden of Anāthapiṇḍika at Sāvatthi, where the Blessed One dwelt and drawing near he saluted the Blessed One and sat down apart and while thus sitting he said to the Blessed One: "My master enquires if there is any slight ailment, etc. (as above . . .)."

"I trust, monk (said the Blessed One) that you bear up, that you are able to carry on, that you have had little fatigue on the journey, that you have not been wearied in quest of alms."

"It is to be borne, Exalted One, there can be carrying on, I have had little fatigue on the journey, I have not wearied myself in quest of alms."

And the Blessed One called the venerable Ānanda to him and said: "Prepare, Ānanda, a sleeping place for this newly arrived monk. The Blessed One desires to share a cell with the venerable Soṇa"; and he prepared a sleeping place for the venerable Soṇa in the cell which the Blessed One occupied. And the Blessed One having spent the greater part of the night sitting in the open air, washed his feet and entered the cell. And the venerable Soṇa, having spent the greater part of the night in the open air, washed his feet and entered the cell.

And the Blessed One arising in the morning, called the venerable Soṇa to him and said: "May the Doctrine become so clear that you may recite it to the monks."

"Be it so," said the venerable Soṇa in assent to the Blessed One, and he intoned all the sixteen chapters of the "Atthăka." [1]

And the Blessed One, at the conclusion of the venerable Soṇa's recitation, expressed his delight, saying: "Excellent, monk, excellent. Those sixteen chapters of the 'Atthăka' have been well grasped, thoroughly thought out, and understood; you are gifted with a sweet voice, distinct and faultless, and are able to explain the meaning of things. How many years have you been ordained?"

"One year, sir."

"Why, monk, did you delay it so long?"

"For a long time, sir, I saw the worthlessness of sense-desires; moreover the householder's life is crowded with business and many anxieties."

And the Blessed One, in this connection, on that occasion, breathed forth this solemn utterance:

> "He who has seen the perils of the world,
> Has learnt the Norm and cannot be reborn,
> He, Ariyan, in evil finds no joy;
> In evil lies no pleasure for the pure."

[1] The Octet, or fourth section of the canonical book "Sutta Nipāta".

Exhortation

(*SAṂYUTTA-NIKĀYA XVI, § 7*)

(*As translated by Mrs. Rhys Davids,* Kindred Sayings, *Vol. II*)

At Rājagaha at the Bamboo Grove :—

Now the venerable Mahā-Kassapa came into the presence of the Exalted One . . . To him seated the Exalted One said this : " Exhort the brethren, Kassapa. Give them discourse on doctrine, Kassapa. Either I or thou must exhort the brethren. Either I or thou must give them discourse on doctrine."

" Just now, lord, it is difficult to speak to the brethren. They are in a state that makes it difficult to speak to them. They are intractable, they pay no deference to instruction. For instance, lord, I saw Bhanda, the brother who is the colleague of Ānanda, and Abhinjika who is the colleague of Anuruddha out-talking each other thus : ' Come, brother, which will speak the more ? which will speak the better ? which will speak the longer ? ' "

Then the Exalted One addressed a brother : " Come thou, brother, tell my word to Bhanda the brother who dwelleth with Ānanda and Abhinjika, the brother who dwelleth with Anuruddha : ' The Master would speak to you.' "

" Even so, lord," responded that brother, and delivered the message.

" Even so, brother," responded those brethren, and came into the presence of the Exalted One, saluted him, and sat down beside him. To them thus seated the Exalted One said this : " Is it true what they say, brethren, that ye have been out-talking each other : ' Which of us will speak the more, the better, the longer ? ' "

" Even so, lord."

" Do ye affirm, brethren, that I have been teaching you to out-talk each other in this way : ' Come brother, which of us will speak the more, which will speak better, which will speak longer ? ' "

" Not so, lord."

" If as you say, brethren, ye do not affirm that I have been teaching you thus, whatever then, futile men that ye are, have ye come to know, have ye come to see, in a Doctrine and a Discipline so well declared, wherein ye are in orders, that ye should be out-talking each other as to what ye have learnt, saying: 'Come brother, which of us will speak the more, the better, the longer?' "

Then those brethren, falling prone at the feet of the Exalted One, spake thus: "Transgression hath overcome us, lord, so foolish, so stupid, so wrong were we, in that we, who are in orders under a Doctrine and Discipline so well declared, did out-talk one another therein saying: 'Come, brother, which of us will talk more, will talk better, will talk longer?' May the Exalted One accept this our confession, lord, for restraint in the future."

"Verily, brethren, hath transgression overcome you, so foolish, so stupid, so wrong were ye in that ye, who are in orders under a Doctrine and Discipline so well declared, did out-talk each other after this fashion. But inasmuch as ye, brethren, have seen your transgression as transgression, and have made confession, as is right, we do accept this from you. For this, brethren, it is to grow in the Ariyan Discipline, when having seen transgression as transgression we make confession as is right, and in future practise self-restraint."

SAND-CASTLES

(*SAMYUTTA-NIKĀYA III*)

(*Trans.*: *F. L. Woodward, under the title* "*A Being*", Kindred Sayings, *Vol. III*)

At Sāvatthi. (Then the venerable Rādha came to the Exalted One.) Seated at one side the venerable Rādha thus addressed the Exalted One:

"'A being. A being,'" they say lord. "Pray, lord, how far is one called a being?"

"That desire, Rādha, that lust, that lure, that craving, which is concerned with body, entangled thereby, fast entangled thereby, therefore is one called a being.

"That desire, that lust, that craving, that lure which is concerned with feeling, with perception, the activities, consciousness, entangled thereby, fast entangled thereby, therefore is one called a being.

"Just as when, Rādha, boys or girls play with little sand-castles. So long as they are not rid of lust, not rid of desire, not rid of affection, thirst, feverish longing and craving for those little sand-castles, just so long do they delight in them, are amused by them, set store by them, are jealous of them.

"But, Rādha, as soon as those boys or girls are rid of lust, of desire and affection, are rid of thirst, feverish longing and craving for those little sand-castles, straightway with hand and foot they scatter them, break them up, knock them down, cease to play with them.

"Even so, Rādha, do you scatter body, break it up, knock it down, cease to play with it, apply yourself to destroy craving for it. So also with feeling, perception, the activities . . . do you scatter consciousness, Rādha, break it up, knock it down, cease to play with it, apply yourself to destroy craving for it.

"Verily, Rādha, the destruction of craving is Nibbāna."

THE BLESSED ONE SEEKS SOLITUDE

(*FROM THE UDĀNA, IV*, 5)

(*Closely following trans. by Maj. Strong*)

Thus have I heard. On a certain occasion the Blessed One dwelt at Kosambi, in the Ghosita monastery.

Now at that time the Blessed One was living surrounded by a crowd of monks and nuns, of male and female lay disciples, of kings and their ministers, as well as by heretical sects and their pupils, and he suffered annoyance and discomfort.

And this thought occurred to him: "Surrounded by a crowd of monks and nuns, male and female votaries, of kings and their ministers, as well as by heretical sects and their pupils, I suffer annoyance and discomfort. What if I were to live alone, remote from the crowd?"

And the Blessed One, robing himself in the forenoon and taking his alms-bowl and robe, entered Kosambi for alms. Having walked about Kosambi for alms, he returned from his rounds and after finishing his meal, he himself put in order his sleeping place, and taking his alms-bowl and robe, and without informing his servitor or giving notice to the Brethren he departed, alone, without a companion, in the direction of Palileyyaka, and wandering from place to place, he reached Palileyyaka, and took up his abode there.

And the Blessed One sojourned in the dense grove Rakkhilā, in the vicinity of Palileyyaka, at the foot of the Bhadda Sāl tree.

Now a certain noble elephant lived there, who was much worried by a crowd of male and female elephants, young elephants and elephant calves. He had to feed on blades of grass with their tips broken off, and they ate the young branches which he himself had broken down. He had also to drink water that had been polluted and when he plunged (into the water) to cross over, the female elephants rubbed their bodies against him. In consequence of this crowd he was annoyed and lived ill at ease.

And this thought occurred to the noble elephant: "Surrounded by a crowd of male elephants, female elephants, young elephants and elephant calves, I have to feed on blades of grass with their tips broken off and they eat the young branches I myself have broken down. I have also to drink water that has been polluted and when I plunge to cross over, the female elephants rub their bodies against me. In consequence of this crowd I am annoyed and live ill at ease. What if I were to live alone, remote from the crowd?"

And the noble elephant leaving the herd went to the deep groves of Rakkhilā in the vicinity of Palileyyaka, to the foot of the Bhadda Sāl tree, where the Blessed One was. And when he arrived there, he removed the grass from the spot which the Blessed One occupied, and brought with his trunk drinking water for the Blessed One.

And as the Blessed One was rejoicing in the calm of solitude and isolation this thought arose: "Formerly I lived a life of annoyance and discomfort surrounded by monks and nuns . . . Now no longer surrounded by monks and nuns . . . I live in comfort and at ease."

And in the mind of the noble elephant this thought arose: "Formerly, I lived a life of annoyance and discomfort surrounded by male elephants and female elephants . . . Now no longer surrounded I live in comfort and at ease."

And the Blessed One, with reference to his own solitude, and perceiving what was passing in the mind of that noble elephant, breathed forth this solemn utterance:

"The heart of the noble elephant (with tusks like plough-poles)
Is at one with the heart of the Noble One
In that alone he delights in the forest."

Reprimanding Cruelty

(*FROM THE UDĀNA, V, 4*)

(*Closely following trans. by Maj. Strong*)

Thus have I heard. On a certain occasion the Blessed One dwelt at Sāvatthi, in the Jetavana, the garden of Anāthapiṇḍika.

Now at that time a number of young men, between Sāvatthi and the Jetavana, were ill-treating some fish.

And the Blessed One, robing himself in the forenoon and taking his alms-bowl and robe, entered Sāvatthi for alms. And the Blessed One beheld these young men, between Sāvatthi and the Jetavana, ill-treating the fish and when he saw them, he went to where the young men were and drawing near, said to them: "Young men, have you yourselves a dread of pain, is pain hateful to you?"

"Yes, sir, we dread pain, pain is hateful to us."

And the Blessed One, in this connection, on that occasion, breathed forth this solemn utterance:

"If pain is hateful to you, perform no evil deed openly or in secret.
If you should do, or do now an evil action,
There is no escape for you from pain tho' ye flee and run away."

Māra Would Tempt Buddha with Worldly Power

(FROM SAṂYUTTA-NIKĀYA, I-IV, § 10)

(Trans. by Mrs. Rhys Davids, Kindred Sayings, *Vol. I)*

The Exalted One was once staying among the Kosalese in the Himālaya regions, dwelling in a leaf-hut.

Now as the Exalted One was meditating in privacy, this thought arose in his heart: "Is it possible to exercise governance without smiting nor letting others slay, without conquering nor causing others to conquer, without sorrowing nor making others sorrow righteously?"

Then Māra the evil one, discerning what was in the mind of the Exalted One, drew near to him, and said: "Let the Exalted One, lord, exercise governance, let the Blessed One rule without smiting nor letting others slay, without conquering nor causing others to conquer, without sorrowing nor making others sorrow, and therewithal ruling righteously."

"Now what, O evil one, hast thou in view, that thou speakest thus to me: 'Let the Exalted One exercise governance. Let the Blessed One rule righteously?'"

"Lord, the four stages to potency have by the Exalted One been developed, repeatedly practised, made a vehicle, established, persevered in, persisted in, well applied. Thus if the Exalted One were to wish the Himālaya, king of the mountains, to be gold, he might determine it to be so, and the mountain would become a mass of gold."

(The Exalted One)

"And were the mountain all of shimmering gold,
Not e'en twice reckoned would it be enough
For one man's wants. This let us learn
To know, and shape our lives accordingly.
He that hath suffering seen, and whence its source—
How should that man to sense-desires incline?
If he but understand rebirth's substrate
And know; here hangs the world bound fast alway,
He fain must work the bonds to eliminate."

Then Māra the evil one thought: "The Exalted One knows me. The Blessed One knows me," and sad and sorrowful he vanished there and then.

How the Blessed One Met Censure and Cautioned New Converts

(*VINAYA TEXTS MAHĀVAGGA VI*, 31)

(*Abridged*)

Once many important Licchavis were assembled in their town-hall and in various ways they praised the Buddha, the Dhamma, and the Sangha. At that time Sīha, their general-in-chief, a follower of the Nigantha sect, was sitting with them. And he thought: "Surely the Blessed One must be an Arahant Buddha, for these many important Licchavis assembled here in their town-hall in various ways praise the Buddha, the Dhamma, and the Sangha. Suppose I go to visit him, the Arahant Buddha."

Then the General Sīha went and said to Nigantha Nātaputta: "I wish, lord, to go and visit the Samana Gotama."

"Why should you, Sīha, who believe in effective action (morally merited) go to visit the Samana Gotama, who denies effective action? . . . he teaches a dhamma of non-effective action; and in this dhamma he trains his disciples." Then the wish to visit the Blessed One abated in the General Sīha.

(A second and third time these circumstances occurred as above related. Then Sīha reflected): "What will the Niganthas do to me whether they approve or not? Suppose I were to go, without consulting the Niganthas, to visit the Blessèd One, the Arahant Buddha."

. . . Then Sīha went to the Blessed One and having respectfully saluted him, he sat down near him and said: "I have heard, lord, that the Samana Gotama denies effective action; he teaches a dhamma of non-effective action, and in this dhamma he trains his disciples. Do they who speak thus speak the words of the Blessed One, or do they not slander him falsely, are they declaring a dhamma in conformity with his dhamma? As it is our wish, lord, to avoid making false accusations against the Blessed One, there is nothing blameworthy in a discussion like this concerning matters of the dhamma."

"There is a way, Sīha, in which one could truly say of me: 'The Samana Gotama denies effective action; he teaches the doctrine of non-effective action; and in this doctrine he trains his disciples.' But also, Sīha, there is a way on which one could truly say of me: 'The Samana Gotama teaches effective action; he teaches the dhamma of action; and in this dhamma he trains his disciples.'

"Also, Sīha, there is a way in which one could truly say of me: 'The Samana Gotama maintains annihilation, disgust, suppression, ascetic ardour, non-rebirth, and courage.'

"In what way is it, Sīha, that one truly could say of me (these things)? . . . I teach, Sīha, the not doing of such actions as are unrighteous by deed, by word, by thought; I teach the not bringing about of the many states, which are evil and not good. In this way, Sīha, one truly could say of me: 'The Samana Gotama teaches non-action.' And in what way is it Sīha, that one truly speaking could say of me: 'The Samana Gotama teaches action and so trains his disciples'? I teach, Sīha, the doing of such actions as are righteous by deed, word and thought; I teach the doing of manifold dhammas which are good . . .

"And in what way is it, Sīha, that one truly could say of me: 'The Samana Gotama teaches annihilation'? I teach the annihilation of the manifold dhammas which are evil and not good.

"And in what way is it, Sīha, that one truly could say of me: 'The Samana Gotama teaches disgust'? Verily I am disgusted at unrighteous actions whether of deed or word or thought. I teach a dhamma of disgust at the bringing to pass of dhammas which are evil, not good . . .

"And in what, Sīha, could one say truly of me: 'The Samana Gotama teaches suppression'? Verily, I teach, Sīha, a dhamma of the suppression of greed, hatred and delusion. I teach a dhamma for the suppression of manifold dhammas which are evil and not good . . . And in what way is it, Sīha, that one truly could say of me: 'The Samana Gotama, teaches ascetic ardour'? I teach, Sīha, the burning away of dhammas which are evil and not good, and all unrighteous actions, in deed, word or thought. He for whom dhammas which are evil and not good are to be burnt away, are put away, are rooted out as a palm-tree made baseless, so that they are made never to become again and cannot arise in the future, him I call an ascetic.

"Now the Tathāgata, Sīha . . . is such an one.

"And in what way is it, Sīha, one truly could say of me: 'The Samana Gotama is not for rebirth'! He who has freed himself from the necessity of returning in the future into a mother's womb, and of being reborn into new becomings, who has rooted out rebirth, and has done away with it as a palm-tree made baseless, so that it is made never to become again, such a person do I call 'not for rebirth'. Now the Tathāgata, Sīha, is such an one.

"And in what way is it, Sīha, that one could truly say of me: 'The Samana Gotama is courageous'? I am courageous, Sīha, by the highest courage, therefore I teach courage and train my disciples in it . . ."

Then when he had spoken thus, Sīha, the general, said to the Blessed One: "Glorious, lord, glorious, lord. As though one were to set up what had been overthrown, or should manifest what had been hidden, or should indicate the way to one who had lost his way, or should bring a lamp into the darkness, that those who had eyes might see visible things, so has the Blessed One taught the dhamma in many ways.

"I take my refuge, lord, in the Blessed One, and in the Dhamma, and in the Bhikkhu-Sangha, may the Blessed One receive me from this day hence as long as my life lasts as a disciple who has taken refuge."

"Consider first, Sīha, that which you are doing. It is proper that well-known people like you, should consider."

"Lord, by this, my joy and satisfaction in the Blessed One still has increased, because the Blessed One thus advises me . . . If the other Titthiya teachers had made me their disciple, they would carry banners through all Vesāli (calling): 'Sīha, the general, has become our disciple.' Yet the Blessed One says to me: 'Consider first . . .' For the second time I take my refuge in the Blessed One, in the Dhamma, and in the Sangha; may the Blessed One receive me from this day hence as long as my life lasts as a disciple who has taken refuge."

"For long, Sīha, your family has been a well-spring to the Niganthas. You should consider it right therefore in the future to give them food when they come."

"Lord, by this, my joy and satisfaction in the Blessed One still has increased, because the Blessed One (thus advises me) . . .

"I have been told, lord: The Samana Gotama says: 'To me alone gifts should be given. To my disciples alone gifts should be given; to no one else's disciples gifts should be given. Solely what is given to me has great reward; what is given to others has no great reward. Solely what is given to my disciples has great reward; what is given to the disciples of others has not great reward.' But the Blessed One urges me to give also to the Niganthas. Well, lord, we will see what will be seasonable. For the third time, lord, I take my refuge in the Blessed One, the Dhamma and the Sangha . . ."

Holding in Reverence

(*SAṂYUTTA-NIKĀYA I, VI, § 2*)

(*Mrs. Rhys Davids's trans.*, Kindred Sayings, *Vol. I*)

Thus have I heard: The Exalted One was once staying at Uruvelā, on the banks of the river Neranjarā, beneath the Goatherd's Banyan, just after he had become fully enlightened.

And to the Exalted One, as he meditated in privacy, the thought arose in his mind: "It is ill to live paying no one the honour and obedience due to a superior. What recluse or brahman is there under whom I could live paying him honour and respect?"

Then the Exalted One thought: "For the perfecting of the moral code (if) imperfectly carried out, I should live under another recluse or brahman, paying him honour and respect. But I see not anywhere in the worlds of devas,

Māras, Brahmās, not among recluses and brahmans, not among the whole race, human or divine, any other recluse, or any brahman more accomplished in moral conduct than myself, and under whom I might live, paying him honour and respect.

"So, too, for the perfecting of concentrative studies, for the perfecting of studies in insight, for the perfecting of study in emancipation, for the perfecting in contemplation of the knowledge of (my) emancipation (if) imperfectly achieved, I should live under another recluse or a brahman, paying him honour and respect. But I see not anywhere in the world of devas, Māras, Brahmās, nor among recluses and brahmans, not among the whole race, human or divine, any other recluse or brahman more accomplished in any of these branches than myself and under whom (for that reason) I should live, paying him honour and respect.

"This Norm then, wherein I am supremely enlightened—what if I were to live under it, paying it honour and respect?"

Thereupon Brahmā Sahampati, becoming aware in thought of the thoughts of the Exalted One, even like a strong man stretching his bent arm out, or drawing together his outstretched arm, vanished from the Brahmā world and appeared before the Exalted One and Brahmā Sahampati draping his outer robes over one shoulder, raised his joined hands towards the Exalted One and said:

"Even so, Exalted One, Even so, Blessed One, they, lord, who in time past were Arahants, Buddhas Supreme, those Exalted Ones did also live only under the Norm, honouring and respecting it. They also, lord, who in time to come will be Arahants, Buddhas Supreme, they will live only under the Norm, honouring and respecting it. Let the Exalted One also, lord, who now is Arahant Buddha live only under the Norm, honouring and respecting it."

Thus spake Brahmā Sahampati, and thereafter he spake thus:

"They who were Buddhas in the days of yore,
And they who will be Buddhas yet to come,
And he who Buddha is in this our day,
Slayer of griefs for many multitudes:

All these have ever lived or now do live
Holding in reverence the holy Norm.
Ay, in the days to come so will they live.
Wherefore let whoso fain is for his good,
Aspiring to be numbered 'mong the great,
Hold ever holy Norm in reverence,
Remembering the Buddhas' ordinance."

THE TEACHER AS WAY-SHOWER

(*AJJHIMA-NIKĀYA II, p. 4*)

(*Trans. by Mrs. Rhys Davids*)

Then the brahman Moggallāna the accountant said: "Why, Master Gotama, is it, seeing that there is a Nibbana and a way to it and Gotama as director, that some of his disciples under his teaching win Nibbana in uttermost fulfilment and some do not?"

"As to that, brahman, it is thee that herein I will question. As thou mayest see fit, so answer. What thinkest thou? Art *thou* wise in the way that leads to Rājagaha?"

"Yes, master, I am."

"Suppose then a man were to come fain to go to Rājagaha, and were to ask thee to direct him. Thou mightest say to him: 'Good, my man! This way goes to Rājagaha; go for a while along it, then wilt thou see such a village. Go for a while, then wilt thou see a certain township. Go for a while, then wilt thou see a lovely park, a lovely grove, a lovely plain, a lovely pool.' He by thee thus bidden may take a wrong road and go the reverse way. Then a second man might come and be fain even so, and be even so bidden, and he might go safe to Rājagaha. Why is it that, seeing there is a Rājagaha and a way to it and thou director, that one man goes wrong, and one goes right?"

"What can I do here, master Gotama? Way-shower am I."

"Even so, brahman, what can I do here? Way-shower am I."

"He, brahman," said Ānanda, "the Exalted One, is one who is discoverer of the undiscovered way, revealer of the unrevealed way, declarer of the undeclared way, knower of the way, wise in the way, skilled in the way."

DISSENSION IN THE ORDER

(FROM THE VINAYA-TEXTS; SEVENTH KHANDHAKA OF THE CHULLAVAGGA)

(Following closely Rhys Davids's and Oldenberg's translation, S.B.E., the first part somewhat abridged)

Now at that time the Blessed One was staying at Anupiya, a town belonging to the Mallas. Then the most distinguished young men of the Sakyan clan had renounced the world in imitation of the Blessed One.

There were the two Sakyan brothers, Anuruddha, who had been very delicately nurtured, and Mahānāma.

And Mahānāma went to Anuruddha saying:

"Either do you renounce the world, or I will do so." (And Anuruddha replied) "I am delicate. It is impossible for me to go forth from the household life into the homeless state. Do you do so."

"But come now, dear Anuruddha, I will tell you what is incident to the household life. First, you have to get your fields ploughed. When that is done, you have to get them sown. When that is done, you have to get the water led down over them. When that is done, you have to get the water led off again. When that is done, you have to get the weeds pulled up. When that is done, you have to get the crop reaped. When that is done, you have to get the crop carried away. When that is done, you have to get it arranged into bundles. When that is done, you have to get it trodden out. When that is done, you have to get the straw picked out. When that is done, you have to get all the chaff removed. When that is done, you have to get it winnowed. When that is done, you have to get the harvest garnered. When that is done, you have to do just the same next year, and the same all over again the year after that.

"The work is never over; one sees not the end of one's labour. O, when shall our work be over? When shall we see the end of our labours? When shall we, still possessing and retaining the pleasures of our five senses yet dwell at rest? Yes, the work, dear Anuruddha, is never over;

no end appears to our labours. Even when our fathers and forefathers had completed their time, even then was their work unfinished.

"Then do you take thought for the household duties. I will go forth from the household life into the houseless state."

And Anuruddha the Sakyan went to his mother, and said to her:

"I want, mother, to go forth from the household life into the houseless state. Grant me thy permission to do so."

And when he had thus spoken, his mother replied to Anuruddha the Sakyan, and said: "You two, dear Anuruddha, are my two sons, near and dear to me, in whom I find no evil. Through death I shall some day, against my will, be separated from you; but how can I be willing, whilst you are still alive, that you should go forth from the household life into the houseless state?"

(And a second time, Anuruddha the Sakyan made the same request, and received the same reply. And a third time Anuruddha the Sakyan made the same request to his mother.)

Now at that time Bhaddiya the Sakyan Rāja held rule over the Sakyans; and he was a friend of Anuruddha the Sakyan's. And the mother of Anuruddha the Sakyan, thinking that that being so, the Rāja would not be able to renounce the world, said to her son: "If, dear Anuruddha, Bhaddiya the Sakyan rāja will renounce the world, you also may go forth into the houseless state."

Then Anuruddha the Sakyan went to Bhaddiya the Sakyan rāja, and said to him: "My renunciation of the world, dear friend, is being obstructed by you."

"Then let that obstruction, dear friend, be removed. I am with you. Renounce the world according to your wish."

"Come, dear friend, let us both renounce the world together."

"I am not capable, dear friend, of giving up the household life. Whatsoever else you can ask of me, that will I do. Do you go forth (alone)."

"My mother, dear friend, has told me that if you do so, I may. And you have even now declared 'If your renunciation be obstructed by me, then let that obstruction be removed. Even with you will I renounce the world according to your wish.' Come, then, dear friend, let us both renounce the world."

Now at that time men were speakers of truth, and keepers of their word, which they had pledged. And Bhaddiya the Sakyan Rāja said to Anuruddha the Sakyan: "Wait, my friend, for seven years. At the end of seven years we will renounce the world together."

"Seven years are too long, dear friend. I am not able to wait for seven years."

Anuruddha finds the offers of six years and so on down to one year, of seven months and so on down to one month, and a fortnight, too long a time to wait. Then the rāja says:

"Wait, my friend, for seven days, whilst I hand over the kingdom to my sons and my brothers."

"Seven days is not too long. I will wait thus far" (*was the reply*).

So Bhaddiya the Sakyan Rāja, and Anuruddha, and Ānanda, and Bhagu, and Kimbila, and Devadatta—just as they had so often previously gone out to the pleasure-ground with fourfold array—even so did they now go out with fourfold array, and Upāli the barber went with them, making seven in all.

And when they had gone some distance, they sent their retinue back, and crossed over into the neighbouring district, and took off their fine things, and wrapped them in their robes, and made a bundle of them, and said to Upāli the barber: "Do you now, good Upāli, turn back, these things will be sufficient for you to live upon."

But as he was going back, Upāli the barber thought: "The Sakyans are fierce. They will think that these young men have been brought by me to destruction, and they will slay me. But since now these young men of the Sakyan clan can go forth from the household life into the houseless state, why indeed should not I?" And he let down the bundle (from his back), and hung the bundle on a tree, saying: "Let whoso finds it take it, as a gift" and returned to the place where the young Sakyans were.

And the Sakyan youths saw him coming from afar, and on seeing, they said to him: "What have you come back for, good Upāli?"

Then he told them (and they replied):

"Thou hast done well, good Upāli, in that thou didst not return; for the Sakyans are fierce, and might have killed thee."

And they took Upāli the barber with them to the place where the Blessed One was. And on arriving there, they bowed down before the Blessed One, and took their seats on one side. And so seated they said to the Blessed One: "We Sakyans, lord, are haughty. And this Upāli, the barber, has long been an attendant, lord, upon us. May the Blessed One admit him to the Order before us, so that we may render him respect and reverence, and bow down with outstretched hands before him (as our senior), and thus shall the Sakyan pride be humbled in us Sakyans."

Then the Blessed One received first Upāli, the barber, and afterwards those young men of the Sakya clan, into the ranks of the Order. And the venerable Bhaddiya, before the rainy season was over, bacame master of the Threefold Wisdom; and the venerable Anuruddha acquired clairvoyance; and the venerable Ānanda realised the effect of having entered upon the Stream; and Devadatta attained to the kind of psychic power which is attainable even by those who have not entered upon the Excellent Way.

Now at that time the venerable Bhaddiya, who had retired into the forest to the foot of a tree, into solitude, gave utterance over and over again to this ecstatic exclamation: "O happiness! O happiness!" And a number of monks went up to the place where the Blessed One was, and bowed down before him, and took their seats on one side. And, so seated, they (told the Blessed One of this), and added: "For a certainty lord, the venerable Bhaddiya is not contented as he lives the life of purity; but rather it is when calling to mind the happiness of his former sovereignty, that he gives vent to this saying."

Then the Blessed One addressed a certain monk, and

said: "Do you go, monk, and in my name call Bhaddiya the monk, saying: 'The Teacher, venerable Bhaddiya, is calling for you.'"

"Even so, lord," said the monk, in assent to the Blessed One. And he went to Bhaddiya, and called him.

"Very well," said the venerable Bhaddiya, in assent to the monk, and he came to the Blessed One, and bowed down before him, and took his seat on one side. And when he was so seated the Blessed One said to the venerable Bhaddiya:

"Is it true, as they say, that you Bhaddiya, when retired into the forest to the foot of a tree, into solitude, have given utterance over and over again to this ecstatic exclamation: 'O happiness! O happiness!' What circumstance was it, O Bhaddiya, that you had in your mind when you acted thus?"

"Formerly, lord, when I was a king, I had a guard completely provided both within and without my private apartments, both within and without the town, and within the (borders of my) country. Yet though, lord, I was thus guarded and protected, I was fearful, anxious, distrustful, and alarmed. But now, lord, even when in the forest, at the foot of a tree, in solitude, I am without fear or anxiety, trustful and not alarmed; I dwell at ease, subdued, secure, with mind as peaceful as an antelope's. It was when calling this fact to mind, lord, that I gave utterance over and over again to that cry: 'O happiness! O happiness!'"

Then the Blessed One, on hearing that, gave utterance at that time to this song:—

> "The man who harbours no harsh thoughts within him,
> Who cares not whether things are thus or thus,
> His state of joy, freedom from grief or care,
> The very gods obtain not to behold."

Now when the Blessed One had stayed at Anupiyā as long as he thought fit, he set out on his journey towards Kosambi. And journeying straight on he arrived in due course at Kosambi, and there, at Kosambi, he stayed at the Ghosita Ārāma.

Now the following thought occurred to Devadatta, when

he had retired into solitude, and was plunged in meditation: "Whom now can I so gain over that, he being well pleased with me, much gain and honour may result to me?" And it occurred to him, "Now this prince Ajātasattu is young, and has a lucky future before him. Let me gain him over; and he being well pleased with me, much gain and honour will result."

Then Devadatta folded up his sleeping-mat, and set out, fully bowled and robed, for Rājagaha; and in due course he arrived at Rājagaha. Then he laid aside his own form, and took upon himself the form of a child clad in a girdle of snakes, and appeared on the lap of prince Ajātasattu. Then was prince Ajātasattu terrified, and startled and anxious, and alarmed.

And Devadatta said to prince Ajātasattu, "Are you afraid of me, O prince?"

"Yes, I am. Who are you?"

"I am Devadatta."

"If you, Sir, are really the worthy Devadatta, be good enough to appear in your own shape."

Then Devadatta, laying aside the form of the child, appeared there before prince Ajātasattu with his inner and outer robes on, and with his bowl in his hand. And prince Ajātasattu was well pleased with Devadatta by reason of this marvel of psychic power, and morning and evening he used to go in five hundred chariots to wait upon him, and food was brought and laid before him in five hundred dishes.

Then there arose in Devadatta's mind, possessed and vanquished by gain and favours and fame, some such thought as this: "It is I who ought to lead the Bhikkhu-sangha." And as the idea rose up within him (that moment) was Devadatta deprived of his psychic power.

Now at that time the Blessed One was seated preaching the dhamma, and surrounded by a great multitude, including the king and his retinue. And Devadatta arose from his seat, and arranging his upper robe over one shoulder stretched out his joined hands to the Blessed One, and said to the Blessed One:

"The Blessed One, lord, is now grown aged, he is old and stricken in years, he has accomplished a long journey, and his term of life is nearly run. Let the Blessed One now dwell at ease in the enjoyment of happiness, reached even in this world. Let the Blessed One give up the Bhikkhu-sangha to me, I will be its leader."

"Enough, Devadatta. Desire not to be the leader of the Bhikkhu-sangha."

(Again Devadatta makes the same request and receives the same reply. After the third time the Blessed One says):

"I would not give over the Bhikkhu-sangha, Devadatta, even to Sāriputta and Moggallāna. How much the less, then, to you, vile spittle-dribbler!"

Then Devadatta thought: "Before the king and his retinue the Blessed One denies me, calling me 'spittle-dribbler', and exalts Sāriputta and Moggallāna." And angry and displeased he bowed down before the Blessed One, and keeping him to the right hand as he passed him, he departed thence.

This was the first time that Devadatta bore malice against the Blessed One.

And the Blessed One said to the monks: "Let then the Sangha, monks, carry out against Devadatta the act of Proclamation in Rājagaha, to the effect that whereas the nature of Devadatta used to be of one kind it is now of another kind, and that whatsoever he shall do, either bodily or verbally, in that neither shall the Buddha be recognised, nor the Dhamma, nor the Sangha, but only Devadatta."

And the Blessed One said to the venerable Sāriputta, "Do you then, Sāriputta, proclaim Devadatta throughout Rājagaha."

"In former times, lord, I have sung the praises of Devadatta in Rājagaha, saying, 'Great is the psychic power of the son of Godhi. Great is the might of the son of Godhi.' How can I now proclaim him throughout Rājagaha?"

"Was it not truth that you spoke, Sāriputta when you (so) sang his praises?"

"Yea, lord."

"Even so, Sāriputta, do you now, speaking the truth, proclaim Devadatta throughout Rājagaha."

"Even so, lord," said Sāriputta in assent to the Blessed One . . .

. . . Then Sāriputta, being so appointed, entered Rājagaha with a number of monks, and proclaimed Devadatta accordingly. And thereupon those people who were unbelievers, without devotion or insight, spake thus: "They are jealous, these Sakyan Samanas. They are jealous of the gain and hospitality that fall to Devadatta." But those who were believers, full of devotion, able, and gifted with insight, spake thus: "This cannot be any ordinary affair, in that the Blessed One has had Devadatta proclaimed throughout Rājagaha."

And Devadatta went to Ajātasattu the prince, and said to him: "In former days, people were long-lived, but now their term of life is short. It is quite possible, therefore, that you may end your life while you are still a prince. So do you, prince, kill your father, and become the Rāja, and I will kill the Blessed One, and become the Buddha."

And prince Ajātasattu thought: "This worthy Devadatta has great powers and might; he will know." And fastening a dagger against his thigh, he entered with violence and at an unusual hour, though fearful, anxious, excited. and alarmed, the royal chamber. And when the ministers, who were in attendance in the private chamber saw that, they seized him. And when, on searching him, they found the dagger fastened on his thigh, they asked him:

"What were you going to do, O prince?"

"I wanted to kill my father."

"Who incited you to this?"

"The worthy Devadatta."

Then some of the ministers advised: "The prince should be slain, and Devadatta, and all the monks." Others of them advised: "The monks ought not to be slain, for they have done no wrong; but only the prince and Devadatta." Others of them again said: "Neither should the prince be slain, nor Devadatta, nor the monks." But the king should be told of this and we should do as the king shall command."

So these ministers, taking the prince with them, went to the Rāja of Magadha, to Seniya Bimbisāra and told him what had happened.

" What advice, my friends, did the ministers give ? " . . . (*When they had told him all as before*) he said :

" What, my friends, can the Buddha, or the Sangha, or the Dhamma have to do with this ? Has not the Blessed One had a proclamation already made throughout Rājagaha concerning Devadatta, to the effect that whereas his nature used to be of one kind, it is now of another ; and that whatsoever he shall do, either in act or word, in that shall neither the Buddha, nor the Dhamma, nor the Sangha be required, but only Devadatta ? "

Then those ministers who had advised that the prince and Devadatta and all the monks should be slain, them he made incapable (of ever again holding office). And those ministers who had advised that the prince should be slain and Devadatta, them he degraded to lower offices. But those ministers who had advised that neither should the prince be slain, nor Devadatta, nor the monks, but that the king should be informed of it, and his command followed, them he advanced to high positions.

And the Rāja of Magadha, Seniya Bimbisāra, said to the prince Ajātasattu, " Why did you want to kill me, prince ? "

" I wanted the kingdom, king."

" If you then want the kingdom, prince, let this kingdom be yours." And he handed over the kingdom to Ajātasattu, the prince.

Then Devadatta went to prince Ajātasattu, and said : " Give such orders, king, to your men that I may deprive the Samana Gotama of life."

And Ajātasattu, the prince, gave orders to his men : " Whatsoever the worthy Devadatta tells you, that do."

Then to one man Devadatta gave command : " Go, my friend, the Samana Gotama is staying at such and such a place. Kill him, and come back by this path."

Then on that path he placed other two men, telling them,

"Whatever man you see coming along this path, kill him, and return by that path." Then on that he placed other four men (and so on up to sixteen men).

And that man took his sword and shield, and hung his bow and quiver at his back, and went to the place where the Blessed One was, and when at some little distance from the Blessed One, being terrified, anxious, excited, and alarmed, he stood stark still and stiff.

On the Blessed One seeing him so he said to the man: "Come hither, friend, be not afraid."

Then that man laid aside his sword and his shield, took off his bow and his quiver, and went up to the Blessed One; and falling at his feet, he said to the Blessed One: "Transgression, lord, has overcome me even according to my folly, my stupidity, and my unrighteousness, in that I have come hither with evil and with murderous intent. May the Blessed One accept the confession I make of my sin in its sinfulness, to the end that in future I may restrain myself therefrom."

"Verily, my friend, transgression has overcome you . . . But since you, my friend, look upon your sin as sin, and duly make amends for it, we do accept (your confession of) it. For this, friend, is progress in the discipline of the Noble One, that he who has seen his sin to be sin, makes amends for it as is meet, and becomes able in future to restrain himself therefrom."

Then the Blessed One discoursed to that man in due order, that is to say he spake to him of giving, of righteousness, of heaven, of the danger, the vanity, and the defilement of lusts, and of the advantages of renunciation. And when the Blessed One saw that the man had become prepared, and upraised and believing in heart, then he proclaimed that, which is the special doctrine of the Buddhas; that is to say, Suffering, its Origin, its Cessation, and the Path. And just as a clean cloth from which all stain has been washed away will readily take the dye, just even so did that man obtain, even while sitting there, the pure and spotless Eye of the Truth (that is to say, the knowledge that) whatsoever is an arising thing all that is a ceasing thing. Thus did the man see, and master, and understand, and penetrate the Truth; and he overcame uncertainty, and dispelled all doubts, and gained full knowledge, becoming dependent upon no one else for his knowledge of the doctrine of the Teacher. And he addressed the Blessed One and said:

"Most excellent, lord (are the words of your mouth) most excellent. Just as if a man were to set up that which is thrown down, or were to reveal that which is hidden away, or were to point out the right road to him who has gone astray, or were to bring a light into the darkness so that those who had eyes could see visible forms—just even so, lord, has the Dhamma been made known to me, in many a figure, by the Blessed One. May the Blessed One accept me as a disciple as one who, from this day forth as long as life endures, has taken refuge in him."

And the Blessed One said to the man: "Do not, my friend, leave me by that path. Go by this path," and so dismissed him by another way.

But the two men thought: "Where now can that man be, who was to come alone? He is delaying long." And as they were going to meet him, they caught sight of the Blessed One sitting at the foot of a certain tree. On seeing him they went up to the place where he was and saluted him, and took their seats on one side. To them also the Blessed One discoursed (and they were converted as the other man had been, and he sent them back by another way. And the same thing occurred as to the four, and the eight, and the sixteen men).

And the one man returned to Devadatta, and said to him: "I cannot, lord, deprive the Blessed One of life. Great is the psychic power and might of the Blessed One."

"That will do, friend, you need not do so. I will slay the Blessed One myself."

Now at that time the Blessed One was walking up and down (meditating) in the shade below the mountain called the Vulture's Peak. And Devadatta climbed up the Vulture's Peak, and hurled down a mighty rock with the intention of depriving the Blessed One of life. But two mountain peaks came together and stopped that rock, and only a splinter falling from it made the foot of the Blessed One bleed.

Then the Blessed One, looking upwards said to Devadatta: " Great, foolish man is the demerit you have brought forth for yourself, in that with evil and murderous intent you have caused the blood of the Tathāgata to flow."

And the Blessed One said to the monks: " This is the first time that Devadatta has heaped up (against himself) a deed which will work out its effect in the immediate future, in that with evil and murderous intent he has caused the blood of the Tathāgata to flow."

And the monks having heard that Devadatta was compassing the death of the Blessed One, walked round and round the Vihāra, making recitation in high and loud tones, for a protection and guard to the Blessed One. On hearing that noise the Blessed One asked the venerable Ānanda what it was. And when Ānanda (told him) the Blessed One said: " Then, Ānanda, call the monks in my name, saying: 'The teacher sends for the venerable ones.' "

And he (did so) and they came, and saluted the Blessed One, and took their seats on one side. And when they were so seated, the Blessed One said to the monks: " This, monks, is an impossible thing, and one that cannot occur, that one should deprive a Tathāgata of life by violence. The Tathāgatas, monks, are extinguished in due and natural course. . . . Go, therefore, monks, each one to his vihāra, for the Tathāgatas require no protection."

Now at that time there was at Rājagaha an elephant named Nālāgiri, fierce and a manslayer. And Devadatta went into Rājagaha, and to the elephant stables, and said to the elephant-keepers: " I, my friends, am a relative of the rāja's, and am able to advance a man occupying a low position to a high position, and to order increase of rations or of pay. Therefore, my friends, when the Samana Gotama shall have arrived at this carriage-road, then loose the elephant Nālāgiri, and let him go down the road."

"Even so, sir," said those elephant-keepers in assent to Devadatta.

And when the Blessed One early in the morning had dressed himself, he entered Rājagaha duly bowled and robed, and with a number of monks, for alms; and he entered upon that road. On seeing him the elephant-keepers loosed Nālāgiri, and let it go down the road. And the elephant saw the Blessed One coming from the distance; and as soon as it saw him, it rushed towards the Blessed One with uplifted trunk, and with its tail and ears erect.

When those monks saw the elephant Nālāgiri coming in the distance, they said to the Blessed One: "This elephant lord, Nālāgiri, is fierce, and a manslayer, and it has got into this road. Let the Blessed One, lord, turn back; let the Wellfarer turn back!"

"Come on, monks, be not alarmed. There is, monks, no possibility. This, monks, is an impossible thing, and one that cannot occur, that one should deprive a Tathāgata of life by violence. The Tathāgatas, monks, are extinguished in due and natural course."

(*The monks appealed to him a second and third time, receiving the same reply.*)

Then at that time the people climbed up and sat on the upper storeys of the houses, and on to the balconies, and on to the roofs. And those of them who were unbelievers, and without faith, or insight, said: "Truly the great Samana is beautiful; the elephant will do him hurt." But those who were believers, full of devotion, able, and having understanding said: "At last elephant will wage war with elephant." [1]

And the Blessed One caused the sense of his love to pervade the elephant Nālāgiri, and the elephant, touched by the sense of his love, put down his trunk, and went up to the place where the Blessed One was, and stood still before him. And the Blessed One, stroking the elephant's forehead with his right hand, addressed him in these stanzas:

[1] *Nāga, nāgena*: the word means both elephant and great man.

> "Touch not, O elephant, the elephant of men; for sad, O elephant, is such attack,
> For no bliss is there, O elephant, when he is passed from hence, for him who strikes the elephant of men.
> Be not then mad, and neither be thou careless, for the careless enter not into a state of bliss,
> Rather do thou thyself so act, that to a state of bliss thou mayest go."

And Nālāgiri the elephant took up with his trunk the dust from off the feet of the Blessed One, and sprinkled it over its head, and retired, bowing backwards the while it gazed upon the Blessed One.

And Nālāgiri the elephant returned to the elephant stables, and stood in its appointed place and became once more the tame Nālāgiri. And at that time the people sung these verses:

> "They can be tamed by sticks and goads and whips,
> But the great Sage has tamed this elephant without a weapon or a stick."

The people were angry, murmured and became indignant, saying: "How wicked is this Devadatta, and how wretched, in that he can go about to slay the Samana Gotama, who is so mighty and so powerful." And the gain and honour of Devadatta fell off, while that of the Blessed One increased.

Now at that time, when the gain and honour of Devadatta had fallen off, he went, surrounded by monks, to people's houses, appealing for alms. The people were angry and murmured, and became indignant, saying: "How can the Sakyaputtiya Samana live on food that they ask for at people's houses? Who is not fond of well-cooked food? Who does not like sweet things?"

The monks heard of this and told the matter to the Blessed One. The Blessed One said to the monks: "Therefore do I lay down this rule, monks, for the monks that (not more than) three shall enjoy an alms (together) at people's houses—and this for the sake of three reasons (to wit); for the restraint of the evil-minded, and for the ease of the good, lest those who have evil desires should, in reliance upon a particular party (among the monks), break up the Sangha, and (lastly) out of compassion for the laity. (A monk) who shall enjoy an alms in parties of more than three, shall be dealt with according to law."

Now Devadatta went to the place where Kokālika and Kātamoraka-tissaka, and the son of Khanda-devī and Samuddadatta were, and said to them: "Come, sirs, let us stir up a division in the Samana Gotama's Sangha, and in the body of his adherents."

When he had thus spoken, Kokālika said to Devadatta: "The Samana Gotama, sir, is mighty and powerful. How can we (do such a thing)?"

"Come, sirs, let us go to the Samana Gotama, and make the following five demands, saying: 'The Blessed One, lord, has declared in many a figure the advantages of the man who wishes for little, who is easy to satisfy in the matter of support and nourishment, who has eradicated evil from his mind, has quelled his passions, and is full of faith, of reverence, and of the exercise of zeal. The following five things, lord, conduce to such a condition. It would be good, lord, if the monks should be lifelong dwellers in the woods. He who were to go to the neighbourhood of a village would thereby commit an offence. It would be good if they should, their lives long, beg for alms. He who should accept an invitation, would thereby commit an offence. It would be good if they should clothe themselves, their lives long, in cast-off rags. He who should accept a gift of robes of a layman, would thereby commit an offence. It would be good if they should dwell, their lives long, under the trees. He who should (sleep) under a roof, would thereby commit an offence. It would be good, if they should, their lives long, abstain from fish. He who should eat fish, would thereby commit an offence.' The Samana Gotama will not grant these things. Then will we gain over the people by means thereof.

"Yes. It is possible so to stir up divisions in the Sangha, and in the party of the Samana Gotama. For the people believe in ascetic measures."

And Devadatta, went to the Blessed One, surrounded by his friends, and made these demands (in the words just set out.)

"No, Devadatta. Whosoever wishes to do so, let him dwell in the woods; whosoever wishes to do so, let him dwell in the neighbourhood of a village; whosoever wishes to do so, let him beg for alms; whosoever wishes to do so, let him accept invitations from the laity; whosoever wishes to do so, let him dress in rags; whosoever wishes to do so, let him receive gifts of robes from laymen. Sleeping under trees has always been allowed by me, Devadatta, for eight months in the year; and the eating of fish that is pure in the three points: to wit, that the eater has not seen, or heard, or suspected that it has been caught for that purpose."

And Devadatta, pleased and delighted that the Blessed One had refused the five demands, arose from his seat, and keeping him on his right hand as he passed him, departed thence with his friends. And he entered Rājagaha, and urged his view upon the people by means thereof, saying: "Such and such things did we ask, sirs, of the Samana Gotama. He would not allow them, but we live in accordance with them."

Then those of the people who were unbelievers, and without reverence or insight, said: "These Sakyan Samanas have eradicated evil from their minds, and have quelled their passions, while on the other hand the Samana Gotama is luxurious and his mind dwells on abundance. But those of the people who were believers, and full of reverence and insight, were indignant, became vexed, and murmured, saying: "How can Devadatta go about to stir up division in the Sangha of the Blessed One, and in the party that is subject to him?"

The monks, hearing them so murmuring, told the matter to the Blessed One.

"Is it true, Devadatta, as they say, that thou goest about to stir up division in the Sangha, and in the body of my adherents?"

"It is true, lord."

"Enough, Devadatta. Let not a division in the Sangha seem good to thee; grievous is such division. Whosoever, Devadatta, breaks up the Sangha, when it is at peace, he gives birth to a fault (the effect of) which endures for a kalpa, and for a kalpa is he boiled in niraya. But whosoever, Devadatta, makes peace in the Sangha, when it has been divided, he gives birth to the highest merit, and for a kalpa is he happy in heaven. Thou hast gone far enough, Devadatta. Let not a division in the Sangha, Devadatta, seem good to thee. Grievous, Devadatta, is such division."

Now the venerable Ānanda, having dressed himself early in the morning, went duly bowled and robed into Rājagaha for alms. And Devadatta saw the venerable Ānanda proceeding through Rājagaha for alms. On seeing that he went up to the venerable Ānanda, and said to him: "At once, from this day forth, friend Ānanda, I intend to perform Uposatha, and to carry out the formal proceedings of the Order, without either the Blessed One or the Monk-Sangha."

And when the venerable Ānanda had gone through Rājagaha for alms, and had returned from his rounds, and had finished his meal, he went to the Blessed One, and bowed down before him, and took his seat on one side. And when he was seated, he told the Blessed One: "This very day, lord, Devadatta will break up the Sangha."

Then the Blessed One, when he heard that, gave utterance at that time to this expression of strong emotion:

"Easy is a good act to the good, a good act is hard to the wicked;

"Easy is evil to the evil, but evil is hard for the Noble Ones to do."

IV

Now Devadatta on that day, which was Uposatha, arose from his seat, and gave out voting-tickets, saying: "We went, sirs, to the Samana Gotama and asked for the Five Points, saying: (as above). These the Samana Gotama will not allow; but we live in accordance therewith. Whosoever of the venerable ones approves of the Five Things, let him take a ticket."

Now at that time there were five hundred monks, Vesāliyans and belonging to the Vajjians, who had but recently joined the Order, and were ignorant of what he had in hand. These took the voting-tickets, believing (the Five Points to be according to) the Dhamma, and the Vinaya, and the teaching of the Master. And Devadatta, having thus created a division in the Sangha, went out to the hill Gayā Head, taking those five hundred monks with him.

Then Sāriputta and Moggallāna went to the Blessed One, and bowed down before him, and took their seats on one side. And when they were so seated, Sāriputta said to the Blessed One: "Devadatta, lord, has gone forth to Gayā Head, taking five hundred monks with him."

"Verily, Sāriputta and Moggallāna, there must be a feeling of kindness towards those young monks among you both. Go therefore, both of you, before they have fallen into entire destruction."

"Even so, lord," said Sāriputta and Moggallāna, in assent to the Blessed One. And rising from their seats, they bowed down before him, and keeping him on their right hand as they passed him, they set out for Gāya Head.

Then at that time a certain monk, standing not far from the Blessed One began to weep, and the Blessed One said to him: "Why, monk, dost thou weep?"

"Those lord, who are the Blessed One's chief disciples, Sāriputta and Moggallāna, even they have gone to Devadatta's side, approving the dhamma of Devadatta."

"That, monk, would be impossible, that Sāriputta and Moggallāna should approve his teachings. They are gone only to gain those monks over again."

Now at that time Devadatta, surrounded by a great number of adherents, was seated, preaching the dhamma. And when he saw from afar Sāriputta and Moggallāna coming towards him, he said to the monks: "See, monks, how well preached must be my doctrine, in that even the two chief disciples of the Samana Gotama—Sāriputta and Moggallāna—are coming to join me being pleased with my dhamma."

When he had thus spoken, Kokālika said to Devadatta: "Venerable Devadatta, trust not Sāriputta and Moggallāna, for they are inclined towards evil, and under the influence of evil desires."

"Nay, my friend, let us bid them welcome since they take pleasure in my dhamma."

And Devadatta invited Sāriputta to share his own seat, saying: "Come, friend Sāriputta. Sit thou here."

"Nay," said Sāriputta, and taking another seat, he sat down on one side. And Devadatta instructed and incited and aroused and gladdened the monks far into the night with religious discourse; and then made request to Sāriputta, saying: "The assembly, friend Sāriputta, is still alert and sleepless. Will you, friend Sāriputta, be so good as to think of some religious discourse to address to the Bhikkhus? My back is tired and I would stretch myself a little."

"Even so, friend," said the venerable Sāriputta, in assent to Devadatta. And Devadatta spread his waist-cloth folded in four on the ground, and lay down on his right side. And in a moment even sleep overcame him who was tired, and had lost his presence of mind and his self-consciousness.

Then the venerable Sāriputta taught and exhorted the monks in a religious discourse touching the marvels of preaching; and the venerable Moggallāna taught and exhorted the monks in a religious discourse touching the marvels of psychic power. And whilst they were being taught and exhorted those monks obtained the pure and spotless dhamma-eye (that is the knowledge that) "whatsoever is an arising thing all that is a ceasing thing". Then the venerable Sāriputta addressed the Bhikkhus, and said: "Let us go, my friends, to the Blessed One's side. Whosoever approves of his dhamma, let him come."

And Sāriputta and Moggallāna went back to the Veḷuvana, taking those five hundred monks with them. But Kokālika awoke Devadatta, and said: "Arise, friend Devadatta. Your monks have been led away by Sāriputta and Moggallāna. Did I not tell you, Devadatta, not to trust Sāriputta and Moggallāna, in that they were inclined towards evil and were under the influence of evil desires?"

Then hot blood came forth from Devadatta's mouth.

But Sāriputta and Moggallāna went to the place where the Blessed One was, and bowed down before him, and took their seats on one side. And when they were so seatec Sāriputta said to the Blessed One:

"It were well, lord, that monks who have turned asid to schism should be ordained afresh."

"Nay, Sāriputta, let not the reordination of schismatica monks seem good to thee. But rather cause such monk to confess that they have committed a transgression And how, Sāriputta, did Devadatta treat you?"

"When Devadatta, lord, had instructed and aroused anc incited and gladdened the monks far into the night witł religious discourse, he then made the request to me, saying 'The assembly, friend Sāriputta, is still alert and sleepless. Will you, friend Sāriputta, think of some religious discourse to address to the monks? My back is tired, and I would stretch myself a little.' This, lord, was the way in which Devadatta behaved to me."

Then the Blessed One addressed the monks, and said:

"Once upon a time, monks, there was a great pond in a forest region. Some elephants dwelt beside it; and they, plunging into the pond, plucked with their trunks the edible stalks of the lotus plants, washed them till they were quite clean, masticated them without any dirt, and so ate them up. And that produced in them both beauty and strength, and by reason thereof, they neither went down into death, nor into any suffering like unto death.

"Now among those great elephants, monks, there were young elephants, calves, who also, in imitation of those others, plunged into that pond, and plucked with their trunks the edible stalks of the lotus plants; but they did not wash them till they were clean, but masticated them, dirt and all, and so ate them up. And that produced in them neither beauty nor strength; and by reason thereof they went down into death, and into suffering like unto death. Just so, monks, will Devadatta die who, poor creature, is emulating me.

"Like the elephant calf who eateth mud in imitation of the great beast—that shakes the earth, and eats the lotus plant, and watches through the night among the waters—so will he poor creature die that emulateth me.

" A monk who is possessed of eight qualifications is worthy, monks, to do the work of an emissary. And what are the eight ? The monk must be able to hear and to make others listen, able to learn, able to bear in mind, able to discern, and to make others discern, skilful to deal with friends and foes, and no maker of quarrels. These are the eight qualifications of which when a monk is possessed, he is worthy, monks, to do the work of an emissary.

" Sāriputta, monks, being possessed of eight qualifications, is worthy to do the work of a messenger. What are the eight (etc. as in last paragraph.) ?

" He who on entering a company that is violent of speech,
Fears not, forgoes no word, disguises not his message,
Is unambiguous in what he says, and being questioned angers not,
Of such is surely the monk worthy to go on a mission.

" Devadatta, monks, being overcome, his mind being taken up by eight evil conditions, is irretrievably (doomed to) remain for a kalpa in states of suffering and woe. And what are the eight ? He is overcome, his mind is obsessed, by gain, by want of gain, by fame, by want of fame, by honour, by want of honour, by his having wicked desires, and by his having wicked friends. These, monks, are the eight evil conditions by which Devadatta being overcome, and his mind being obsessed, he is irretrievably (doomed to) remain for a kalpa in states of suffering and woe.

" It would be well, monks, that monks should continue in complete ascendency over any gain or loss, any fame or the reverse, any honour or dishonour, any evil longing or evil friendship, that may accrue to them. And for what reason ? For as much, monks, that bad influences—āsavas—arise, full of vexation and distress, to one who is not continuing in complete ascendency over each of these eight things ; but to one, who is so continuing such influences arise not. This is the reason, monks, why it would be well (etc., as before).

" Let us then, monks, continue in complete ascendency, over any gain or loss, any fame or the reverse, any honour or dishonour, any evil longing or evil friendship, that may accrue to us. And thus, monks, should you train yourselves.

"There are three evil conditions, monks, by which Devadatta being overcome, and his mind being taken up, he is irretrievably doomed to remain for a kalpa in states of suffering and woe. And what are the three? His having wicked desires, and his having wicked friends, and his having come to a stop on the way because he had already attained to some lesser distinction. These are the three (etc., as before):

"Verily, let no wicked desire whatever arise within you.
Know rather from this what is the outcome thereof.
Known was he as wise, reputed to be trained;
Aglow with glory did Devadatta stand (thus have I heard).
He gave himself to vanity, to attacking the Tathāgata:
He fell into the Avichi hell, guarded fourfold and terrible.
The injurer of the good, of the man who does no wrong,
Him sin pervades, the man of cruel heart, and void of love.
Though one should think the ocean to befoul with but one poison pot,
Yet could he not befoul it, for awful is the sea, and great;
Just so though one would injure the Tathāgata by words—
That perfect one, that peaceful heart—against him the words would not avail.
Let the wise bhikkhu make a friend of, and resort to him
By following whose way he will come to the end of griefs."

A Description of the Buddha given by one Brahman to other Brahmans

(Dīgha-Nikāya, IV)

(Transl. by Rhys Davids, in Dialogues of the Buddha, *Vol. I)*

"Truly, sirs, the venerable Gotama is well born on both sides, of pure descent through the mother and the father back through seven generations, with no slur put upon him and no reproach in respect of birth.

"Truly, sirs, the Samana Gotama has gone forth (into the religious life) giving up the great clan of his relations.

"Truly, sirs, the Samana Gotama has gone forth (into the religious life) giving up much money and gold, treasure both buried and above the ground.

"Truly, sirs, the Samana Gotama, while he was still a young man, without a grey hair on his head, in the beauty of his early manhood, has gone forth from the household life into the homeless state.

"Truly, sirs, the Samana Gotama, though his father and mother were unwilling, and wept, their cheeks being wet with tears, nevertheless cut off his hair and beard, and donned the yellow robes, and went out from the household life into the homeless state.

"Truly, sirs, the Samana Gotama is handsome, pleasant to look upon, inspiring trust, gifted with great beauty of complexion, fair in colour, fine in presence, stately to behold.

"Truly, sirs, the Samana Gotama is virtuous with the virtue of the Arahants, good and virtuous, gifted with goodness and virtue.

"Truly, sirs, the Samana Gotama hath a pleasant voice, and a pleasing delivery, he is gifted with polite address, distinct, not husky, suitable for making clear the matter on hand."

Advice to a Brahman.

(*MAJJHIMA NIKĀYA I*)

(*Closely following Lord Chalmers in Further Dialogues of the Buddha, I*)

Thus have I heard. Once when the Lord was staying at Sāvatthī in Jeta's grove in Anāthapiṇḍika's pleasaunce, he addressed the monks as follows:

"Even as a foul and dirty piece of cloth, if dipped by the fuller in blue, yellow, red, or pink dye would take the dye badly and not come out a good colour, and that because of the cloth's impurity; even so, monks, when a man's heart is impure, woe must be expected to ensue; and, conversely, just as cloth in the fuller's hands takes the dye well if it be pure and clean, so, when a man's heart is pure, bliss may be expected to ensue.

"Now, what are the heart's impurities? They are avarice and covetise, malevolence, anger, malice, rivalry, jealousy, grudging, envy, hypocrisy, deceit, imperviousness, outcry, pride, arrogance, inflation, and indolence. Recognizing that each in turn of these is an impurity of the heart, a monk puts them from him; and when at last he has put them all from him, he comes to full belief in the Enlightened One and to recognition of him as the Lord, Arahant all-enlightened, walking by knowledge, blessed, understanding all worlds, the matchless tamer of the human heart, teacher of gods and men, the Lord of Enlightenment; he comes to full belief in the Doctrine and to recognition of it as having been excellently expounded by the Lord, as being here and now and immediate, with a welcome to all and with salvation for all, to be comprehended of each man of understanding; he comes to belief in the Lord's Confraternity and to recognition of it as schooled aright and as walking uprightly, trained in all propriety and in duty, the Brotherhood of the conversion with its four pairs making up the eight classes of the converted, right worthy to receive gifts, hospitality, donations and reverence, unrivalled throughout the world as the field for garnering merit. To the uttermost, every form of self-seeking is renounced, spewed out, discharged, discarded and abandoned. Realizing that he has come to full belief in the Enlightened One—and in his Doctrine—and in his Confraternity—the Brother reaches fruition of spiritual welfare and of its causes together with the gladness attendant thereon; from such gladness is born zest, bringing tranquillity to the body; with his body now tranquil, he experiences satisfaction, wherein he finds peace for his heart. A monk who has reached this pitch in virtue, character and lore, may, without harm or hurt, eat the choicest rice with all manner of sauces and curries. Just as a foul and filthy cloth, if plunged in clear water, becomes pure and clean, and just as silver, if passed through the furnace, becomes pure and clean; even so can such a monk eat as he will without harm or hurt.

"With radiant thoughts of love, of pity, of sympathy, and of poised equanimity, his mind pervades each of the world's four quarters, above, below, across, everywhere; the whole length and breadth of the wide world is pervaded by the radiant thoughts of a mind all-embracing, vast, and boundless, in which no hate dwells nor malevolence.

"Thus much is so, says he to himself; there is a lower and there is yet a higher stage; Deliverance lies beyond this realm of consciousness. When he knows and sees this, his heart is delivered from the Cankers of sensuous pleasure, of continuing existence, of ignorance; and to him thus Delivered comes knowledge of his Deliverance in the conviction: Rebirth is no more; I have lived the highest life; my task is done; and now for me there is no hereafter. Such a monk is said to be inly washen."

Now at this time there was sitting near the brahmin Sundarika-Bhāradvāja who asked whether the Lord went to the river Bāhukā to bathe.

"What boots the river Bāhukā, brahmin? What can it do?"

"It is reputed to cleanse and give merit; many have their burthen of evil borne away in its waters."

Thereupon, the Lord addressed the brahmin in these lines:

"*In Bāhukā, at Adhikakka's ghât,*
Gayā, Sundarikā, Sarassatī,
Bāhumatī, Payāga, there the fool
may bathe and bathe, yet never cleanse his heart.
Of what avail are all these ghâts and streams?
—They cleanse not heart or hand of guilt.
For him whose heart is Cleansed, each day is blest,
each day is hallowed; pure of heart and mind,
he hallows each new day with vows renewed.
So hither, brahmin, come and Bathe as I!
Love all that lives, speak truth, slay not nor steal,
no niggard be but dwell in faith, and then—
why seek Gayā?—'Tis but a pool for thee."

Hereupon the brahmin said to the Lord: "Excellent, Gotama, excellent! It is just as if a man should set upright again what had been cast down, or reveal what had been hidden away, or tell a man who had gone astray which was his way, or bring a lamp into darkness so that those with eyes to see might see the things about them; even so, in many a figure, has the reverend Gotama made his plan clear. I come to Gotama as my refuge and to his Doctrine and to his Confraternity. I ask him to admit me as a disciple and to confirm me therein."

Ānanda

(*THERA-GĀTHĀ CCLX*)

(*Transl. by Mrs. Rhys Davids*, Psalms of the Brethren)

For five-and-twenty years a learner I;
No sensual consciousness arose in me.
O see the seemly order of the Norm!
For five-and-twenty years a learner I;
No hostile consciousness arose in me.
O see the seemly order of the Norm!
For five-and-twenty years on the Exalted One
I waited, serving him by loving deeds,
And like his shadow followed after him.
For five-and-twenty years on the Exalted One
I waited, serving him with loving speech,
And like his shadow followed after him.
For five-and-twenty years on the Exalted One
I waited, serving him with loving thoughts,
And like his shadow followed after him.
When pacing up and down, the Buddha walked,
Behind his back I kept the pace alway;
And when the Norm was being taught, in me
Knowledge and understanding of it grew.
But I am one who yet has work to do,
A learner with a mind not yet matured;
And now the Master hence hath passed away,
Who e'er to me such sweet compassion showed.

Grieving at the Death of the Beloved Teacher

The firmament on every hand
Grows dim, yea all confusèd stand
The truths I seemed to understand.
Gone is the noble friend we love [1]
And dark is earth and heaven above.

[1] According to the Commentary, this refers not to Gotama, but to Sāriputta, who predeceased Gotama. It is conceivable that the editors found the allusion too familiar. But it is just this touch—the word of one who knew Gotama personally and intimately—that has *for us* the ring of a genuine reference to the Master.

And is the comrade passed away?
And is the Master gone from hence?
No better friend is left, methinks,
Than to mount guard o'er deed and sense.
They of the older time are gone
The new men suit mo not at all.
Alone to-day this child doth brood,
Like nesting bird when rain doth fall.

SUNĪTA

THERAGĀTHĀ CCXLII

Humble the clan wherein I took my birth,
And poor was I and scanty was my lot;
Mean task was mine, a scavenger of flowers.
One for whom no man cared, despised, abused,
My mind I humbled and I bent the head
In deference to a goodly tale of folk.
And then I saw the All-Enlightened come,
Begirt and followed by his bhikkhu-train,
Great champion ent'ring Magadha's chief town.
I laid aside my baskets and my yoke,
And came where I might due obeisance make,
And of his loving kindness just for me,
The chief of men halted upon his way.
Low at his feet I bent, then standing by,
I begged the Master's leave to join the Rule
And follow him, of every creature chief.
Then he whose tender mercy watcheth all
The world, the Master pitiful and kind,
Gave me my answer: Come, almsman, he said.
Thereby to me was ordination given.

Lo, I alone in forest depths abode.
With zeal unfaltering wrought the Master's word,
Even the counsels of the Conqueror.
While passed the first watch of the night there rose
Long memories of the bygone line of lives.
While passed the middle watch, the heav'nly eye,
Purview celestial, was clarified.
While passed the last watch of the night, I burst
Asunder all the gloom of ignorance.
Then as the night wore down at dawn
And rose the sun, came Indra and Brahmā,
Yielding me homage with their claspèd hands:
Hail unto thee, thou nobly born of men.
Hail unto thee, thou highest among men:
Perished for thee are all th'intoxicants;
And thou art worthy, noble sir, of gifts.

The Master, seeing me by troop of gods
Begirt and followed, thereupon a smile
Revealing, by this utterance made response:
"By discipline of holy life, restraint
And mastery of self: hereby a man
Is holy; this is holiness supreme."

CHULLA-PANTHĂKA

THERAGĀTHĀ CCXXXVI

Sluggish and halt the progress that I made,
And therefore was I held in small esteem.
My brother judged I should be turned away,
And bade me, saying: "Now do thou go home."
So I, dismissed and miserable, stood
Within the gateway of the Brethren's Park,
Longing at heart within the Rule to stay.
And there he came to me, the Exalted One,
And laid his hand upon my head; and took
My arm and to the garden led me back.
To me the Master in his kindness gave
A napkin for the feet and bade me thus:
"Fix thou thy mind on this clean thing, the while
Well concentrated thou dost sit apart."

And I who heard his blessed Word abode
Fain only and alway to keep his Rule.
Achieving concentrated thought and will,
That I might win the crown of all my quest.
And now I know the where and how I lived,
And clearly shines the eye celestial;
The threefold wisdom have I made my own,
And what the Buddha bids us do is done.
In thousand different shapes did Panthăka
Himself by power abnormal multiply;
And seated in the pleasant Mango-Grove,
Waited until the hour should be revealed.
Then did the Master send a messenger,
Who came revealer of the hour to me,
And at th' appointed time I flew to him.
Low at his feet I worshipped; then aside
I sat me down, and me so seated near
Whenas he had discerned, the Master then
Suffered that men should do him ministry.[1]
High altar he where all the world may give,
Receiver of th' oblations of mankind,
Meadow of merit for the sons of men,
He did accept the gifts of piety.

[1] Panthăka had not been called to the lunch given to the Buddha and several of his disciples. The Master having left him meditating on purity by the clean towel as object-lesson, refused to eat until Panthăka had been sent for, and served first.

PART V

LAST EVENTS IN THE LIFE OF THE BUDDHA

Last Events in the Life of the Buddha

I

COMPILER'S NOTE

(In the Maha-Parinibbāna Suttanta, which is part XVI of the Dīgha-Nikāya, we have what seems to be a successive history of the last months of the Buddha's life, similarly as we find in the Mahāvagga of the Vinaya Texts an account of his life immediately following the Enlightenment.

The Buddha becomes aware that it is his last journey among his disciples, and we find him delivering sermons on the same heads at various places. From the nature and succession of the events here recorded it would seem that this Suttanta gives also a fair picture of what was the daily life of the Buddha, during those more than forty years of his ministry.

Rhys Davids remarks that this Suttanta covers ninety-six pages in the Pali-Text, and that only about one-third is not found elsewhere in the Canon, in nearly identical words, and that that proportion would be still reduced if one were to include passages of similar tendency or of shorter length.

The selections in the following chapter are adapted from this Suttanta as translated by Rhys Davids in Volume II " Dialogues of the Buddha ".)

The Exalted One is Consulted on Matters of State

Thus have I heard. The Exalted One was once dwelling in Rājagaha, on the hill called the Vulture's Peak. Now at that time Ajātasattu, the son of the queen-consort of the Videha clan, the king of Magadha, had made up his mind to attack the Vajjians; and he said to himself, " I will strike at these Vajjians, mighty and powerful though they be, I will root out these Vajjians, I will destroy these Vajjians, I will bring these Vajjians to utter ruin."

So he spake to the brahmin Vassakāra (the Rain-maker) prime-minister of Magadha, and said "Come you, brahmin, do you go to the Exalted One, and bow down in homage at his feet on my behalf, and inquire in my name whether he is free from illness and suffering, and in the enjoyment of ease and comfort, and vigorous health. Then tell him that Ajātasattu, son of the Vedehi, the king of Magadha, in his eagerness to attack the Vajjians, has resolved 'I will strike at these Vajjians, mighty and powerful though they may be, I will root out these Vajjians, I will destroy these Vajjians, I will bring these Vajjians to utter ruin'. And bear carefully in mind whatever the Exalted One may predict, and repeat it to me. For the Buddhas speak nothing untrue."

Then the brahmin Vassakāra, the Rain-maker, hearkened to the words of the king, saying: "Be it as you say." And ordering a number of state carriages to be made ready, he mounted one of them, left Rājagaha with his train, and went to the Vulture's Peak, riding as far as the ground was passable for carriages, and then alighted and proceeded on foot to the place where the Exalted One was. On arriving there he exchanged with the Exalted One the greetings and compliments of politeness and courtesy, sat down respectfully by his side . . . (and then delivered to him the message even as the king had commanded).

Now at that time the venerable Ānanda was standing behind the Exalted One, and fanning him. And the Blessed One said to him: "Have you heard this, Ānanda, that the Vajjians foregather often and frequent the public meetings of their clan?"

"Lord, so I have heard," replied he.

"So long, Ānanda," rejoined the Blessed One, "as the Vajjians foregather thus often, and frequent the public meetings of their clan; so long may they be expected not to decline, but to prosper.

" . . . So long, Ānanda, as the Vajjians meet together in concord, and rise in concord, and carry out their undertakings in concord, so long as they enact nothing, not already established, abrogate nothing that has been already enacted, and act in accordance with the ancient institutions of the Vajjians, as established in former days—so long as they honour and esteem and revere and support the Vajjian elders, and hold it a point of duty to hearken to their words—so long as no women or girls of respectable families are detained among them by force or abduction—so long as they honour and esteem and revere and support the Vajjian shrines in town and country, and allow not the proper offerings and rites, as formerly given and performed, to fall in disuetude—so long as the rightful protection, defence and support shall be fully provided for the Arahants among them, so that Arahants from a distance may enter the realm and the Arahants therein may live at ease—so long may the Vajjians be expected not to decline, but to prosper."

Then the Exalted One addressed Vassakāra the brahmin and said:

"When I was once staying, brahmin, at Vesāli at the Sarandada Shrine, I taught the Vajjians these conditions of welfare; and so long as these conditions shall continue to exist among the Vajjians, so long as the Vajjians shall be well instructed in those conditions, so long may we expect them not to decline, but to prosper."

"We may expect, then," answered the brahmin, "the welfare and not the decline of the Vajjians when they are possessed of any one of these conditions of welfare, how much more so when they are possessed of all the seven. So, Gotama, the Vajjians cannot be overcome by the king of Magadha; that is, not in battle, without diplomacy or breaking up their alliance. And now, Gotama, we must go; we are busy and have much to do."

"Whatever you think most fitting, brahmin," was the reply. And the brahman, Vassakāra, the Rain-maker, delighted and pleased with the words of the Exalted One, rose from his seat, and then went his way.

The Exalted One Speaks on the Welfare of his Disciples

Now soon after (Vassakāra) had gone, the Exalted One addressed the venerable Ānanda, and said: "Go now, Ānanda, and assemble in the Service Hall such of the monks as live in the neighbourhood of Rājagaha."

And he did so; and returned to the Exalted One, and informed him, saying: "The company of monks, lord, is assembled, let the Exalted One do as seemeth to him fit."

And the Exalted One arose, and went to the Service Hall; and when he was seated, he addressed the monks and said:

"I will teach you, seven conditions of the welfare of a community. Listen well and attend, and I will speak."

"Even so, lord," said the monks, in assent, to the Exalted One; and he spake as follows:

"So long, monks, as the brethren[1] foregather oft, and be frequently in assembly—so long as they meet together in concord, and end their meeting in concord, and carry out in concord the duties of the Order—so long as the brethren shall establish nothing that has not been already prescribed, and abrogate nothing that has been already established, and act in accordance with the rules of the Order as now laid down—so long as the brethren honour and esteem and revere and support the elders of experience and long standing, the fathers and leaders of the Order, and hold it a point of duty to hearken to their words—so long as the brethren fall not under the influence of that craving which, springing up within them, would give rise to renewed existence—so long as the brethren delight in forest abodes—so long as the brethren so train their minds in self-possession that good men among their fellow-disciples shall come to them, and those who have come shall dwell at ease—so long may growth be expected of the brethren, not decline.

"So long as these seven conditions shall continue to exist among the brethren, so long as they are well-instructed in these conditions, so long may growth be expected of the brethren, not decline.

[1] Brethren = monks = bhikkhū.

"Other seven conditions of welfare will I teach you, O brethren. Listen well, and attend, and I will speak."

And on their expressing their assent, he spake as follows:

"So long as the brethren shall not engage in, or be fond of, or be connected with business—so long as the brethren shall not be in the habit of, or be fond of, or be partakers in idle talk—so long as the brethren shall not be addicted to, or be fond of, or indulge in slothfulness—so long as the brethren shall not frequent, or be fond of, or indulge in society—so long as the brethren shall neither have, nor fall under the influence of wrong desires—so long as the brethren shall not become friends, companions, or intimates of evil-doers—so long as the brethren shall not come to a stop in mid-way, because they have attained to any lesser thing—so long may the brethren be expected not to decline, but to prosper.

"So long as these conditions shall continue to exist among the brethren—so long as they are instructed in these conditons—so long may growth be expected of the brethren, not decline.

"Other seven conditions of welfare will I teach you, O brethren. Listen well, and attend, and I will speak."

And on expressing their assent, he spake as follows:

"So long as the brethren shall be full of faith, modest in heart, afraid of blame, full of learning, strong in energy, shall have presence of mind and wisdom, so long may growth be expected of the brethren, not decline.

"So long as these conditions shall continue to exist among the brethren—so long as they are instructed in these conditions—so long may growth be expected of the brethren, not decline.

"Other seven conditions of welfare will I teach you, O brethren listen well and attend, and I will speak."

And on their expressing their assent, he spake as follows:

"So long as the brethren shall exercise themselves in the sevenfold higher wisdom, that is to say, in mental activity, search after truth, energy, joy, peace, earnest contemplation, and equanimity of mind—so long may the brethren be expected not to decline, but to prosper.

"So long as these conditions shall continue to exist among the brethren—so long as they are instructed in these conditions—so long may growth be expected of the brethren not decline.

"Other seven conditions of welfare will I teach you, O brethren. Listen well, and attend, and I will speak."

And on their expressing their assent, he spake as follows:

"So long as the brethren shall create in themselves the idea of impermanence, the idea of no unchanging principle, the idea of corruption, of danger, of riddance, of passionlessness, of ceasing, so long may growth be expected of the brethren, not decline. . . .

"Six conditions of welfare will I teach you, O brethren. Listen well and attend, and I will speak."

And on their expressing their assent, he spake as follows:

"So long as the brethren shall persevere in kindness of action, speech, and thought among their fellow-disciples, both in public and in private—so long as they shall divide without partiality, and share in common with their upright companions, all such things as they receive in accordance with the just provisions of the Order, down even to the mere contents of a begging-bowl—so long as the brethren shall live among the saints in the practice, both in public and in private, of those virtues which, unbroken, intact, unspotted, unblemished, are productive of freedom, and praised by the wise; which are untarnished and which are conducive to concentration of heart—so long as the brethren shall live among the saints cherishing, both in public and in private, that noble and saving view which leads to the complete destruction of the sorrow of him who acts according to it—so long may the brethren be expected not to decline, but to prosper . . ."

What May be Said of all Buddhas

Now the venerable Sāriputta came to the place where the Exalted One was, and having saluted him, took his seat respectfully at his side, and said: "Lord, such faith have I in the Exalted One, that methinks there never has been, nor will there be, nor is there now any other, whether wanderer or brahmin, who is greater and wiser than the Exalted One, that is to say, as regards enlightenment."

"Grand and bold are the words of thy mouth, Sāriputta; verily, thou hast burst forth into a song of ecstasy—of course then, thou hast known all the Exalted Ones who in long ages of the past have been Arahants, Awakened Ones, comprehending their minds by thine, and aware what their conduct was, what their wisdom, what their mode of life, and what the emancipation they attained to."

"Not so, O lord."

"Of course then thou hast perceived all the Exalted Ones who in long ages of the future shall be Arahants, Awakened Ones comprehending (in the same manner their minds with thine)?"

"Not so, O lord."

But at least then, Sāriputta, thou knowest me as the Arahant, Awakened One now alive, and hast penetrated my mind (in the manner I have mentioned).

"Not even that, O lord."

"Thou seest then, Sāriputta, that thou knowest not the hearts of the Arahants, Awakened Ones of the past and of the future. Why therefore are thy words so grand and bold? Why dost thou burst forth into such a song of ecstasy?"

"O lord. I have not the knowledge of the hearts of the Arahants, Awakened Ones that have been, and are to come, and now are. I only know the lineage of the faith.

"Just, lord, as a king might have a border city, strong in its foundations, strong in its ramparts and towers, and with only one gate; and the king might have a watchman there, clever, expert, and wise, to stop all strangers and admit only men well-known. And he, on patrolling in his sentry walks over the approaches all round the city, might not so observe all the joints and crevices in the ramparts of that city as to know where even a cat could get out. He might well be satisfied to know that all living things of larger size that entered or left the city, would have to do so by that gate. Thus only is it, lord, that I know the lineage of faith.

"I know that the Arahants, Awakened Ones of the past, putting away all hankering after the world, ill-will, sloth, worry and perplexity—those five hindrances, mental faults which make the understanding weak—training their minds in the four kinds of mental activity; thoroughly exercising themselves in the sevenfold higher wisdom, received the full fruition of Enlightment. And I know that the Arahants, Awakened Ones of the time to come will (do the same). And I know that the Exalted One, the Arahant, Awakened One of to-day, has (done so) now."

A Frequently Repeated Text

(*The following text is delivered so often, during these last months of the Buddha's life, as he travelled from place to place, that it may well be regarded as part of his farewell message. Note is made of it having been given in eleven of the fourteen places he is mentioned as having visited: it is repeated each time in the original, like a recurring theme in music.*) Compiler.

There too at Nālandā in the Pāvārika mango grove the Exalted One held that comprehensive religious talk with the brethren, saying:—

"Such and such is upright conduct; such and such is earnest contemplation, such and such is wisdom. Great becomes the fruit, great the advantages of earnest contemplation, when it is set round with upright conduct. Great becomes the fruit, great the advantage of wisdom when it is set round with earnest contemplation. The mind set round with wisdom is set quite free from the delusions, that is to say, from the delusion of sensuality, from the delusion of re-birth, from the delusion of opinion, from the delusion of ignorance."

A Sermon to Householders

Now when the Exalted One had sojourned as long as he thought fit at Nālandā, he addressed the venerable Ānanda, and said: "Come, Ānanda, let us go on to Pāṭaligāma."

"So be it, lord," said Ānanda, in assent, to the Exalted One.

Then the Exalted One proceeded, with a great company of the brethren to Pāṭaligāma.

Now the disciples at Pāṭaligāma heard of his arrival there, and they went on to the place where he was, took their seats respectfully beside him, and invited him to their rest-house. And the Exalted One signified, by silence his consent.

Then the Pāṭaligāma disciples seeing that he had accepted the invitation, rose from their seats, and went away to the rest-house, bowing to the Exalted One and keeping him on their right as they passed him. On arriving there, they strewed all the rest-house with fresh sand, placed seats in it, set up a water-pot, and fixed an oil lamp. Then they returned to the Exalted One and saluting him they stood beside him, and told him what they had done and said: "It is time for you to do what you deem most fit."

And the Exalted One robed himself, took his bowl and other things, went with the brethren to the rest-house, washed his feet, entered the hall, and took his seat against the centre pillar, with his face towards the east. And the brethren also, after washing their feet, entered the hall, and took their seats round the Exalted One, against the western wall, and facing the east. And the Pāṭaligāma disciples too, after washing their feet entered the hall, and took their seats opposite the Exalted One, against the eastern wall, and facing towards the west.

Then the Exalted One addressed the Pāṭaligāma disciples, and said "Fivefold, O householders, is the loss of the wrong-doer through his moral failure. In the first place the wrong-doer failing in morals falls into great poverty through carelessness; in the next place his evil repute gets noised abroad; thirdly, whatever society he enters—whether of nobles, brahmins, heads of houses, or men of a religious order—he enters with diffidence and confused; fourthly, he is confused in mind when he dies; and lastly, on the dissolution of the body, after death he is reborn into some unhappy state of suffering or woe. This, O householders, is the fivefold loss of the evil-doer."

Fivefold, O householders, is the gain of the well-doer through his moral development. In the first place the well-doer, morally developed, acquires great wealth through his industry; in the next place good reports of him are spread abroad; thirdly, whatever society he enters, whether of nobles, brahmins, heads of houses, or members of a religious order, he enters confident, and self-possessed; fourthly, he dies not confused in mind; and lastly, on the dissolution of the body, after death, he is reborn into some happy state in heaven. This O householders is the fivefold gain of the well-doer.

When the Exalted One had thus taught the lay disciples at Pāṭaligāma, and incited them, and roused them, and gladdened them, far into the night with religious discourse, he dismissed them saying:

"The night is far spent, O householders. It is time for you to do what you deem most fit."

"Even so, lord," answered the disciples of Pāṭaligāma, and they rose from their seats, and bowing to the Exalted One, and keeping him on their right hand as they passed him, they departed thence.

(While at Pāṭaligāma we are told that the Buddha saw thousands of devas, unseen by others, encouraging the building of a new city Pāṭaliputta, concerning which the Buddha prophesied its greatness, but he adds that the danger of fire, and water, and dissension among friends hung over the city; this prophecy seems to have been fulfilled. He is invited by the chief ministers of Magadha to take his meal with them; and when he leaves the city they propose to name after him the gate through which he passes and the ferry at which he crosses the river. But when the Buddha reaches the river

"as instantaneously as a strong man would stretch forth his arm, or draw it back again when he had stretched it forth", he vanished from the one side, and stood on the further bank with the company of monks.)

The Exalted One Speaks on the Four Noble Truths

Now the Exalted One addressed the venerable Ānanda and said: "Come, Ānanda, let us go on to Koṭigāma."

"So be it, lord," said Ānanda, in assent, to the Exalted One. The Exalted One proceeded with a great company of the brethren to Koṭigāma; and there he stayed in the village itself.

And at that place the Exalted One addressed the brethren, and said: "It is through not understanding and penetrating four Aryan Truths, O brethren, that we have run so long, wandered so long both you and I."

"And what are these four?"

"The Aryan truth about sorrow; the Aryan truth about the cause of sorrow, the Aryan truth about the cessation of sorrow; and the Aryan truth about the path that leads to that cessation. But when these Aryan truths are understood and penetrated, the craving for future life is rooted out, that which leads to renewed becoming is destroyed, and then there is no more birth. "Thus spake the Exalted One; and when the Happy One had thus spoken, then again the Teacher said:

By not seeing the Aryan Truths as they really are,
Long is the path that is traversed through many a birth;
When these are seen, the cause of rebirth is removed,
The root of sorrow uprooted, then is no more becoming.

The Mirror of Truth

Now when the Exalted One had remained as long as he thought fit at Koṭigāma, he addressed the venerable Ānanda, and said: "Come, Ānanda, let us go on to the Nādikas."

"So be it, lord," said Ānanda, in assent, to the Exalted One. And the Exalted One proceeded to the Nādikas with a great company of the brethren; and there at Nādika, the Exalted One stayed in the Brick Hall.

And the venerable Ānanda went to the Exalted One and paid him reverence and took his seat beside him. And when he was seated, he addressed the Exalted One, and said: "The brother named Sālha has died at Nādika lord. Where has he been reborn, and what is his destiny? The sister named Nandā has died, lord, at Nādika. Where is she reborn, and what is her destiny?" (And in the same terms he inquired concerning the lay disciple Sudatta and the devout lady Sugatā, the lay disciples Kakudha, and Kālinga, and Nikata, and Katissabha, and Tuttha, and Santuttha, and Bhadda and Subhadda.)

The brother named Sālha, Ānanda, by the destruction of the delusions has by himself, and in this world, known and realised and attained to Arahantship, to emancipation of heart and to emancipation of mind. The sister named Nandā, Ānanda, has, by the complete destruction of the five bonds that bind people to these lower worlds of lust, become an inhabitant of another world, there to pass entirely away, thence never to return. The lay-brother, Sudatta, Ānanda, by the complete destruction of the three bonds, and by the reduction to a minimum of lust, ill-will, and stupidity, has become a once-returner, who on his only return to this world will make an end of sorrow. The lay-sister Sujātā, Ānanda, by the complete destruction of the three bonds, has become converted, is no longer liable to be reborn in a state of suffering, and is assured of hereafter attaining to enlightenment. The lay-brother Kakudha, Ānanda, by the complete destruction of the five bonds that bind people to these lower worlds of lust, has become an inhabitant of another world, there to pass entirely away, thence never to return. (The same of Kālinga, Nikata, Katissabha, Tuttha Santuttha, Bhadda, and Subhadda and with more than fifty lay-brethren in Nādika.)

More than ninety lay-brethren in Nādika, who have died, Ānanda, have by the complete destruction of the three bonds, and by the reduction of lust, ill-will, and stupidity, become once-returners, who on their only return to this world will make an end of sorrow. More than five hundred lay-brethren of Nādika who have died, Ānanda, have by the complete destruction of the three bonds become converted, are not longer liable to be reborn in a state of suffering, and are assured of hereafter attaining enlightenment.

Now there is nothing strange in this, Ānanda, that a human being should die; but that, as each one does so, you should come to me, and inquire about them in this manner, that is wearisome to me. I will, therefore, teach you a way of truth, called the Mirror of Truth, which if a disciple of the noble ones possess he may, if he should desire, himself predict of himself: "Purgatory is destroyed for me, and rebirth as an animal, or a ghost, or in any place of woe. I am converted, I am no longer liable to be reborn in a state of suffering, and am assured of hereafter attaining to enlightenment."

What then Ānanda, is this Mirror of Truth? (It is the consciousness that) the disciple of the Arahants is in the world possessed of faith in the Buddha—believing the Exalted One to be the Arahant, the Fully-Enlightened One, Wise, Upright,. Wellfarer, Worldknowing, Supreme, the Bridler of men's wayward hearts, the Teacher of gods and men, the Exalted and Awakened One. And that he (the disciple) is possessed of faith in the Truth—believing the Truth to have been proclaimed by the Exalted One, as being here and now and immediate, welcoming all, leading to salvation, and to be attained to by the wise, each one for himself. And that he (the disciple) is possessed of faith in the Order—believing the multitude of the disciples of the Exalted One who are walking in the four stages of the noble eightfold path, the righteous, the upright, the just, the law-abiding—believing this Order of the Exalted One to be worthy of honour, of hospitality, of gifts, and of reverence; to be the supreme sowing-ground of merit for the world; to be possessed of the virtues beloved by the good, virtues unbroken, intact, unspotted, unblemished, virtues which make men truly free, virtues which are praised by the wise, are untarnished by the desire of future life or by the belief in the efficacy of outward acts, and are conducive to concentration of heart.

This, Ānanda, is the way the Mirror of Truth, which a disciple of the noble ones possess he may, if he should so desire, himself predict of himself: " Purgatory is destroyed for me; and rebirth as an animal, or a ghost, or in any place of woe. I am converted; I am no longer liable to be reborn in a state of suffering, and am assured of finally attaining to enlightenment."

The Courtezan Ambapāli Appears

Now when the Exalted One had remained as long as he wished at Nādika he addressed Ānanda, and said: " Come, Ānanda, let us go on to Vesāli."

" So be it, lord," said Ānanda, in assent, to the Exalted One.

Then the Exalted One proceeded, with a great company of the brethren to Vesāli; and there at Vesāli, the Exalted one stayed at Ambapāli's grove.

Now there the Exalted One addressed the brethren and said: " Let a brother, monks, be mindful and self-possessed; this is our instruction to you." [1]

" And how does a brother become mindful?"

"Herein, monks, a brother continues as to the body, so to look upon the body that he remains strenuous, self-possessed and mindful, having overcome both the hankering and the dejection common in the world. (And in the same way as to feeling, moods, or ideas, he continues so to look upon each) that he remains strenuous, self-possessed, and mindful, having overcome both the hankering and the dejection, common in the world."

" And how does a brother become self-possessed?"

" He acts, monks, in full presence of mind whatever he

[1] This is a frequently occurring subject in Buddhist teaching, but here the commentator Buddhaghosa suggests it is due to the imminent approach of the beautiful courtezan. The meeting with Ambapāli also occurs in the Vinaya Texts. Ambapāli means ' Row of Mangoes.'

may do, in going out or coming in, in looking forward or looking round, in bending in his arm or in stretching it forth, in wearing his robes or in carrying his bowl, in eating or drinking, in masticating or swallowing, in obeying the calls of nature, in walking or standing or sitting, in sleeping or waking, in talking and in being silent.

"Thus let a brother, monks, be mindful and self-possessed; this is our instruction to you."

Now the courtezan Ambapāli heard that the Exalted One had arrived at Vesāli, and was staying there at her mango grove. And ordering a number of state vehicles to be made ready; she mounted one of them, and went forth with her train from Vesāli towards her garden. She went in the carriages as far as the ground was passable for carriages; there she alighted; and she proceeded on foot to the place where the Exalted One was, and took her seat respectfully on one side. And when she was thus seated the Exalted One instructed, aroused, incited, and gladdened her with religious discourse.

Then she—instructed, aroused, incited and gladdened with his words—addressed the Exalted One, and said:

"May the Exalted One do me the honour of taking his meal, together with the brethren, at my house to morrow?"

And the Exalted One gave, by silence, his consent. Then when Ambapāli the courtezan saw that the Exalted One had consented, she rose from her seat and bowed down before him, and keeping him on her right hand as she passed him, she departed thence.

Now the Licchavis of Vesāli heard that the Exalted One had arrived at Vesāli, and was staying at Ambapāli's grove. And ordering a number of state carriages to be made ready; they each mounted one of them and went forth with their train from Vesāli. Some of them were dark, dark in colour, and wearing dark clothes and ornaments; some of them were fair, fair in colour, and wearing light clothes and ornaments; some of them were red, ruddy in colour, and wearing red clothes and ornaments; some of them were white, pale in colour, and wearing white clothes and ornaments.

And Ambapāli drove up against the young Licchavis, axle to axle, wheel to wheel, and yoke to yoke, and the Licchavis said to Ambapāli the courtezan, "How is it, Ambapāli, that thou drivest up against us thus?"

"My lords, I have just invited the Exalted One and his brethren for their morrow's meal," said she.

"Ambapāli, give up this meal to us for a hundred thousand," said they.

"My lords, were you to offer all Vesāli with its subject territory, I would not give up so honourable a feast."

Then the Licchavis cast up their hands, exclaiming: "We are outdone by this mango girl. We are out-reached by this mango girl," and they went on to Ambapāli's grove.

When the Exalted One saw the Licchavis approaching in the distance, he addressed the brethren, and said: "Brethren, let those of the brethren who have never seen the next world devas, gaze upon this company of the Licchavis, behold this company of the Licchavis, compare this company of the Licchavis—for they are even as a company of next world devas."

And when they had ridden as far as he ground was passable for carriages the Licchavis alighted there, and then went on foot to the place where the Exal ed One was, and took their seats respectfully by his side. And when they were thus seated the Exalted One instructed and roused and incited and gladdened them with religious discourse.

Then they—instructed, and roused and incited, and gladdened with his words—addressed the Exalted One, and said: "May the Exalted One do us the honour of taking his meal, together with the brethren, at our house to-morrow?"

"I have promised, Licchavis, to dine to-morrow with Ambapāli the courtezan," was the reply."

Then the Licchavis cast up their hands, exclaiming: "We are outdone by this mango girl, we are outreached by this mango girl." And expressing their thanks and approval of the words of the Exalted One, they rose from their seats and bowed down before the Exalted One, and keeping him on their right hand as they passed him, they departed thence.

And at the end of the night Ambapāli the courtezan made ready in her mansion sweet rice and cake, and announced the time to the Exalted One saying: "The hour, lord, has come, and the meal is ready."

And the Exalted One who had dressed himself early in the morning, took his bowl, and his robe, and went with the brethren to the place where Ambapāli's mansion was; and when he had come there he seated himself on the seat prepared for him. And Ambapāli the courtezan set the sweet rice and cakes before the Order, with the Buddha at their head, and waited upon them till they refused any more.

And when the Blessed One had quite finished his meal, and had cleansed the bowl and his hands, the courtezan had a low stool brought, and sat down at his side, and addressed the Exalted One, and said:

"Lord, I present this pleasaunce to the order of monks, of whom the Buddha is the chief." And the Exalted One accepted the gift; and after instructing, and rousing, and inciting, and gladdening her with religious discourse, he rose from his seat and departed thence.

The Enlightened One is attacked by Sickness but Delivers a Sublime Discourse

Now when the Exalted One had remained so long as he wished at Ambapāli's grove, he addressed Ānanda, and said: "Come, Ānanda, let us go on to Beluva."

"So be it, lord," said Ānanda, in assent, to the Exalted One.

Then the Exalted One proceeded with a great company of the brethren to Beluva, and there the Exalted One stayed in the village itself.

Now the Exalted One there addressed the brethren, and said: "Monks, do you take up your abode round about Vesāli, each according to the place where his friends, acquaintances, and intimates may live, for the retreat in the rainy season (for Vassa). I shall enter upon the rainy season here at Beluva."

"So be it, lord," said these brethren, in assent, to the Exalted One. And they entered upon the rainy season round about Vesāli, each according to the place where his friends, acquaintances, and intimates lived, whilst the Exalted One stayed even here at Beluva.

Now when the Exalted One had thus entered upon the rainy season, there fell upon him a dire sickness, and sharp pains came upon him, even unto death. But the Exalted One, mindful and self-possessed, bore them without complaint. Then this thought occurred to the Exalted One: "It would not be right for me to pass away without addressing the disciples, without taking leave of the Order. Let me now, by a strong effort of the will, bend this sickness down again, and keep my hold on life, till the allotted time be come."

And the Exalted One, by a strong effort of will, bent that sickness down again, and kept his hold on life till the time he fixed upon should come. And the sickness abated upon him.

Now very soon after the Blessed One began to recover. And when he had quite got rid of his sickness, he came out from his lodging, and sat down in the shadow thereof on a seat spread out there. And the venerable Ānanda went to the place where the Exalted One was, and saluted him, and took a seat respectfully on one side, and addressed the Exalted One, and said:

"I have beheld, lord, how the Exalted One was in health, and I have beheld now how the Exalted One had to suffer. And though at the sight of the sickness of the Exalted One my body became weak as a creeper, and the horizon became dim to me, and my faculties were no longer clear, yet notwithstanding I took some little comfort from the thought that the Exalted One would not pass away until at least he had left instructions as touching the Order."

"What then, Ānanda, does the Order expect of me? I have preached the dhamma without making it either inner or outer; for in respect of doctrines, Ānanda, the

Tathāgata has no such thing as the teacher's (closed) fist. Surely should there be any one who harbours the thought: 'It is I who will lead the brotherhood,' or, 'The Order is dependent upon me,' it is he who should lay down instructions in any matter concerning the Order. Now the Tathāgata, Ānanda, thinks not that it is he who should lead the brotherhood, or that the Order is dependent upon him. Why then should he leave instructions in any matter concerning the Order?

But I, Ānanda, am now grown old, and full of years, my journey is drawing to its close, I have reached my sum of days, I am in the years eighty and more of age; and just as a worn-out cart, Ānanda, can be kept going only with the help of thongs, so, methinks, the body of the Tathāgata can only be kept going by bandaging it up. It is only, Ānanda, when the Tathāgata, by ceasing to attend to any outward thing, becomes plunged by the cessation of any separate sensation in that concentration of heart, which is concerned with no material object, it is only then that the body of the Tathāgata is at ease.

"Therefore, O Ānanda, be ye lamps[1] unto yourselves. Be ye a refuge to yourselves. Betake yourselves to no external refuge. Hold fast to the dhamma as a lamp.[1] Hold fast as a refuge to the dhamma. Look not for refuge to any one besides yourselves. And how, Ānanda, is a brother to be a lamp[1] unto himself, a refuge to himself, betaking himself to no external refuge, holding fast to the dhamma as a lamp,[1] holding fast as a refuge to the dhamma, looking not for refuge to any one besides himself?

"Herein, monks, a brother continues, as to the body, so to look upon the body that he remains strenuous, self-possessed, and mindful, having overcome both the hankering and the dejection common in the world. (And in the same way) as to feeling . . . moods . . . ideas, he continues so to look upon each that he remains strenuous, self-possessed, and mindful, having overcome both the hankering and the dejection common in the world.

"And whosoever, Ānanda, either now or after I am dead,

[1] *Dīpā* may be translated also as islands.

shall be a lamp unto themselves, and a refuge unto themselves, shall betake themselves to no external refuge, but holding fast to the dhamma as their lamp, and holding fast as their refuge to the dhamma, shall look not for a refuge to any one besides themselves, it is they, Ānanda, among my Bhikkhus, who shall reach the very topmost Height, whosoever of them are anxious to learn."

The Buddha Decides when to Pass Away

Now the Exalted One robed himself early in the morning, and taking his bowl in the robe, went into Vesāli for alms. When, after he had returned from his round for alms, he had finished eating the rice, he addressed the venerable Ānanda, and said: "Take up the mat, Ānanda, I will go and spend the day at the Chāpāla Shrine."

"So be it, lord," said the venerable Ānanda, in assent, to the Exalted One. And taking up the mat, he followed step for step behind the Exalted One.

So the Exalted One proceeded to the Chāpāla Shrine, and when he had come there he sat down on the mat spread out for him, and the venerable Ānanda took his seat respectfully beside him. Then the Exalted One addressed the venerable Ānanda, and said:

"How delightful a spot, Ānanda, is Vesāli, and how charming the Udena Shrine and the Gotamaka Shrine, and the Shrine of the Seven Mangoes, and the Shrine of Many Sons, and the Sārandad Shrine, and the Chāpāla Shrine.

"Ānanda, whosoever has developed, practised, dwelt on, expanded and ascended to the very heights of the four paths of Iddhi, and so mastered them as to be able to use them as a vehicle, and as a basis, he, should he desire it, could remain in the same birth for an æon or for that portion of the æon which had yet to run. Now the Tathāgata has thoroughly practised and developed them, and he could, therefore, should he desire it, live on yet for an æon, or for that portion of the æon which has yet to run."

But even though a suggestion so evident and a hint so clear were thus given by the Exalted One, the venerable Ānanda was incapable of comprehending them; and he besought not the Exalted One, saying: "Vouchsafe, lord, to remain during the æon. Live on through the æon, O happy One. For the good and the happiness of the great multitudes, out of pity for the world for the good and the gain and the weal of gods and men." So far was his heart possessed by the Evil One.

A second and a third time did the Exalted One (say the same thing, and a second and a third time was Ānanda's heart thus hardened).

Then the Exalted One addressed the venerable Ānanda, and said:

"You may leave me, Ānanda, a while, and do whatsoever now seemeth to you fit." "So be it, lord," said the venerable Ānanda, in assent, to the Exalted One, and passing him on the right sat down at the foot of a certain tree not far off thence.

Now not long after the venerable Ānanda had been gone, Māra, the Evil One, approached the Exalted One and stood beside him. And so standing there, he addressed the Exalted One in these words:

"Pass away now, lord, let the Exalted One now die. Now is the time for the Exalted One to pass away, even according to the word which the Exalted One spoke when he said: 'I shall not die, Evil One, until the brethren and sisters of the Order, and until the lay-disciples of either sex shall have become true hearers, wise and well trained, ready and learned, carrying the doctrinal books in their memory, masters of the lesser corollaries, that follow from the larger doctrine, correct in life, walking according to the precepts, until they, having thus themselves learned the doctrine shall be able to tell others of it, preach it, make it known, establish it, open it, minutely explain it, and make it clear, until they, when others start vain doctrine easy to be refuted by the truth, shall be able in refuting it, to spread the wonder-working truth abroad.

"And now, lord, the brethren and sisters of the order

and the lay-disciples of either sex have become (all this), are able to do (all this). Pass away now therefore, lord, let the Exalted One now die. The time has come for the Exalted One to pass away, even according to the word which he spake when he said: 'I shall not die, O Evil One, until this pure religion of mine shall have become successful, prosperous, wide-spread, and popular in all its full extent—until, in a word, it shall have been well proclaimed among men. And now, lord, this pure religion of thine has become (all this). Pass away now therefore, lord; let the Exalted One now die. The time has come for the Exalted One to pass away."

And when he had thus spoken, the Exalted One addressed Māra, the Evil One, and said: "Make thyself happy, Evil One, the death of the Tathāgata shall take place before long. At the end of three months from this time the Tathāgata will pass away."

Thus the Exalted One while at the Shrine of Chāpāla deliberately and consciously emptied (himself of) the conditions of life.[1] And on his so rejecting there arose a mighty earthquake, awful and terrible, and the thunders of heaven burst forth. And when the Exalted One beheld this, he broke out at that time into this hymn of exultation:

> His sum of life the sage renounced :—
> The cause of life immeasurable or small;
> With inward joy and calm he broke,
> Like coat of mail, his life's own cause.

Between this and the following account we omit discourses on eight proximate and eight remote causes of earthquakes, the eight kinds of assemblies, the eight powers of mastery, the eight stages of deliverance.

[1] *Āyu-sankhāra.*

Ānanda Petitions the Buddha not to Pass Away

(The Enlightened One has just recounted to Ānanda the two appearances of Mara when he begged the Buddha to pass away)

"And now again, Ānanda, the Tathāgata has to-day at Chāpāla's Shrine consciously and deliberately rejected the rest of his allotted term of life."

And when he had thus spoken the venerable Ānanda addressed the Exalted One, and said: "Vouchsafe, lord, to remain during the æon; live on through the kalpa, O Exalted One. For the good and the happiness of the great multitudes, out of pity for the world, for the good and the gain and the weal of gods and men."

"Enough now, Ānanda, beseech not the Tathāgata," was the reply. "The time for making such request is past."

And again, the second time, the venerable Ānanda besought the Exalted One (in the same words). And he received from the Exalted One the same reply.

And again, the third time, the venerable Ānanda besought the Exalted One (in the same words).

"Hath thou faith, Ānanda, in the wisdom of the Tathāgata?"

"Even so, lord."

"Now why then, Ānanda, dost thou trouble theTathāgata even until the third time?"

"From his own mouth have I heard from the Exalted One, from his own mouth have I received this saying: 'Whoever has developed, practised, dwelt on, expanded, and ascended to the very heights of the four paths to Iddhi, and so mastered them as to be able to use them as a vehicle and as a basis, he, should he desire it, could remain in the same birth for an æon, or for that portion of the æon which is yet to run.' Now the Tathāgata has thoroughly practised and developed them (in all respects as just now fully described) and he could, therefore, should he desire it, live on yet for an æon, or for that portion of the æon which has yet to run.

"Hast thou faith, Ānanda?"

"Even so, lord."

"Then, O Ānanda, thine is the fault, thine is the offence, in that when a suggestion so evident and a hint so clear were thus given thee by the Tathāgat, thou wast yet incapable of comprehending them, and thou besoughtest not the Tathāgata, saying: 'Vouchsafe, lord, to remain during the æon for the good and the happiness of the great multitudes, out of pity for the world, for the good and the gain and the weal of gods and men.' If thou shouldst then have so besought the Tathāgata, the Tathāgata might have rejected the appeal even to the second time, but the third time he would have granted it. Thine, therefore, O Ānanda, is the fault, thine is the offence."

(Here occurs with much repetition a list of several occasions when Ānanda failed to ask the Buddha to remain for an æon, or the remainder of one.)

"But now, Ānanda, have I not formerly declared to you that it is in the very nature of all things, near and dear unto us, that we must divide ourselves from them, leave them, sever ourselves from them? How, then, Ānanda, can this be possible where as anything whatever born, brought into being and organized, contains within itself the inherent necessity of dissolution, how then can this be possible that such a being should not be dissolved? No such condition can exist. And that which, Ānanda, has been relinquished, cast away, renounced, rejected, and emptied out by the Tathāgata—the remaining sum of life surrendered by him—verily with regard to that the word has gone forth from the Tathāgata, saying: 'The passing away of the Tathāgata shall take place before long. At the end of three months from this time the Tathāgata will die.' That the Tathāgata for the sake of living should repent him again of that saying, this can no wise be."

The Buddha Gives a Summary of His Teachings

(Then the Exalted One said):

"Come, Ānanda, let us go to the Kutāgāra Hall, to the Mahāvana."

"Even so, lord," said the venerable Ānanda, in assent to the Exalted One.

Then the Exalted One proceeded, and Ānanda with him, to the Mahāvana, to the Kutāgāra Hall; and when he had arrived there he addressed the venerable Ānanda, and said:

"Go now, Ānanda, and assemble in the Service Hall such of the brethren as reside in the neighbourhood of Vesāli."

"Even so, lord," said the venerable Ānanda, in assent, to the Eaxlted One. And when he had assembled in the Service Hall such of the brethren as resided in the neighbourhood of Vesāli, he went to the Exalted One and saluted him and stood beside him. And standing beside him, he addressed the Exalted One, and said:

"Lord, the assembly of the brethren has met together. Let the Exalted One do even as seemeth to him fit."

Then the Exalted One proceeded to the Service Hall, and sat down there on the mat spread out for him. And when he was seated the Exalted One addressed the brethren, and said:

"Therefore, brethren—ye to whom the truths I have perceived have been made known by me—having thoroughly made yourselves masters of them, practise them, meditate upon them, and spread them abroad; in order that pure religion may last long and be perpetuated, in order that it may continue to be for the good and the happiness of the great multitudes, out of pity for the world, to the good and the gain and the weal of gods and men.

"Which then, brethren, are the truths which, when I had perceived I made known to you, which when you have mastered it, behoves you to practise, meditate upon, and spread abroad, in order that pure religion may last long and be perpetuated, in order that it may continue, to be for the good and the happiness of the great multitudes, out of pity for the world, to the good and the gain and the weal of gods and men.

"They are these:—

The four earnest meditations,
The fourfold right struggle,
The four stages of psychic power,

The five moral powers,
The five organs of spiritual sense.
The seven kinds of wisdom, and
The Aryan eightfold path.

"These, brethren, are the truths which, when I had perceived, I made known to you, which when you have mastered it behoves you to practise, meditate upon, and spread abroad, in order that pure religion may last long, and be perpetuated, in order that it may continue to be for the good and the happiness of the great multitudes, out of pity for the world, to the good and the gain and the weal of gods and men."

And the Exalted One exhorted the brethren, and said :—

"Behold now, brethren, I exhort you saying: 'All component things must grow old. Accomplish with diligence. The final extinction of the Tathāgata will take place before long. At the end of three months from this time the Tathāgata will die.

"'My age is now full ripe, my life draws to its close ;
I leave you, I depart, relying on myself alone.
Be earnest then, O brethren, holy, full of thought.
Be steadfast in resolve. Keep watch o'er your own hearts.
Who wearies not, but holds fast to this truth and law,
Rid of this sea of birth, shall make an end of grief.'"

(Then the Exalted One visits five other places, delivering mostly discourses which have been given above.)

The Four Great Authorities

Now there at Bhoga-nagara the Exalted One stayed at the Ānanda Shrine.

There the Exalted One addressed the brethren and said : "I will teach you, O brethren, these four Great Authorities. Listen thereto, and give good heed, and I will speak."

"Even so, lord," said the brethren, in assent, to the Exalted One, and the Exalted One spoke as follows :

"In the first place, brethren, a brother may say thus : 'From the mouth of the Exalted One himself have I heard, from his own mouth have I received it. This is the truth, this the law, this the teaching of the Master . . .'

"Again, brethren, a brother may say thus: 'In such and such a dwelling-place there is a company of the brethren with their elders and leaders. From the mouth of that company have I heard, face to face have I received. This is the truth, this the law, this the teaching of the Master.'

"Again, brethren, a brother may say thus: 'In such and such a dwelling-place there are dwelling many elders of the Order, deeply read, holding the faith as handed down by tradition, versed in the truths, versed in the Regulations of the Order, versed in the summaries of the doctrines of the law. From the mouth of those elders have I heard, from their mouth have I received it. This is the truth, this the law, this the teaching of the Master . . .'

"Again, brethren, a brother may say: 'In such and such a dwelling-place there is there living a brother, deeply read, holding the faith as handed down by tradition, versed in the truths, versed in the regulations of the Order, versed in the summaries of the doctrines and the law. From the mouth of that elder have I heard, from his mouth have I received it. This is the truth, this the law, this the teaching of the Master.'

"The word spoken, brethren, by that brother (and of each of the other brethren) should neither be received with praise nor treated with scorn. Without praise and without scorn every word and syllable should be carefully understood, and then put beside the Suttas and compared with the rules of the Order. If when so compared they do not harmonize with the Suttas, and do not fit in with the rules of the Order, then you may come to the conclusion: 'Verily, this is not the word of the Exalted One, and has been wrongly grasped by that brother.' Therefore, brethren, you should reject it. But if they harmonize with the Suttas and fit in with the rules of the Order, then you may come to the conclusion: 'Verily, this is the word of the Exalted One, and has been grasped well by that brother . . .'

"These, brethren (you should receive as) . . . the Four Great Authorities."

The Buddha Accepts Food from Chunda

Now when the Exalted One had remained as long as he desired at Bhogagāma, he addressed the venerable Ānanda, and said: "Come, Ānanda, let us go on to Pāvā."

"Even so, lord," said the venerable Ānanda, in assent to the Exalted One. And the Exalted One proceeded with a great company of the brethren to Pāvā. And there at Pāvā the Exalted One stayed at the Mango Grove of Chunda, who was by family a worker in metals.

Now Chunda, the worker in metals, heard that the Exalted One had come to Pāvā, and was staying there in his Mango Grove.

And Chunda, the worker in metals, went to the place where the Exalted One was, and saluting him took his seat respectfully on one side. And when he was thus seated, the Exalted One instructed, aroused, incited and gladdened him with religious discourse.

Then he, instructed, aroused, incited and gladdened by the religious discourse, addressed the Exalted One, and said: "May the Exalted One do me the honour of taking his meal together with the brethren, at my house to-morrow?"

And the Exalted One signified by silence his consent.

Then seeing that the Exalted One had consented, Chunda, the worker in metals, rose from his seat and bowed down before the Exalted One and keeping him on his right hand as he passed him, departed thence.

Now at the end of the night, Chunda, the worker in metals, made ready in his dwelling-place sweet rice and cakes, and a quantity of truffles. And he announced the hour to the Exalted One, saying: "The hour, lord, has come and the meal is ready."

And the Exalted One robed himself early in the morning, and taking his bowl, went with the brethren to the dwelling-place of Chunda, the worker in metals. When he had come hither he seated himself on the seat prepared for him. And when he was seated he addressed Chunda, the worker in metals, and said: "As to the truffles, you have made ready, serve me with them, Chunda; and as to the other food, the sweet rice and cakes, serve the brethren with it."

"Even so, lord," said Chunda, the worker in metals, in assent, to the Blessed One. And the truffles he had made ready he served to the Exalted One; whilst the other food, the sweet rice and cakes, he served to the members of the Order.

Now the Exalted One addressed Chunda, the worker in metals, and said: "Whatever truffles, Chunda, are left over to thee, those bury in a hole. I see no one, Chunda, in earth nor in Māra's heaven, nor in Brahmā's heaven, no one among samanas and brahmins among gods and men, by whom, when he has eaten it, that food can be properly assimilated, save by a Tathāgata."

"Even so, lord," said Chunda, the worker in metals, in assent, to the Exalted One. And whatever truffles remained over those he buried in a hole. And he went to the place where the Exalted One was; and when he had come there, took his seat respectfully on one side. And when he was seated, the Exalted One instructed, and aroused and incited and gladdened Chunda, the worker in metals, with religious discourse. And the Exalted One then rose from his seat and departed thence.

Now when the Exalted One had eaten the rice prepared by Chunda, the worker in metals, there fell upon him a dire sickness, the disease of dysentery, and sharp pain came upon him, even unto death. But the Exalted One, mindful and self-possessed, bore it without complaint. And the Exalted One addressed the venerable Ānanda, and said: "Come, Ānanda, let us go on to Kusinārā."

"Even so, lord," said Ānanda, in assent, to the Exalted One.

The Clarifying of a Stream

Now the Exalted One went aside from the path to the foot of a certain tree, and when he had come there he addressed the venerable Ānanda, and said: "Fold, I pray you,

Ānanda, the robe in four ; and spread it out for me. I am weary, Ānanda and must rest awhile."

"Even so, lord," said the venerable Ānanda, in assent, to the Exalted One, and spread out the robe folded in fourfold

And the Exalted One seated himself on the seat prepared for him ; and when he was seated, he addressed the venerable Ānanda, and said : "Fetch me, I pray you Ānanda, some water. I am thirsty, Ānanda, and would drink."

When he had thus spoken, the venerable Ānanda said to the Exalted One : "But just now, lord, about five hundred carts have gone over. That water stirred up by wheels has become shallow and flows fouled and turbid. This river Kakuttha, lord, not far off is clear and pleasant, cool and transparent, easy to get down into, and delightful. There the Exalted One may both drink the water and cool his limbs."

Again the second time the Exalted One (made his request). And again the second time the venerable Ānanda replied as before. . . . But after a third request from the Exalted One, Ānanda said : "Even so, lord . . . and taking a bowl he went down to the streamlet. And lo, the streamlet which stirred up by the wheels, was but just now become shallow, and was flowing fouled and turbid, had begun, when the venerable Ānanda came up to it, to flow clear and bright and free from all turbidity.

Then Ānanda thought : "How wonderful, how marvellous is the great might and power of the Tathāgata. For this streamlet which stirred up by the wheels was but just now become shallow and was flowing foul and turpid, now as I come up to it, is flowing clear and bright and free from all turbidity."

And taking the water in the bowl he returned towards the Exalted One ; and when he had come where the Exalted One was he said to him : "How wonderful, how marvellous is the great might and power of the Tathāgata For this streamlet which, stirred up by the wheels, was but just now become shallow and was flowing foul and turbid, now, as I come up to it is flowing clear and bright and free from all turbidity.

"Let the Exalted One drink the water. Let the Happy One drink the water."

Then the Exalted One drank of the water.

Stories Concerning Concentration

Now at that time a man named Pukkusa, a young Mallian, a disciple of Alārā-Kālāma, was passing along the high road from Kusinārā to Pāvā. And Pukkusa, the young Mallian, saw the Exalted One seated at the foot of the tree. On seeing him, he went up to the place where the Exalted One was, and when he had come there, he saluted the Exalted One, and took his seat respectfully on one side. And when he was seated, Pukkusa, the young Mallian, said to the Exalted One: "How wonderful a thing it is lord, and how marvellous, that those, who have gone forth out of the world, should pass their time in a state of mind so calm.

"Formerly, lord, Alārā-Kālāma was once walking along the high road; and leaving the road he sat himself down under a certain tree to rest during the heat of the day. Now, lord, five hundred carts passed by, one after the other, each close to Alārā-Kālāma. And a certain man, who was following close behind that caravan of carts, went up to the place where Alārā-Kālāma was, and when he was come there he spake as follows to Alārā-Kālāma:

"'But, lord, did you see those five hundred carts go by?'

"'No, indeed, friend, I saw them not.'

"'But, lord, did you hear the sound of them?'

"'No, indeed, friend, I heard not their sound.'

"'But, lord, were you then asleep?'

"'No, friend, I was not asleep.'

"'But, lord, were you then conscious?'

"'Even so, friend.'

"'So that you, lord, though you were both conscious and awake, neither saw nor heard the sound of five hundred carts passing by, one after the other, and each close to you. Why, lord, even your robe was sprinkled over with the dust of them.'

" 'It is even so, friend.'

"Then thought the man: 'How wonderful a thing it is, and how marvellous that those who have gone forth out of the world, should pass their time in a state of mind so calm. So much so that a man though being both conscious and awake, neither sees, nor hears, the sound of five hundred carts, passing by, one after the other, and each close to him.'

"And after giving utterance to his deep faith in Ālārā-Kālāma, he departed thence."

"Now what think you, Pukkusa, which is the more difficult thing either to do or to meet with, that a man, being conscious and awake, should neither see nor hear the sound of five hundred carts passing by, one after the other, close to him; or that a man, being conscious and awake, should neither see nor hear the sound thereof when the falling rain goes on beating and splashing and the lightnings are flashing forth, and the thunderbolts are crashing?"

"What in comparison, lord, can these five hundred carts do, or six or seven or eight or nine hundred, yea, even hundreds and thousands of carts?

"That certainly is more difficult, both to do and to meet with, that a man, conscious and awake, should neither see, nor hear the sound thereof when the falling rain goes on beating and splashing, and the lightnings are flashing forth, and the thunderbolts are crashing.

"Now on one occasion, Pukkusa, I was dwelling at Atumā, and was at the Threshing-floor. And at that time the falling rain began to beat and to splash, and the lightnings to flash forth, and the thunderbolts to crash; and two peasants, brothers, and four oxen were killed. Then, Pukkusa, a great multitude of people went forth from Atumā, and went up to the place where the two peasants, brothers, and the four oxen were killed.

"Now at that time, Pukkusa, I had gone forth from the threshing-floor, and was walking up and down thinking at the entrance of the threshing-floor. And a certain man, Pukkusa, came out of that great multitude of people, up to the place where I was, and when he came up he saluted me, and took his place respectfully on one side. And as he stood there, Pukkusa, I said to the man :

"'Why then, friend, is this great multitude of people assembled together ?'

"'But just now, the falling rain began to beat and to splash, and the lightnings to flash forth, and the thunderbolts to crash ; and two peasants, brothers, were killed, and four oxen. Therefore is this great multitude of people gathered together. But where, lord, were you ?'

"'I, friend, have been here all the while.'

"'But, lord, did you see it ?'

"'I, friend, saw nothing.'

"'But, lord, did you hear it ?'

"'I, friend, I heard nothing.'

"'Were you then, lord, asleep ?'

"'I, friend, was not asleep.'

"'Were you then conscious, lord ?'

"'Even so, friend.'

"'So that you, lord, being conscious and awake, neither saw, nor heard the sound thereof when the falling rain went on beating and splashing, and the lightnings were flashing, and the thunderbolts were crashing.'

"'That is so, sir.'

"Then, Pukkusa, the thought occurred to that man :

"'How wonderful a thing is it, and marvellous, that those who have gone forth out of the world should pass their time in a state of mind so calm, so that a man, being conscious and awake, neither sees, nor hears the sound thereof when the falling rain is beating and splashing, and the lightnings are flashing forth, and the thunderbolts are crashing.' And after giving utterance to his deep faith in me, he departed from me (with the customary demonstrations of respect)."

And when he had thus spoken, Pukkusa, the young Mallian, addressed the Blessed One in these words : "Now I, lord, as to the faith that I had in Alārā Kālāma, that I winnow away as in a mighty wind, and wash it away as in a swiftly running stream. Most excellent, lord, are the words of thy mouth, most excellent. Just as if a man were to set up that which is thrown down or were to reveal that which is hidden away; or were to point out the right road to him who has gone astray, or were to bring a lamp into the darkness so that those who have eyes can see visible forms, just even so, lord, has the dhamma been made known to me, in many a figure, by the Exalted One. And I, even I, betake myself, lord, to the Exalted One as my refuge, to the Dhamma and to the Brotherhood. May the Exalted One accept me as a disciple, as a true believer, from this day forth, as long as life endures."

Pukkusa Presents the Buddha and Ānanda with Robes of Gold

Now Pukkusa, the young Mallian, addressed a certain man and said: "Fetch, I pray you, my good man, a pair of robes of cloth of gold, burnished and ready for wear."

"So be it, sir," said that man in assent, to Pukkusa, the young Mallian, and he brought a pair of robes of cloth of gold, burnished and ready for wear.

And the Mallian Pukkusa presented the pair of robes of cloth of gold, burnished and ready for wear, to the Exalted One, saying: "Lord, this pair of robes of burnished cloth of gold is ready for wear. May the Exalted One show me favour and accept it at my hands."

"In that case, Pukkusa, robe me in one, and Ānanda in one."

"Even so, lord," said Pukkusa, in assent, to the Exalted One; and in one he robed the Exalted One, and in one, Ānanda.

Then the Exalted One instructed and aroused and incited and gladdened Pukkusa, the young Mallian, with religious discourse. And Pukkusa, the young Mallian, when he had been instructed and aroused and incited and gladdened by the Exalted One with religious discourse, arose from his seat, and bowed down before the Exalted One; and keeping him on his right hand as he passed him, departed thence.

Now not long after the Mallian Pukkusa had gone, the

venerable Ānanda compared that pair of robes of cloth of gold, burnished and ready for wear, to the body of the Exalted One; and when it was so compared to the body of the Exalted One it appeared to have lost its splendour.

And the venerable Ānanda said to the Exalted One: "How wonderful a thing it is, lord, and how marvellous that the colour of the skin of the Exalted One should be so clear, so exceeding bright. For when I compared even this pair of robes of burnished cloth of gold and ready for wear to the body of the Exalted One, lo, it seemed as if it had lost its splendour."

"It is even so, Ānanda, there are two occasions, Ānanda, on which the colour of the skin of a Tathāgata becomes clear and exceeding bright. What are the two?

"On the night, Ānanda, on which a Tathāgata attains to the supreme and perfect insight and on the night in which he passes finally away in that utter passing away which leaves nothing whatever to remain, on these two occasions the colour of the skin of the Tathāgata becomes clear and exceeding bright.

"And now this day, Ānanda, at the third watch of the night, in the Upavattana of Kusinārā, in the Sala Grove of the Mallians, between the twin Sāla-trees, the utter passing away of the Tathāgata will take place.

"Come, Ānanda, let us go on to the river Kakuttha."

"Even so, lord," said the venerable Ānanda, in assent, to the Exalted One. . . .

The Exalted One Speaks of Chunda

Now the Exalted One with a great company of the brethren went on to the river Kakuttha; and when he had come there, he went down into the water, and bathed and drank. And coming up out again on the other side he went on to the Mango-Grove.

And when he was come there he addressed the venerable Chundaka and said: "Fold, I pray you, Chundaka, a robe in four and spread it out. I am weary, Chundaka, and would lie down."

"Even so, lord," said the venerable Chundaka, in assent, to the Exalted One. And he folded a robe in four, and spread it out.

And the Exalted One laid himself down on his right side, with one foot resting on the other; and calm and self-possessed he meditated, intending to rise up again in due time. And the venerable Chundaka seated himself there in front of the Exalted One. . . .

And the Exalted One addressed the venerable Ānanda, and said: "Now it may happen, Ānanda, that some one should stir up remorse in Chunda the smith, saying: 'This is evil of thee, Chunda, and loss to thee, in that when the Tathāgata had eaten his last meal from thy provision, then he died.' Any such remorse, Ānanda, in Chunda the smith should be checked by saying: 'This is good to thee, Chunda, and gain to thee, in that when the Tathāgata had eaten his last meal from thy provision, then he died.' From the very mouth of the Exalted One, Chunda, have I heard, from his own mouth have I received this saying: 'These two offerings of food are of equal fruit, and of equal profit, and of much greater fruit and much greater profit than any other, and which are the two?

"'The offering of food which, when the Tathāgata has eaten, he attains to supreme and perfect insight and the offering of food which, when a Tathāgata has eaten, he passes away by that utter passing away in which nothing whatever remains behind—these two offerings of food are of equal fruit and of equal profit, and of much greater fruit and much greater profit than any others. There has been laid up by Chunda the smith a karma redounding to length of life, redounding to good birth, redounding to good fortune, redounding to good fame, redounding to the inheritance of heaven, and of sovereign power.' In this way, Ānanda, should be checked any remorse in Chunda the smith."

UNDER THE TWIN SĀLA-TREES

Now the Exalted One addressed the venerable Ānanda, and said: "Come, Ānanda, let us go on to the Sāla Grove of the Mallas, the Upavattana of Kusinārā on the further side of the river Hiranyavatī."

"Even so, lord," said the venerable Ānanda, in assent, to the Exalted One.

And the Exalted One proceeded with a great company of the brethren to the Sāla Grove of the Mallas, the Upavattana of Kusinārā, on the further side of the river Hiranyavatī, and when he had come there he addressed the venerable Ānanda and said:

"Spread for me, I pray you, Ānanda, the couch with its head to the north, between the twin Sāla-trees. I am weary, Ānanda, and would lie down."

"Even so, lord," said the venerable Ānanda, in assent, to the Exalted One. And he spread a covering over the couch with its head to the north, between the twin Sāla-trees. And the Exalted One laid himself down on his right side, with one leg resting on the other; and he was mindful and self-possessed.

Now at that time the twin Sāla-trees were all one mass of bloom with flowers out of season; and all over the body of the Tathāgata these dropped and sprinkled and scattered themselves out of reverence for the successor of the Buddhas of old. And heavenly Mandārava flowers too, and heavenly sandal-wood powder came falling from the sky, and all over the body of the Tathāgata, they descended and sprinkled and scattered themselves, out of reverence for the successor of the Buddhas of old. And heavenly music was sounded in the sky, out of reverence for the successor of the Buddhas of old. And heavenly songs came wafted from the skies, out of reverence for the successor of the Buddhas of old.

Then the Exalted One addressed the venerable Ānanda, and said: "The twin Sāla-trees are all one mass of bloom with flowers out of season; all over the body of the Tathāgata these drop and sprinkle and scatter themselves out of reverence for the successor of the Buddhas of old. And heavenly Mandārava flowers too, and heavenly sandal-wood powder come falling from the sky, and all over the body of the Tathāgata they descend and sprinkle and scatter themselves, out of reverence for the successor of the Buddhas of old. And heavenly music sounds in the sky, out of reverence for the successor of the Buddhas of old. And heavenly songs come wafted from the skies out of reverence for the successor of the Buddhas of old (in text, Tathāgata.)

"Now it is not thus, Ānanda, that the Tathāgata is rightly honoured, reverenced, venerated, held sacred or revered. But the brother or the sister, the devout man or the devout woman, who continually fulfills all the great and lesser duties, who is correct in life, walking according to the precepts, it is he who rightly honours, reverences, venerates, holds sacred, and reveres the Tathāgata, with the worthiest homage. Therefore, Ānanda, be ye constant, in the fulfilment of the greater and of the lesser duties, and be ye correct in life walking according to the precepts; and thus, Ānanda, should it be taught."

Now at that time the venerable Upavāna was standing in front of the Exalted One, fanning him. And the Exalted One was not pleased with Upavāna and he said to him: "Stand aside, brother, stand not in front of me."

Then this thought sprang up in the mind of the venerable Ānanda: "This venerable Upavāna had long been in close personal attendance and service on the Exalted One. And now, at the last moment, the Exalted One is not pleased with Upavāna, and has said to him: 'Stand aside, brother, stand not in front of me.' What may be the cause and what the reason that the Exalted One is not pleased with Upavāna, and speaks thus with him?"

And the venerable Ānanda said to the Exalted One: "This venerable Upavāna has long been in close personal attendance and service on the Exalted One. And now at the last moment, the Exalted One is not pleased with Upavāna, and has said to him: 'Stand aside, brother, stand not in front of me.' What may be the cause and what the reason that the Exalted One is not pleased with Upavāna, and speaks thus with him ? "

" In great numbers, Ānanda, are the devas of the ten-world-systems assembled together to behold the Tathāgata. For twelve leagues, Ānanda, around the Sāla Grove of the Mallas, the Upavattana of Kusinārā, there is no spot in size even as the pricking of the point of the tip of a hair which is not pervaded by powerful devas. And the devas, Ānanda, are murmuring and say : ' From afar have we come to behold the Tathāgata. Few and far between are the Tathāgatas, the Arahant Buddhas who appear in the world ; and now to-day in the last watch of the night, the death of a Tathāgata will take place ; and this eminent brother stands in front of the Tathāgata, concealing him, and in his last hour we are prevented from beholding the Tathāgata ' ; thus, Ānanda, do the devas murmur."

" But of what kind of devas is the Exalted One thinking ? "

" There are devas, Ānanda, in the air, but of earthly mind, who dishevel their hair and weep, who stretch forth their arms and weep, who fall prostrate on the ground, and roll to and fro in anguish at the thought : ' Too soon will the Exalted One die. Too soon will the Exalted One pass away. Full soon will the light of the world vanish away.'

" There are devas, too, Ānanda, on the earth, and of earthly mind, who tear their hair and weep, who stretch forth their arms and weep, who fall prostrate on the ground, and roll to and fro in anguish at the thought : ' Too soon will the Exalted One die. Too soon will the Wellfarer pass away. Full soon will the Eye of the world disappear from sight.'

" But the devas who are free from passion bear it, calm and self-possessed mindful of the saying which begins : ' Impermanent indeed are all component things. How then were it possible ? ' [1] "

[1] The saying is more fully stated in the section above, on p. 196.

Places to be Reverenced

"In times past, lord, the brethren, when they had spent the rainy season in different districts, used to come to see the Tathāgata, and we used to receive those very reverend brethren to audience, and to wait upon the Exalted One. But, lord, after the passing away of the Exalted One, we shall not be able to receive those very reverend brethren to audience, and to wait upon the Exalted One."

"There are these four places, Ānanda, which the believing clansman should visit with feelings of reverence. Which are the four?

"The place, Ānanda, at which the believing man can say 'Here the Tathāgata was born.'

"The place, Ānanda, at which the believing man can say: 'Here the Tathāgata attained to the supreme and perfect insight,' is a spot to be visited with feelings of reverence.

"The place, Ānanda, at which the believing man can say: 'Here the kingdom of righteousness set on foot by the Tathāgata,' is a spot to be visited with feelings of reverence.

"The place, Ānanda, at which the believing man can say: 'Here the Tathāgata passed finally away in that utter passing away which leaves nothing whatever to remain behind,' is a spot to be visited with feelings of reverence. These are the four places, Ānanda, which the believing clansman should visit with feelings of reverence.

"And there will come, Ānanda, to such spots, believers, brethren and sisters of the Order, or devout men and devout women, and will say: 'Here was the Tathāgata born,' or, 'Here did the Tathāgata attain to the supreme and perfect insight,' or, 'Here was the kingdom of righteousness set on foot by the Tathāgata,' or, 'Here the Tathāgata passed away, in that utter passing away which leaves nothing whatever to remain behind.'

"And they, Ānanda, who shall die while they, with believing heart, are journeying on such pilgrimage, shall be reborn after death, when the body shall dissolve, in the happy realms of heaven."

The Monk's Conduct Towards Women

"How are we to conduct ourselves, lord, with regard to womankind?"

"As not seeing them, Ānanda."

"But if we should see them, what are we to do?"

"No talking, Ānanda."

"But if they should speak to us, lord, what are we to do?"

"Keep wide awake, Ānanda."

Ananda Questions Regarding the Remains of the Buddha

"What are we to do, lord, with the remains of the Tathāgata?"

"Hinder not yourselves, Ānanda, by honouring the remains of the Tathāgata. Be zealous, I beseech you, Ānanda, in your own behalf. Devote yourselves to your own behalf. Be earnest, be zealous, be intent on your own good. There are wise men, Ānanda, among the nobles, among the brahmans, among the heads of houses, who are firm believers in the Tathāgata; and they will do due honour to the remains of the Tathāgata."

"But what should be done, lord, with the remains of the Tathāgata?"

"As men treat the remains of a king of kings, so, Ānanda, should they treat the remains of a Tathāgata."

"And how, lord, do they treat the remains of a king of kings?"

"They wrap the body of a king of kings, Ānanda, in a new cloth. When that is done they wrap it in carded cotton wool. When that is done they wrap it in a new cloth, and so on till they have wrapped the body in five hundred successive layers of both kinds. Then they place the body in an oil vessel of iron, and cover that close up with another oil vessel of iron. They then build a funeral pyre of all kinds of perfume, and burn the body of the king of kings.

"And then at the four cross roads they erect a cairn to the king of kings.

"This, Ānanda, is the way in which they treat the remains of a king of kings.

"And as they treat the remains of a king of kings, so, Ānanda, should they treat the remains of the Tathāgata. At the four cross roads a cairn should be erected to the Tathāgata. And whosoever shall there place garlands or perfumes, or paints, or make salutation there or become in its presence calm in heart that shall long be to them for a profit and a joy.

"The men, Ānanda, worthy of a cairn, are four in number, Which are the four?

"A Tathāgata, an Able Awakened One, is worthy of a cairn. One awakened for himself alone [1] is worthy of a cairn. A true hearer of the Tathāgata is worthy of a cairn. A king of kings is worthy of a cairn.

"And on account of what circumstance, Ānanda, is a Tathāgata, an Able Awakened One, worthy of a cairn?

"At the thought, Ānanda, 'This is the cairn of that Exalted One, of that Able Awakened One,' the hearts of many shall be made calm and happy; and since they there had calmed and satisfied their hearts, they will be reborn after death, when the body has dissolved, in the happy realms of heaven. It is on account of this circumstance, Ānanda, that a Tathāgata, an Able Awakened One is worthy of a cairn . . ."

(*The same circumstances on account of which one is worthy of a cairn is repeated for the one awakened for himself alone, the true hearer, and the king of kings.*)

Regarding Ānanda

Now the venerable Ānanda went into the Vinara, and stood leaning against the lintel of the door, and weeping at the thought: "Alas! I remain still but a learner, one

[1] A Paccheka-buddha.

who has yet work to do. And the Master is about to pass away from me—he who is so kind."

Now the Exalted One called the brethren, and said: "Where then, brethren, is Ānanda?"

"The venerable Ānanda, lord, has gone into the Vihara, and stands leaning against the lintel of the door, and weeping at the thought: 'Alas! I remain still but a learner, one who has yet work to do. And the Master is about to pass away from me—he who is so kind.'"

And the Exalted One called a certain brother, and said: "Go now, brother, and call Ānanda in my name, and say, 'Brother Ānanda, the Master calls for thee.'"

"Even so, lord," said the brother, in assent, to the Exalted One. And he went up to the place where the venerable Ānanda was, and when he had come there, he said to the venerable Ānanda: "Brother Ānanda, the Master calls for thee." "Very well, brother," said the venerable Ānanda, in assent, to that brother. And he went up to the place where the Exalted One was, and when he had come there, he bowed down before the Exalted One, and took his seat respectfully on one side.

Then the Exalted One said to the venerable Ānanda, as he sat there by his side: "Enough! Ānanda. Grieve not; lament not! Have I not already, on former occasions, told you that it is in the very nature of all things most near and dear unto us, that we must divide ourselves from them, leave them, sever ourselves from them?

How, then, Ānanda, can this be possible—whereas anything whatever born, brought into being, and organized contains within itself the inherent necessity of dissolution; how, then can this be possible, that such a being should not dissolve? No such condition can exist. For a long time Ānanda, have you been very near to me by acts of love, kind and good, that never varies, and is beyond all measure. For a long time, Ānanda, have you been very near to me by words of love, kind and good, that never varies, and is beyond all measure. For a long time, Ānanda, have you been very near to me by thoughts of love, kind and good, that never varies, and is beyond all measure. You have done well, Ānanda, be earnest in effort, and you shall soon be free from the Cankers."

Then the Exalted One addressed the brethren, and said: "Whosoever, brethren, have been Able Awakened Ones through the long ages of the past, they also had servitors, just as devoted to those Exalted Ones as Ānanda has been to me.

"He is a clever man, brethren, is Ānanda, and wise, he knows when it is the right time for the brethren or for the sisters of the Order, for devout men and devout women for a king or for a king's ministers, or for other teachers, or for their disciples to come and visit the Tathāgata.

"Brethren, there are these four wonderful and marvellous qualities in Ānanda. Which are the four?

"If brethren, a number of the brethren of the Order should come to visit Ānanda, they are filled with joy on beholding him; and if Ānanda should then preach the dhamma to them, they are filled with joy at the discourse; while the company of brethren is ill at ease, brethren, when Ānanda is silent.

"If, brethren, a number of the sisters of the Order . . . or devout men . . . or of devout women, should come to visit Ānanda, they are filled with joy on beholding him; and if Ānanda should then preach the dhamma to them, they are filled with joy at the discourse; while the company of sisters is ill at ease, brethren, when Ānanda is silent.

"Brethren, there are these four wonderful and marvellous qualities in a king of kings. What are the four?

"If, brethren, a number of nobles, or brahmans, or heads of houses, or members of a religious order should come to visit a king of kings, they are filled with joy on beholding him; and if the king of kings should then speak, they are filled with joy at what he said; while they are ill at ease, brethren, when the king of kings is silent.

"Just so, brethren, are the four wonderful and marvellous qualities in Ānanda.

"If, brethren, a number of the brethren of the Order, or of the sisters of the Order, or of devout men, or of devout women should come to visit Ānanda, they are filled with joy on beholding him; and if Ānanda should then preach the dhamma to them, they are filled with joy at the discourse; while the company of brethren is ill at ease, when Ānanda is silent.

"Now these, brethren, are the four wonderful and marvellous qualities that are in Ānanda."

The Mallas come to Pay their Respects

When he had thus spoken, the venerable Ānanda said to the Exalted One:

"Let not the Exalted One die in this little wattle-and-daub town, in this town in the midst of the jungle, in this branch township. For, lord, there are other great cities, such as Champā, Rājagaha, Sāvatthi, Sāketa, Kosambi. Let the Exalted One die in one of them. There there are many wealthy nobles and brahmans, and heads of houses, believers in the Tathāgata, who will pay due honour to the remains of the Tathāgata."

"Say not so, Ānanda. Say not so, Ānanda, that this is but a small wattle-and-daub town, a town in the midst of the jungle, a branch township.

"Long ago, Ānanda, there was a king, by name Mahā-Sudassana, a king of kings, a righteous man who ruled in righteousness, lord of the four quarters of the earth, conqueror, the protector of his people, possessor of the seven royal treasures. This Kusinārā, Ānanda, was the royal city of King Māha-Sudassana, under the name of Kusāvatī, and on the east and on the west it was twelve leagues in length, and on the north and on the south it was seven leagues in breadth.

"That royal city Kusāvatī, Ānanda, was mighty and prosperous, and full of people, crowded with men, and provided with all things for food. Just, Ānanda, as the royal city of the gods, Ālakamandā, by name, is mighty, prosperous, and full of people, crowded with devas, and provided with all kinds of food, so, Ānanda, was the royal city Kusāvatī mighty and prosperous, full of people, crowded with men and provided with all kinds of food.

" Both by day and night, Ānanda, the royal city Kusāvatī resounded with the ten cries ; that is to say, the noise of elephants, and the noise of horses, and the noise of chariots ; the sounds of the drum, of the tabor, and of the lute ; the sound of singing, and the sounds of the cymbal and of the gong ; and lastly, with the cry, ' Eat, drink, and be merry.'

" Go now, Ānanda, and enter into Kusinārā, and inform the Mallas of Kusinārā, saying : This day, O Vāsetthas, in the last watch of the night, the final passing away of the Tathāgata will take place. Be favourable herein, O Vāsetthas, be favourable ! Give no occasion to reproach yourselves here after saying : ' In your village did the death of our Tathāgata take place and we took not the opportunity of visiting the Tathāgata in his last hours."

" Even so, lord," said the venerable Ānanda, in assent, to the Exalted One, and he robed himself and taking his bowl, he entered into Kusinārā attended by another member of the Order.

Now at that time the Mallas of Kusinārā were assembled in the council hall on some (public) affair.

And the venerable Ānanda went to the council hall of the Mallas of Kusinārā ; and when he had arrived there, he informed them, saying : " This day, O Vāsetthas, in the last watch of the night, the final passing away of the Tathāgata will take place. Be favourable, herein O Vāsetthas, be favourable ! Give no occasion to reproach yourselves hereafter, saying : ' In our own village did the death of our Tathāgata take place, and we took not the opportunity of visiting the Tathāgata in his last hours.' "

And when they had heard this saying of the venerable Ānanda, the Mallas with their young men and maidens and their wives were grieved, and sad, and afflicted at heart. And some of them wept, dishevelling their hair, and stretched forth their arms and wept, fell prostrate on the ground, and rolled to and fro in anguish at the thought : " Too soon will the Exalted One die. Too soon will the Wellfarer pass away. Full soon will the Light of the world vanish away."

Then the Mallas, with their young men and maidens and their wives, being grieved, and sad, and afflicted at heart, went to the Sāla Grove of the Mallas, to the Upavattana, and to the place where the venerable Ānanda was.

Then the venerable Ānanda thought: "If I allow the Mallas of Kusinārā one by one, to pay their respects to the Exalted One, the whole of the Mallas of Kusinārā will not have been presented to the Exalted One until this night brightens up into dawn. Let me, now, cause the Mallas of Kusinārā to stand in groups, each family in a group, and so present them to the Exalted One, saying: 'Lord, a Malla of such and such a name with his children, his wives, his retinue, and his friends, humbly bows down at the feet of the Exalted One.'"

And the venerable Ānanda caused the Mallas of Kusinārā to stand each family in groups and so presented them to the Exalted One, and said:

"Lord, a Malla of such and such a name, with his children, his wives, his retinue, and his friends, humbly bows down at the feet of the Exalted One."

And after this manner the venerable Ānanda presented all the Mallas of Kusinārā to the Exalted One in the first watch of the night.

SUBHADDA

Now at that time a Wanderer named Subhadda, who was not a believer, was dwelling at Kusinārā. And the Wanderer Subhadda heard the news: "This very day, they say, in the third watch of the night will take place the final passing away of the Samana Gotama. . . ."

Then the Wanderer Subhadda went to the Sāla Grove of the Mallas to the Upavattana of Kusinārā, to the place where the venerable Ānanda was. And when he had come there he said to the venerable Ānanda: "Thus have I heard from fellow Wanderers, old and well stricken in years, teachers and disciples, when they said: 'Sometimes and full seldom do Tathāgatas appear in the world, the Able Awakened Ones.' Yet this day, in the last watch of the night, the final passing away of the Samana Gotama will take place. Now a certain feeling of uncertainty has sprung up in my mind; and this faith have I in the Samana Gotama, that he, methinks, is able so to present the dhamma that I may get rid of this feeling of uncertainty. O that I, even I, Ānanda, might be allowed to see the Samana Gotama!"

And when he had thus spoken the venerable Ānanda said to the Wanderer Subhadda: "Enough, friend Subhadda, Trouble not the Tathāgata. The Exalted One is weary."

And again the Wanderer Subhadda (a second and third time made the same request in the same words, and received the same reply).

Now the Exalted One overheard this conversation of the venerable Ānanda with the Wanderer Subhadda. And the Exalted One called the venerable Ānanda, and said: "It is enough, Ānanda. Do not keep out Subhadda. Subhadda, Ānanda, may be allowed to see the Tathāgata. Whatever Subhadda may ask of me, he will ask from a desire for knowledge, and not to annoy me. And whatever I may say in answer to his questions, that he will quickly understand."

Then the venerable Ānanda said to Subhadda, the Wanderer: "Enter, friend Subhadda, for the Exalted One gives you leave."

Then Subhadda, the Wanderer, went in to the place where the Exalted One was and saluted him courteously, and after exchanging with him the compliments of esteem and of civility, he took his seat on one side. And when he was thus seated, Subhadda, the Wanderer, said to the Exalted One: "The leaders in religious life who are heads of companies of disciples and students, teachers of students, well known, renowned founders of schools of doctrine, esteemed as good men by the multitude, to wit, Purana Kassapa, Makkhali of the cattle-pen, Ajita of the garment of hair, Kaccnāyana of the Pakudha-tree, Sanjaya, the son of the Belatthi slave-girl, and the Nigantha of the Nāthas, have they all, according to their own assertion, thoroughly understood things or have they not? or are there some of them who have understood, and some who have not?"

"Enough, Subhadda. Let this matter rest whether they, according to their own assertion, have thoroughly understood things, or whether they have not, or whether some of them have understood and some have not. The dhamma, Subhadda, will I teach you. Listen well to that, and give ear attentively, and I will speak."

"Even so, lord," said the Wanderer Subhadda, in assent, to the Exalted One.

And the Exalted One spake: "In whatsoever dhamma and discipline, Subhadda, the Aryan eightfold path is not found, neither in it is there found a man of saintliness (*samana*) of the first, or the second, or of the third, or of the fourth degree. And in whatsoever dhamma and discipline, Subhadda, the Aryan eightfold path is found, in it is found the man of true saintliness of the first, and the second, and the third, and the fourth degree. Now in this dhamma and discipline, Subhadda, is found the Aryan eightfold path, and in it too, are found, Subhadda, the men of true saintliness of all the four degrees. Void are other systems of saints (*samana's*). And in this one, Subhadda, may the brethren live the life that is right, so that the world be not bereft of Arahants.

But twenty-nine was I when I renounced
The world, Subhadda, seeking after Good.
For fifty years and one year more, Subhadda,
Since I went out, a pilgrim have I been
Through the wide realm of System and of Dhamma.
Outside of that there is no 'saint.'

"Yea, not of the first nor of the third, nor of the fourth degree. Void are other systems of saints. But in this one, Subhadda, may the brethren live the perfect life, that the world be not bereft of Arahants."

And when he had thus spoken, Subhadda, the Wanderer, said to the Exalted One: "Most excellent, lord, are the words of thy mouth, most excellent. Just as if a man were to set up that which is thrown down, or were to reveal that which is hidden away, or were to point out the right road to him who has gone astray, or were to bring a lamp into the darkness, so that those who have eyes can see visible forms ; just even so, lord, has the dhamma been made known to me, in many a figure, by the Exalted One. And I, even I, betake myself, lord, to the Exalted One as my refuge, to the Dhamma, and to the Order, I would fain be accepted as a probationer under the Exalted One, as a full member in his Order."

"Whosoever, Subhadda, has formerly been a follower of another doctrine, and thereafter desires to be received into the higher or the lower grade in this dhamma and discipline, he remains on probation for the space of four months and at the end of the four months, the brethren, exalted in spirit, receive him into the lower or into the higher grade of the order. Nevertheless in this case I acknowledge the difference in persons."

"If lord, whosoever has formerly been a follower of another doctrine, and then desires to be received into the higher or the lower grade in this dhamma and discipline, if, in that case, such a person remains on probation for the space of four months ; and at the end of four months, the brethren, exalted in spirit, receive him into the lower or into the higher grade of the Order, I too, then, will remain on probation for the space of four months ; and at the end of the four months let the brethren, exalted in spirit receive me into the lower or into the higher grade of the Order."

But the Exalted One called the venerable Ānanda, and said : "Well then, Ānanda, receive Subhadda into the Order."

"Even so, lord," said the venerable Ānanda, in assent, to the Exalted One.

And Subhadda, the Wanderer, said to the venerable Ānanda : "Great is your gain, friend Ānanda, great is your fortune, friend Ānanda, in that you all have been sprinkled with the sprinkling of discipleship in this brotherhood at the hands of the Master himself."

So Subhadda, the Wanderer, was received into the higher grade of the Order, under the Exalted One ; and from immediately after his ordination the venerable Subhadda remained alone and separate, earnest, zealous, and resolved. And ere long he attained to that supreme goal of the higher life, for the sake of which the clansmen go out from all and every household gain and comfort, to become houseless wanderers, yea, that supreme goal did he, by himself, and while yet in this visible world, bring himself to the knowledge of, and continue to realize, and to see face to face.

And he became conscious that birth was at an end, that the holy life had been fulfilled, that all that should be done had been accomplished, and that after the present life there would be no more of that.

So the venerable Subhadda became yet another among the Arahants ; and he was the last disciple whom the Exalted One himself converted.

The Last Words of the Buddha

Now the Exalted One addressed the venerable Ānanda and said : " It may be, Ānanda, that in some of you the thought may arise : 'The word of the Master is ended, we have no teacher more.' But it is not thus, Ānanda, that you should regard it. The Dhamma, and the Rules of the Order, which I have set forth and laid down for you all, let them, after I am gone, be the Teacher to you.

" Ānanda, when I am gone, address not one another in the way in which the brethren have heretofore addressed each other, with the epithet that is, of 'Āvuso' (Friend). A younger brother may be addressed by an elder with his name, or his family name, or the title 'Friend.' But an elder should be addressed by a younger brother as 'Sir,' or as 'Venerable Sir.'

" When I am gone, Ānanda, let the Order, if it should so wish, abolish all the lesser and minor precepts.[1]

" When I am gone, Ānanda, let the higher penalty be imposed on brother Channa."

[1] The Order refused to avail themselves of this permission.

"But what, lord, is the higher penalty?"

"Let Channa say whatever he may like, Ānanda, the brethren should neither speak to him, nor exhort him, nor admonish him."[1]

Then the Exalted One addressed the brethren, and said: "It may be, brethren, that there may be doubt or misgiving in the mind of some brother as to the Buddha, or the Dhamma, or the Sangha, or the Path, or the Method. Inquire, brethren, freely. Do not have to reproach yourselves afterwards with the thought: 'Our teacher was face to face with us, and we could not bring ourselves to inquire of the Exalted One when we were face to face with him.'"

And when he had thus spoken the brethren were silent.

And again the second and the third time the Exalted One addressed the brethren, and said: "It may be, brethren, that there may be doubt or misgiving in the mind of some brother as to the Buddha, or the Dhamma, or the Sangha, or the Path, or the Method. Inquire, brethren, freely. Do not have to reproach yourselves afterwards with the thought: 'Our teacher was face to face with us, and we could not bring ourselves to inquire of the Exalted One when we were face to face with him.'"

And even the third time the brethren were silent.

Then the Exalted One addressed the brethren, and said: "It may be, brethren, that you put no questions out of reverence for the teacher. Let one friend communicate to another."

And when he had thus spoken the brethren were silent.

And the venerable Ānanda said to the Exalted One: "How wonderful a thing is it, lord, and how marvellous. Verily, I believe, that in this whole assembly of the brethren there is not one brother who has any doubt or misgiving as to the Buddha, or the Dhamma, or the Sangha, or the Path, or the Method."

"It is out of the fullness of faith that thou hast spoken, Ānanda. But, Ānanda, the Tathāgata knows for certain

[1] We are told that this brother was one who had committed some offence against the Order, that the penalty was sufficient to open his eyes to his faults, and that finally he attained the "supreme goal" of the Buddhist faith.

that in this whole assembly of the brethren there is not one brother who has any doubt or misgiving as to the Buddha, or the Dhamma, or the Sangha, or the Path, or the Method. For even the most backward, Ānanda, of all these five hundred brethren has become converted, is no longer liable to be born in a state of suffering, and is assured of hereafter attaining to the Enlightenment (of Arahantship)."

Then the Exalted One addressed the brethren, and said: "Behold now, brethren, I exhort you, saying: 'Decay is inherent in all component things. Accomplish earnestly!'"

This was the last word of the Tathāgata.

The Buddha Attains Parinibbāna

(Passing through the nine states called Anupubba-Vihāras)

Then the Exalted One entered into the first stage of Rapture.[1] And rising out of the first stage he passed into the second. And rising out of the second, he passed into the third. And rising out of the third stage he passed into the fourth. And rising out of the fourth stage of Rapture, he entered into the state of mind to which the infinity of space is alone present. And passing out of the mere consciousness of the infinity of space he entered into the state of mind to which the infinity of thought is alone present. And passing out of the mere consciousness of the infinity of thought, he entered into a state of mind to which nothing at all was specially present. And passing out of the consciousness of no special object he fell into a state between consciousness and unconsciousness. And passing out of the state between consciousness and unconsciousness he fell into a state in which the consciousness both of sensations and of ideas had wholly passed away.

Then the venerable Ānanda said to the venerable Anuruddha: "Lord, Anuruddha, the Exalted One is dead."

"Nay, friend Ānanda, the Exalted One is not dead. He has entered into that state in which both sensations and ideas have ceased to be."

1 = jhāna: rapt interest

Then the Exalted One passing out of the state in which both sensations and ideas have ceased to be, entered into the state between consciousness and unconsciousness. And passing out of the state between consciousness and unconsciousness he entered into the state of mind to which nothing at all is specially present. And passing out of the consciousness of no special object he entered into the state of mind to which the infinity of thought is alone present. And passing out of the mere consciousness of the infinity of thought he entered into the state of mind to which the infinity of space is alone present. And passing out of the mere consciousness of the infinity of space he entered into the fourth stage of Rapture. And passing out of the fourth he entered into the third. And passing out of the third stage he entered into the second. And passing out of the second he entered into the first. And passing out of the first stage of Rapture he entered into the second. And passing out of the second stage he entered into the third. And passing out of the third stage he entered into the fourth stage of Rapture. And passing out of the last stage of Rapture he immediately expired.

Events Immediately following the Passing Away

When the Exalted One died there arose, at the moment of his passing out of existence, a mighty earthquake, terrible and awe-inspiring: and the thunders of heaven burst forth.

When the Exalted One died, Brahmā Sahampati, at the moment of his passing away from existence, uttered this stanza:

"They all, all beings that have life, shall lay
Aside their complex form—that aggregate
Of mental and material qualities,
That gives them, or in heaven or on earth,
Their fleeting individuality.
E'en as the teacher—being such a one,
Unequalled among all the men that are,
Successor of the prophets of old time,
Mighty by wisdom, and in insight clear—
Hath died."

When the Exalted One died, Sakka, the ruler of the devas, at the moment of his passing away from existence, uttered this stanza:

> "They're transient all, each being's part and powers,
> Growth is their very nature, and decay.
> They are produced, they are dissolved again:
> To bring them all into subjection—that is bliss."

When the Exalted One died, the venerable Anuruddha, at the moment of his passing away from existence, uttered these stanzas:

> "When he who from all craving want was free,
> Who to Nibbāna's tranquil state had reached,
> When the great sage finished his span of life,
> No gasping struggle vexed that steadfast heart.
>
> "All resolute, and with unshaken mind,
> He calmly triumphed o'er the pain of death.
> E'en as a bright flame dies away, so was
> The last emancipation of his heart."

When the Exalted One died, the venerable Ānanda, at the moment of his passing away from existence uttered this stanza:

> "Then was there terror.
> Then stood the hair on end.
> When he endowed with every grace—
> The supreme Buddha—died."

When the Exalted One died, of those of the brethren who were not yet free from the passions, some stretched out their arms and wept, and some fell headlong on the ground rolling to and fro in anguish at the thought: "Too soon has the Exalted One died! Too soon has the Wellfarer passed away! Too soon has the Light gone out in the world!"

But those of the brethren who were free from the passions (the Arahants) bore their grief collected and composed at the thought: "Impermanent are all component things. How is it possible that (they should not be dissolved). Then the venerable Anuruddha exhorted the brethren and said: "Enough, my brethren, Weep not, neither lament. Has not the Exalted One formerly declared this to us, that it is in the very nature of all things near and dear unto us, that we must divide ourselves from them, leave them, sever ourselves from them? How then, brethren, can this be possible—that whereas any thing whatever born, brought into being, and organised contains within itself the inherent necessity of dissolution—how then can this be possible that such a being should not be dissolved? No such condition can exist. Even the devas, brethren, will reproach us."

"But of what kind of devas, sir, is the venerable Anuruddha thinking?"

"There are devas, brother Ānanda, in the air, but of earthy mind, who dishevel their hair and weep, and stretch forth their arms and weep, fall prostrate on the ground, and roll to and fro in anguish at the thought: 'Too soon has the Exalted One died. Too soon has the Light gone out in the world.'

"There are, devas, too, Ānanda, on the earth, and of earthy mind, who tear their hair and weep, and stretch forth their arms, and weep, fall prostrate on the ground and roll to and fro in anguish at the thought: 'Too soon has the Blessed One died. Too soon has the Happy One passed away. Too soon has the Light gone out in the world.'

"But the devas who are free from passion bear it, calm and self-possessed, mindful of the saying, which begins: 'Impermanent indeed are all component things. How then is it possible . . . (that such a being should not be dissolved)?'"

Now the venerable Anuruddha and the venerable Ānanda spent the rest of the night in religious discourse. Then the venerable Anuruddha said to the venerable Ānanda: "Go now, brother Ānanda into Kusinārā and inform the Mallas of Kusinārā, saying: 'The Exalted One, O Vāsetthas, has passed away; do, then, whatever seemeth to you fit.'"

"Even so, lord," said the venerable Ānanda, in assent, to the venerable Anuruddha. And having robed himself early in the morning, he took his bowl, and went into Kusinārā with one of the brethren as an attendant. Now at that time the Mallas of Kusinārā were assembled in the council hall concerning that very matter.

And the venerable Ānanda went to the council hall of the Mallas of Kusinārā; and when he had arrived there, he informed them saying: "The Blessed One, O Vāsetthas, has passed away; do, then, whatever seemeth to you fit."

And when they had heard this saying of the venerable Ānanda, the Mallas with their young men and their maidens and their wives, were grieved, and sad, and afflicted at heart. And some of them wept, dishevelling their hair, and some stretched forth their arms and wept; and some fell prostrate on the ground, and some reeled to and fro in anguish at the thought: "Too soon has the Exalted One died. Too soon has the Wellfarer passed away. Too soon has the Light gone out in the world."

Then the Mallas of Kusinārā gave orders to their attendants, saying: "Gather together perfumes and garlands and all the music of Kusinārā." And the Mallas of Kusinārā took the perfumes and garlands, and all the musical instruments, and five hundred suits of apparel, and went to the Upavattana, to the Sāla Grove of the Mallas, where the body of the Exalted One lay. There they passed the day in paying honour, reverence, respect, and homage to the remains of the Exalted One with dancing and hymns, and music, and with garlands and perfumes; and in making canopies of their garments and preparing decoration wreaths to hang thereon.

Then the Mallas of Kusinārā thought:

"It is much too late to burn the body of the Exalted One to-day. Let us now perform the cremation to-morrow." And in paying honour, reverence, respect, and homage to the remains of the Exalted One with dancing, and hymns, and music, and with garlands and perfumes; and in making canopies of their garments, and preparing decoration wreaths to hang thereon, they passed the second day too, and then the third day, and the fourth, and the fifth, and the sixth day also.

Then on the seventh day the Mallas of Kusinārā thought: "Let us carry the body of the Exalted One, by the south and outside, to a spot on the south, and outside of the city, paying honour, and reverence and respect, and homage, with dance and song, and music, with garlands and perfumes, and there, to the south of the city, let us perform the cremation ceremony."

And thereupon eight chieftains among the Mallas bathed their heads, and clad themselves in new garments with the intention of bearing the body of the Exalted One. But, behold, they could not lift it up.

Then the Mallas of Kusinārā said to the venerable Anuruddha: "What, lord, can be the reason, what can be the cause, that eight chieftains of the Mallas who have bathed their heads, and clad themselves in new garments with the intention of bearing the body of the Exalted One, are unable to lift it up?"

"It is because you, O Vāsetthas, have one purpose and the devas have another purpose."

"But what, lord, is the purpose of the devas?"

"Your purpose, O Vāsettha, is this: 'Let us carry the body of the Exalted One by the south and outside, to a spot on the south, and outside the city, paying it honour, and reverence, and respect, and homage, with dance and song, and music with garlands and perfumes, and there, to the south of the city, let us perform the cremation ceremony.' But the purpose of the devas, Vāsettha, is this: 'Let us carry the body of the Exalted One by the north to the north of the city, and entering the city by the north gate, let us bring it through the midst of the city into the midst thereof. And going out again by the eastern gate, paying honour, and reverence, and respect, and homage, to the body of the Exalted One, with heavenly dance, and song, and music, and garlands, and perfumes, let us carry it to the shrine of the Mallas called Makuta-bandhana, to the east of the city, and there let us perform the cremation ceremony.'"

"Even according to the purpose of the devas, so, lord, let it be."

Then immediately all Kusinārā down even to the dust bins and rubbish heaps became strewn knee-deep with Mandārava flowers from heaven, and while both the devas from the skies, and the Mallas of Kusinārā upon earth, paid honour and reverence, and respect, and homage to the body of the Exalted One, with dance, and song, and music, with garlands, and with perfumes, they carried the body by the north to the north of the city; and entering the city by the north gate they carried it through the midst of the city into the midst thereof; and going out again by the eastern gate they carried it to the shrine of the Mallas, called Makuta-bandhana; and there, to the east of the city, they laid down the body of the Exalted One.

Then the Mallas of Kusinārā said to the venerable Ānanda: "What should be done, lord, with the remains of the Tathāgata?"

"As men treat the remains of a king of kings, so, Vāsetthas, should they treat the remains of a Tathāgata."

"And how, lord, do they treat the remains of a king of kings?"

"They wrap the body of a king of kings, Vāsetthas, in a new cloth. When that is done they wrap it in carded cotton wool. When that is done they wrap it in a new cloth, and so on till they have wrapped the body in five hundred successive layers of both kinds. Then they place the body in an oil vessel of iron, and cover that close up with another oil vessel of iron. They then build a funeral pyre of all kinds of perfumes and burn the body of the king of kings. And then at the four cross roads they erect a cairn to the king of kings. This, Vāsetthas, is the way in which they treat the remains of a king of kings.

"And as they treat the remains of a king of kings, so, Vāsetthas, should they treat the remains of the Tathāgata. At the four cross roads a cairn should be erected to the Tathāgata. And whosoever shall there place garlands or perfumes or paint, or make salutation there, or become in its presence calm in heart, that shall long be to them for a profit and a joy."

Therefore the Mallas gave orders to their attendants, saying: "Gather together all the carded cotton wool of the Mallas."

Then the Mallas of Kusinārā wrapped the body of the Exalted One in a new cloth. And when that was done, they wrapped it in carded cotton wool. And when that was done, they wrapped it in a new cloth, and so on till they had wrapped the body of the Exalted One in five hundred layers of both kinds. And then they placed the body in an oil vessel of iron, and covered that close up with another oil vessel of iron. And then they built a funeral pyre of all kinds of perfumes, and upon it they placed the body of the Exalted One.

Now at that time the venerable Mahā Kassapa was journeying along the high road from Pāvā to Kusinārā with a great company of the brethren, with about five hundred of the brethren. And the venerable Mahā Kassapa left the high road, and sat himself down at the foot of a certain tree.

Just at that time a certain naked ascetic who had picked up a Mandārava flower in Kusinārā was coming along the high road to Pāvā.

Now the venerable Mahā Kassapa saw the naked ascetic coming in the distance, and when he had seen him said to that naked ascetic:

"Friend, surely thou knowest our Master?"

"Yea, friend, I know him. This day the Samana Gotama has been dead a week. That is how I obtained this Mandārava flower."

On that of those of the brethren who were not yet free from the passions, some stretched out their arms and wept, and some fell headlong on the ground, and some reeled to and fro in anguish at the thought: "Too soon has the Exalted One died. Too soon has the Wellfarer passed away. Too soon has the Light gone out in the world."

But those of the brethren who were free from the passions (the Arahants) bore their grief self-possessed and composed at the thought: "Impermanent are all component things. How is it possible that (they should not be dissolved)?"

Now at that time a brother named Subhadda,[1] who had been received into the Order in his old age, was seated in that company.

And Subhadda, the recruit in his old age, said to those brethren: "Enough, sirs. Weep not, neither lament. We are well rid of the great Samana. We used to be annoyed

[1] This can not be the same Subhadda who was the last convert under the Buddha.

by being told: 'This beseems you, this beseems you not.' But now we shall be able to do whatever we like; and what we do not like, that we shall not have to do."

But the venerable Mahā Kassapa exhorted the brethren: "Enough, my brethren, Weep not, neither lament. Has not the Exalted One formerly declared this, that it is in the very nature of all things near and dear unto us that we must divide ourselves from them, leave them, sever ourselves from them? How then, brethren, can this be possible, whereas anything whatever born, brought into being, and organized contains within itself the inherent necessity of dissolution—how then can this be possible that such a being should not be dissolved? No such condition can exist."

Now just at that time four chieftains of the Mallas had bathed their heads and clad themselves in new garments with the intention of setting on fire the funeral pyre of the Exalted One. But, behold, they were unable to set it alight."

Then the Mallas of Kusinārā said to the venerable Anuruddha: "What, lord, can be the reason, and what the cause (of this)?"

"The purpose of the devas, O Vāsetthas, is different."

"But what, sir, is the purpose of the devas?"

"The purpose of the devas, O Vāsetthas, is this: 'That venerable brother Mahā Kassapa is now journeying along the way from Pāvā to Kusinārā with a great company of the brethren, with five hundred brethren. The funeral pyre of the Exalted One shall not catch fire until the venerable Mahā Kassapa shall have been able reverently to salute the feet of the Exalted One."

"Even according to the purpose of the devas so, sir, let it be."

Then the venerable Mahā Kassapa went on to Makutabandhana of Kusinārā, to the shrine of the Mallas, to the place where the funeral pyre of the Exalted One was. And when he had come up to it he arranged his robe on one shoulder; and after bowing down with clasped hands, he thrice walked reverently round the pyre, and then, uncovering the feet, he bowed down in reverence at the feet of the Exalted One.

And those five hundred brethren arranged their robes on one shoulder; and bowing down with clasped hands, they thrice walked reverently round the pyre, and then bowed down in reverence at the feet of the Exalted One.

And when the homage of the venerable Mahā Kassapa and of those five hundred brethren was ended, the funeral pyre of the Exalted One caught fire of itself.

Now as the body of the Exalted One burned itself away, from the skin and the integument, and the flesh, and the nerves, and the fluid of the joints, neither soot nor ash was seen. Only the bones remained behind. Just as one sees no soot and ash when ghee or oil is burned; so as the body of the Exalted One burned itself away, from the skin and the integument, and the flesh, and the nerves, and the fluid of the joints, neither soot nor ash was seen. Only the bones remained behind. And of those five hundred pieces of raiment the very innermost and outermost were both consumed.

And when the body of the Exalted One had been burnt up, there came down streams of water from the sky and extinguished the funeral pyre of the Exalted One; and there burst forth streams of water from the storehouse of the waters (beneath the earth), and extinguished the funeral pyre of the Exalted One. The Mallas of Kusinārā also brought water scented with all kinds of perfumes, and extinguished the funeral pyre of the Exalted One.

Then the Mallas of Kusinārā surrounded the bones of the Exalted One in their council hall with a lattice work of spears, and with a rampart of bows; and there for seven days they paid honour, and reverence, and respect, and homage to them with dance, and song, and music, and with garlands and perfumes.

Now the king of Magadha, Ajātasattu, the son of the queen of the Videha clan, heard the news that the Exalted One had died at Kusinārā.

Then the king of Magadha, Ajātasattu, the son of the queen of the Videha clan, sent a messenger to the Mallas, saying: "The Exalted One was a Kshatriya and so am I. I am worthy to receive a portion of the relics of the Exalted

One. Over the remains of the Exalted One will I put up a sacred cairn, and in their honour will I celebrate a feast."

And the Licchavis of Vesāli heard the news that the Exalted One had died at Kusinārā. And the Licchavis of Vesāli sent a messenger to the Mallas, saying: "The Exalted One was a Kshatriya and so are we. We are worthy to receive a portion of the relics of the Exalted One. Over the remains of the Exalted One will we put up a sacred cairn, and in their honour will we celebrate a feast."

And the Sākiyas of Kapila-vatthu heard the news that the Exalted One had died at Kusinārā. And the Sākiyas of Kapila-vatthu sent a messenger to the Mallas, saying: "The Exalted One was the pride of our race. We are worthy to receive a portion of the relics of the Exalted One. Over the remains of the Exalted One will we put up a sacred cairn, and in their honour will we celebrate a feast."

And the Bulis of Allakappa heard the news that the Exalted One had died at Kusinārā. And the Bulis of Allakappa sent a messager to the Mallas, saying: "The Exalted One was a Kshatriya and so are we. We are worthy to receive a portion of the relics of the Exalted One. Over the remains of the Exalted One will we put up a sacred cairn, and in their honour will we celebrate a feast."

And the Koliyas of Rāmagāma heard the news that the Exalted One had died at Kusinārā. And the Koliyas of Rāmagāma sent a messenger to the Mallas, saying: "The Exalted One was a Kshatriya and so are we. We are worthy to receive a portion of the relics of the Exalted One. Over the remains of the Exalted One will we put up a sacred cairn, and in their honour will we celebrate a feast." And the brahmin of Vethadīpa heard the news that the Exalted One had died at Kusinārā. And the brahmin of Vethadīpa sent a messenger to the Mallas, saying: "The Exalted One was a Kshatriya, and I am a brahmin. I am worthy to receive a portion of the relics of the Exalted One. Over the remains of the Exalted One will I put up a sacred cairn, and in their honour will I celebrate a feast." And the Mallas at Pāvā heard the news that the Exalted One had died at Kusinārā.

Then the Mallas of Pāvā sent a messenger to the Mallas, saying: "The Exalted One was a Kshatriya and so are we. We are worthy to receive a portion of the relics of the Exalted One. Over the remains of the Exalted One we will put up a sacred cairn, and in their honour will we celebrate a feast."

When they heard these things the Mallas of Kusinārā spoke to the assembled crowds, saying: "The Exalted One died in our village domain. We will not give away any part of the remains of the Exalted One."

When they thus had spoken, Dona the brahmin addressed the assembled crowds, and said :—

"Hear, gracious sirs, one single word from me.
Forbearance was our Buddha wont to teach.
Unseemly is it that over the division
Of the remains of him who was the best of beings,
Strife should arise, and wounds and war.
Let us all, sirs, with one accord unite
In friendly harmony to make eight portions.
Wide spread let cairns spring up in every land
That in the light of the world mankind may trust."

"Do thou then, O brahmin, thyself divide the remains of the Exalted One equally into eight parts, with fair division."

"Be it so, sirs," said Dona the brahmin, in assent to the assembled brethren. And he divided the remains of the Exalted One equally into eight parts, with fair division. And he said to them: "Give me, sirs, this vessel, and I will set up over it a sacred cairn, and in its honour will I establish a feast."

And they gave the vessel to Dona the brahmin.

And the Moriyas of Pipphalivana heard the news that the Exalted One had died at Kusinārā.

Then the Moriyas of Pipphalivana sent a messenger to the Mallas, saying: "The Exalted One was a Kshatriya and so are we. We are worthy to receive a portion of the relics of the Exalte One. Over the remains of the Exalted One will we put up a sacred cairn and in their honour will we celebrate a feast."

And when they heard the answer, saying: "There is no portion of the remains of the Exalted One left over:

the remains of the Exalted One are all distributed," they took away the embers.

So the king of Magadha, Ajātasattu, the son of the queen of the Videha clan made a cairn in Rājagaha over the remains of the Exalted One, and celebrated a feast.

And the Licchavis of Vesāli made a cairn in Vesāli over the remains of the Exalted One, and celebrated a feast.

And the Sakiyas of Kapila-vatthu made a cairn in Kapila-vatthu over the remains of the Exalted One, and celebrated a feast.

And the Bulis of Allakappa made a cairn in Allakappa over the remains of the Exalted One, and celebrated a feast.

And the Kiloyas of Rāmagāma made a cairn in Rāmgāma over the remains of the Exalted One, and celebrated a feast.

And Vethadīpaka the brahman made a cairn in Vathadīpa over the remains of the Exalted One, and celebrated a feast.

And the Mallas of Pāvā made a cairn over the remains of the Exalted One and celebrated a feast.

And the Mallas of Kusinārā made a cairn in Kusinārā over the remains of the Exalted One, and celebrated a feast.

And Dona the brahmin made a cairn over the vessel (in which the remains had been collected) and celebrated a feast.

And the Moriyas of Pipphavana made a cairn over the embers, and celebrated a feast.

Thus were there eight cairns (thūpas) for the remains, and one for the vessel, and one for the embers.

This is what came to be.

(Eight measures of relics there were of him of the far-seeing eye,
Of the best of the best of men. In India seven are worshipped.
And one measure in Rāmagāma, by the kings of the serpent race.
One tooth, too, is honoured in next world, one in Gandhāra's city,
One in the Kalinga realm, and one more by the Nāga race.
Through their glory the bountiful earth is made bright with offerings painless—
For with such are the Great Teacher's relics best honoured by those who are honoured,
By gods and by Nāgas and kings, yea, thus by the noblest of humans.
Bow down with clasped hands.
Hard, hard is a Buddha to meet with through hundreds of ages !)

End of the Book of the Great Decease.

END

AUTHORITIES

Vinaya-Piṭaka

Sutta-Piṭaka

INDEX